BHA

Karen Sullivan is a bestselling
journalist specialising in natural health and childcare. She has
written over 20 books on health and health issues, including
*Vitamins and Minerals, Healthy Eating, The Complete Illustrated
Guide to Natural Home Remedies, The Common Sense Guide to
Pregnancy* and *Childcare and Natural Healthcare for Children*.
She writes regularly for national newspapers and magazines.
Karen is passionate about natural health and practises what
she preaches with her own two young sons. She lives in
London.

Kids under Pressure

How to raise a stress-free and happy child

KAREN SULLIVAN

PIATKUS

For Cole and Luke

Copyright © 2002 Karen Sullivan

First published in 2002 by
Judy Piatkus (Publishers) Limited
5 Windmill Street
London W1T 2JA
e-mail: info@piatkus.co.uk

The moral right of the author has been asserted

A catalogue record for this book is available from the British Library

ISBN 0 7499 2200 1

Text design Paul Saunders
Edited by Carol Franklin
Illustrated by Lesley Wakerley

This book has been printed on paper manufactured with respect for the environment using wood from managed sustainable resources

Typeset by Palimpsest Book Production Limited,
Polmont, Stirlingshire
Printed and bound in Great Britain by
Biddles Ltd, Guildford & King's Lynn
www.biddles.co.uk

Contents

Acknowledgements

This book simply could not have been written without the enthusiasm, experience, insight and inspiration of many people. A great deal of research has gone into its making, and I have called upon the expertise and resources of more people and organisations than I could possibly mention here. Special thanks are due, however, to Marilyn Glenville, PhD, who set me straight on all the physiological effects of stress; Dr Robert Dato, PhD, NCPsyA, in the US, who showed enormous enthusiasm for the project, giving me lots of ideas and avenues to follow, as well as kindly allowing me to reprint his Dato Stress Inventory; George Marsh, headmaster of Dulwich College Preparatory School in London and chairman of IAPS, for taking the time to share his considerable experience, insight, theories and beliefs; Professor Wes Sime, PhD, MPH, at the University of Nebraska; health journalist and author Sarah Stacey, who put me in touch with all the right people; Margaret DeJong, BA, MDCM, MRCPsych, who provided expert guidance, support and fact-checking; William J. Doherty, PhD; and Tricia Allen, Families First, Professional Association of Teachers in the UK, the American Institute of Stress, the International Stress Management Association, the Child Nutrition Research Center in the US, the NSPCC, Center for Working Families at the University of California, Office for National Statistics, the Institute of Psychiatry, the Maudsley Hospital in London, the Complementary Medical Association, the Association of Reflexologists, Young Minds, MIND, the new Health Development Agency, the Massage for Therapy Council and the Homeopathic Medical Association. Thank you to Dr Michael Apple for checking this book thoroughly for possible medical errors.

Big thanks go to Piatkus Books, who allowed my deadline to slip and slip as I got embroiled in the issues, and who showed great faith and belief in this project. Thanks to Gill Bailey, Rachel Winning, Judy Piatkus, Sandra Rigby and Susan Fleming, all of whom were continually encouraging and supportive. Thanks, too, to Carol Franklin, my favourite copy editor and loyal supporter, and to Jana Sommerlad in publicity, who is capable of performing miracles.

On a personal level, I would like to thank everyone who put up with my enthusiasm for (obsession with) the subject for almost a year, as well as my inability to focus on anything other than the book for just as long! Thanks, then, to Melanie Woollcombe, Gill Paul, Tracey Lawrie, Debbie and Malcolm Gill, Lisa McGown, Ann Abrahams, Helen Owen, JoAnn Thornton, Kellie Jackson, David Boyle, Elaine Gawin and Sonia Henley.

Last but not least, I'd like to thank the many children who gave up their time to complete my survey; not only were they honest (often to their parents' horror) and forthright, but they confirmed my deepest suspicions that today's children are simply under too much pressure. Special thanks to Ilana Newman, Nathan Gawin, Danielle Abrahams, Lucy Lovell, George and Alice Rowell, Casey Partridge, Andrew Penney, Daniel Jackson, Rachel and Kyra Evans, Courtney Turgott, Joe Okore, and my son, Cole, who all made a special effort to explain their feelings. Thanks also to my under-10s football team, who provided invaluable information without cottoning on to the reason why I was suddenly so interested in their home lives. And thank you, Luke, for not getting stressed when I did!

Foreword

Karen Sullivan has written a timely and important book. In recent years, adults have become increasingly aware of the stresses of our modern life, and the negative impact on our personal sense of contentment and fulfilment. It seems that more and more is expected of us, both in the workplace and in our often frenetically busy home life. Many women find themselves struggling to combine career and child-rearing, in a juggling act which has its rewards, but also brings with it many stresses. Similarly, men struggle to find a more comfortable equilibrium. Many experience job demands as overwhelming, and find that they have precious little time to relax with their families.

The strain on families is evident. Increased mobility has brought with it increased isolation, with fewer families benefiting from the support of extended families living nearby. Lack of close family and community support are contributing factors in the high rate of family breakdown and divorce. The increase in numbers of women working has not been matched by increased availability of good-quality child care. The result is that even very young children may be exposed to rapidly changing or inadequate child care, which is likely to lead to increased emotional insecurity.

As Karen Sullivan points out, it has taken us some time to recognise the impact of these numerous stresses on children. Professionals working in the field of child mental health have been faced with skyrocketing demands for their services over the past five to 10 years. But it has only been in recent years that the media has begun to focus on stress in children, and its various manifestations.

Kids Under Pressure has much to offer to the tired, overstretched and sometimes guilt-ridden parents of the new millennium. It is a thoughtful, down-to-earth and practical book, providing guidance on every aspect of a child's daily life. The important role of diet is considered. The impact of stress on sleep problems, as well as on a whole range of physical disorders is described, with a section devoted to herbal and homeopathic remedies. Throughout the book the emphasis is on the importance of the emotional well-being of children.

If busy parents can make the time to read this book, they may find a way to spend more time with their children, and to resist the tendency to put the same sorts of pressures on children that we ourselves experience.

Margaret DeJong, BA, MDCM, FRCPsych (Can),
MRCPsych (UK), Consultant Child and Adolescent
Psychiatrist, Royal Marsden Hospital, London
September 2001

Introduction

Not so very long ago, the concept of stress in children was laughable. Childhood was a time of freedom and development, when children explored their environments and learned life's lessons at an easy, relaxed pace. As adults, many of us look back on our childhood years with fondness; our memories are of fun and play, testing our parental boundaries, schooldays and sports, laughter and an overwhelming sense of timelessness. In contrast to the years that follow, with their inevitable stresses and strains, childhood, in hindsight, appears positively idyllic.

Consider now the lives of our children. Will they look back with the same nostalgia and fond memories? Will they associate their childhood with freedom from responsibility, and relaxing times? Will they recall days and even weeks spent whiling away the hours, with little to do but enjoy being a child?

Chances are they won't. Over the past decade, the nature of childhood has been transformed into a rigorous series of obligatory and challenging activities that not only disrupt a hugely important aspect of growing up, but also threaten the long-term emotional and physical health of our children. Children today are, without a doubt, under pressure, and experiencing what have until now been considered adult patterns of stress-related behaviour and health problems.

One in 10 children in the UK now suffers from a serious mental disorder, and children as young as three are being treated for stress-related and emotional problems. As many as one in 33 children and one in eight adolescents in the USA now suffers from depression. What does that say about the way we are raising our children?

Kids Under Pressure looks at the reasons why childhood has changed so dramatically over the past generations, and how our expectations – on both a societal and a parental level – have altered. While 'stress' undoubtedly became a buzzword for the late 20th century, and beyond, a number of related issues do affect large segments of the adult population and their well-being. But instead of learning from their own mistakes, adults thrust an unsuitable lifestyle and expectations upon their children as part of their culture.

With broad-ranging health and emotional problems in children now becoming the norm, more and more parents are showing concern. And rightly so. This book addresses the very real problems that are affecting children, examining the reasons why their lives have become so stressful, and how their emotional, physical and spiritual health is being damaged by the demands placed upon them. It looks at what children really need to develop into healthy, emotionally stable adults, and questions the values of contemporary society, and the reasons why parents are encouraged to drive their children so hard. We've lost faith in family as a means to provide children with what they need. And we're scheduling activities so tightly that there's no room for playful exchanges with parents, siblings, and peers, all of which are necessary for emotional health. Ball games in the garden have been overtaken by strictly organised sport and competition. Children no longer have the freedom to tinker at a piano; they are expected to pass exams and excel. Where is the fun? In many cases it has been replaced by an overwhelming characteristic of contemporary society: competition, and its inherent component, stress.

Stress manifests itself in children in various ways; their reactions are often very different from those seen in adults. This book aims to show parents how to identify problems before they become serious. It also looks at the lifestyle of the modern family, with a view to making changes that can affect the well-being of all its members. One key element in reducing stress is a stress-free environment, based on social support, the ability to find hope by thinking through solutions, and an ability to anticipate stress and learn ways to avoid it.

Relaxed, happy children feel good about themselves and are better equipped to deal with the competitive adult world. This book examines the importance of preparing children for life in a way that leaves them free to enjoy the pleasures of being a child.

The world around us won't change overnight but the way we bring up our children can. We can teach them resilience and guide them through many difficult situations. We can nurture their emotional health and spirit, giving them the tools they need to survive in an often chaotic world. Most importantly, however, we can make changes to the way we live, and the way we expect them to life, to give them the best possible chance of coping with the demands they will inevitably face.

All parents want the best for their children, and from the earliest days set out to create the best possible life. *Kids Under Pressure* will help you to make practical changes that will do just that. Statements from real children, describing what they consider to be stressful, will help you see problem areas in your own child's life and to find ways to ease your child's path through life. Whether your child is just starting out on life, facing his first days at school, in the middle of a family divorce or separation, coping with exams, finding the competition on the football pitch too much to bear, or simply struggling with an overscheduled lifestyle or the daily grind of school, this book can transform his life.

With two children of my own, this is a subject very close to my heart, and one that has been niggling away at the back of my mind for many years. Most of my friends and colleagues share the same growing concern that all is not well with the way our children are being raised, or rather, forced through life. With this book I am determined to change the way we view our children, and to give them back the childhood they deserve. Every child needs a peaceful, stable and nurturing environment in which to grow – and thrive. This book will show you how to create it.

PART ONE

The Elimination of Childhood

In all our efforts to provide 'advantages' we have actually produced the busiest, most competitive, highly pressured and over-organized generation of youngsters in our history – and possibly the unhappiest. We seem hell-bent on eliminating much of childhood.

EDA J.LE SHAN, *The Conspiracy Against Childhood*, 1967

CHAPTER ONE

Can children be stressed?

The average child today, leading an average lifestyle, is under pressure. Taking that one step further, most children are suffering from stress that could seriously affect their emotional and physical health, both in the long term, and on a day-to-day basis. It affects the way they learn and grow, their ability to fight infection, cope with the rigours of life, and interact with their peers; it undermines confidence, and, most importantly, affects their quality of life.

This is no small-scale problem with a quick-fix solution. Stress in children is on the increase, and is a cause for great concern. Children are the workers and guardians of the future; they will be the leaders of our countries, the parents of our grandchildren, and the payers of pensions. And the ironic thing is that not only is this problem underestimated, but it is often genuinely invisible to caring parents. The fact is that the majority of adults do not expect children to suffer from stress, and often overlook the key signs that indicate a problem.

A modern plague

Many adults in today's society face considerable demands that may lead to stress; some adapt better than others. 'Stress' has become a somewhat overused buzzword, a peg on which to hang a multitude of symptoms and emotions that affect well-being. It has become one of the most common causes of work-related litigation, and we've all bemoaned the huge payouts made to people for reasons of 'stress', who are simply doing their jobs. It's the single most significant reason for 'sick days' and extended periods of time off work. The UK Health and Safety Executive estimates that stress is costing the economy £6.4 billion a year. In the year 2000, 70 per cent of adults reported experiencing stress at work – up from 60 per cent in the previous year. In the US, the situation is not much different: 43 per cent of all adults suffer adverse health effects from stress, while some 75 to 90 per cent of all visits to GPs are for stress-related ailments and complaints. In terms of lost hours due to absenteeism, reduced productivity and workers' compensation benefits, stress costs the American industry more than $300 billion annually, or $7,500 per worker per year.

Stress has become so common that some experts now question whether it is a genuine affliction, or whether we have become accustomed to blaming a collective inability to cope with 21st-century life on external factors.

Why, then, add to the furore by bringing children into the picture? The answer is this: stress is more than a state of tension that can be eased by relaxation; and it's more than an excuse for a day off work or off school. It constitutes a very real physical and emotional condition, which has a dramatic impact on both the short-term and long-term health and well-being of all members of society. And because children as young as three (and in some cases, even babies) are now showing clear symptoms of stress-related disease and emotional problems, for the first time, this syndrome could affect the population as a whole.

Adults are able to recognise and learn to adapt to the effects of pressure. In fact, dealing successfully with stress – a fundamental part of the modern lifestyle – is one of the keys to health and happiness. But children are different. First and foremost, many parents are genuinely unaware of the fact that their children are under pressure; some of them even contribute unknowingly to the demands faced by their children. Secondly, an undiagnosed problem cannot be prevented, and it cannot be treated. If children are not taught to adapt to the demands they face, it is unlikely that they will be any more successful in controlling stress and its ill-effects than the vast majority of their adult counterparts. Even more importantly, children are under more pressure today than ever before. From a physiological point of view, no one really knows what the long-term health ramifications may be. The same goes for the emotional impact.

Adults under pressure burn out, and downshift. Adults experience and accept a lower quality of life in order to meet the demands of their daily life. Adults suffer a host of debilitating physical and emotional symptoms, and often deal with them using quick-fix solutions – alcohol, nicotine, over-the-counter and prescription drugs, 'retail therapy', or a comfortable armchair in front of the television. Children have neither the tools nor the knowledge to understand or to adapt to stress. If they turn to the same comforts that adults seek, what will be the end result? If adults suffer heart disease from prolonged periods of stress, for example, what effect would such pressure have across a childhood? Will we begin to see teenage victims of afflictions that have been traditionally associated with ageing?

In Chapter 2, we'll look at some of the scenarios that could result from long periods of stress, but first it's important to understand the extent of the problem.

Children and stress

Stress manifests itself in different ways, and every child will have a unique combination of symptoms. Some children will adapt easily to a rigorous schedule and intense competition at school or at sports. Others will be set back by relatively minor occurrences, such as failing a test, a change in child care, not being picked for the swimming team, or falling out with a friend. However, all children, even those who adapt well at an early age, experience stress, and it is often those high achievers who ultimately feel the most strain.

Many children are now showing adult patterns of stress-related illness, distress, and an inability to cope with the problems encountered in daily life. But many parents will be surprised to learn that stress in children is a growing issue. A child may not be able to put a name to what he is experiencing, and symptoms are often put down to illness, poor behaviour or even emotional problems. Children have the same physiology as adults. For many reasons, however, they are more susceptible to emotional and physical stress, while at the same time being even less well equipped to adapt to it.

Robert Dato, PhD, NCPsyA, is a US stress expert and pioneer, who developed the 'Law of Stress', and the highly regarded and scientifically validated 'Dato Stress Inventory'. According to Dato, 'Children and adults all have the same hardware. The symptoms of children, however, are often more extreme or frequent under the same pressure because adults have better software in place to manage that pressure. In other words, they are more adaptable.'

What is the scale of the problem?

According to research published in October 2000, children as young as eight describe themselves as 'stressed'. More than 200 interviews conducted by a team from London's City University found unprecedented levels of stress in British people of all ages, and 'worryingly high' levels in children. More than a quarter of those questioned by the researchers said they were often or always stressed. Half were 'occasionally stressed'. 'We were surprised by the extent of the problem, particularly by the amount of stress reported by very young people,' said Professor Stephen Palmer, who led the study. 'If you had asked eight-year-olds about stress 20 years ago, they would have looked blank. Now they understand the concept and a significant number report experiencing it.' They also found that nearly a quarter of the under-18s studied said that they often got stressed, and only one in six never suffered from it.

And according to another survey that was carried out by the Office for National Statistics in partnership with a team at the Institute of Psychiatry and the Maudsley Hospital, a quarter of young people in the UK had felt so unhappy or worried that they asked people for help.

In 1996, on behalf of the National Society for the Prevention of Cruelty to Children (NSPCC), MORI Social Research interviewed a representative quota sample of 998 children aged from eight to 15 in England and Wales. The aim of the survey was to obtain a contemporary picture of children's experiences of, and attitudes towards, family and social life. Among the many surprising things that researchers found (many of which will be covered later in this book) was the fact that stress and anxiety were considered to be normal by almost half of those polled.

When asked about sources and frequencies of worries, academic pressures were the most commonplace (44 per cent) for all except the youngest children. Younger children were generally more likely to say they frequently worried about things and a fifth were classified as 'anxious' on a composite scale, compared with one in 10 of those aged 12 or over.

A recent report by the Mental Health Foundation revealed that one in five people under 20 experiences psychological problems, from anxiety to psychosis. Research by Young Minds, the mental health charity, shows a huge increase in recent years in the number of children, some as young as four, seeking treatment for severe mental health problems.

Statistics are more difficult to obtain in the USA, perhaps underlining a failure to acknowledge the issue. In 2000, the Federal Interagency Forum on Children and Family Statistics published a voluminous document entitled *America's Children: Key National Indictors of Wellbeing*, which delved into the various aspects of childhood that comprise health, happiness and wellbeing. Interestingly, the subject of stress and anxiety did not feature. US stress expert Dr Dato feels that stress is widely underresearched and underplayed in his home country. He says, 'We are only willing to acknowledge stress when it becomes a severe emotional burden to people. We tend to sweep stress under the rug because it is ubiquitous.'

Not surprisingly, statistics relating to child and adolescent emotional-health problems are widely available. As Dr Dato points out, these conditions are very often a result of stress becoming out of control. In the USA, as many as one in 33 children and one in eight adolescents suffers from depression, according to the US Center for Mental Health Services. Thirteen per cent of US children between the ages of nine and 17 suffer from an anxiety disorder, while a MECA Study (Methodology for Epidemiology of Mental Disorders in Children and Adolescents) estimated that almost 21 per cent of US children aged nine to 17 had a diagnosable mental or addictive disorder associated with at least minimum impairment.

One of the problems with assessing the extent of the problem is, of course, the fact that children are not always aware of stress and its inherent symptoms. They experience the symptoms, but they do not know their cause, and they have often not been taught to verbalise their emotions to the extent that they should. Furthermore, parents are unaware of the link between the symptoms, and they tend to try to treat them individually, rather than looking at the root cause.

In researching this book, I gave a questionnaire to 80 schoolchildren between the ages of five and 16, from a variety of different backgrounds, in the UK, Ireland, Canada, the USA and Australia, and interviewed others in addition. While many had a definition for stress (largely inaccurate), and expressed feelings of being out of control and under pressure, few associated the multitude of symptoms they experienced with stress itself. The vast majority suffered from irritability, difficulty getting up in the morning, regular stomach upsets, headaches, digestive discomfort, nervousness and difficulty concentrating, but made no connection between any stress they might be experiencing and their physical and emotional symptoms.

Harry is a nine-year-old boy in the private school system in the UK. He claims that he doesn't experience stress, but when completing my survey he noted that he suffered from regular headaches, stomach upsets, trouble getting to sleep, trouble getting up in the morning, irritability, tearfulness, nervousness, feeling aggressive and angry, finding it difficult to relax, feeling that he isn't as good as his colleagues at school, difficulty concentrating, feeling anxious and out of control, dizziness and frustration. He defines stress as 'anger'.

What is stress?

In the Western world, stress is usually considered to be tension created by intolerable situations, such as demanding work, difficult commuting and traffic jams, financial problems, relationship trouble, or the death of a loved one, for example. Stress is certainly caused by all of those things, but there are many other aspects that you may have not have considered.

How should we define 'stress'? First of all, it is important to understand that stress is a response rather than a cause. Some people respond to external demands (*see below*) well, and experience few or no adverse effects. Their lifestyle could hardly be described as 'stressful'. Other people have a lower 'stress threshold', which means that even the smallest trigger can set off a response, leaving them with a host of unpleasant symptoms. This individual aspect to stress means that it is unique to every one of us. Before deciding how to approach a child's problem, it's vital to gauge what elements of their lifestyle are stressful, or capable of creating a 'stress response'.

Dr Robert Dato (*see* page 10) has developed an equation for analysing the stress response, based on the Law of Stress. This equation works equally well for children as for adults. In his view, 'stress is the difference between Pressure and Adaptability, or $S = P - A$. All children have low adaptability, therefore society only places on them the pressure they can manage successfully. As we reach the prime of life and our highest level of adaptability, society sees fit to put the most pressure on us. And as we age, and lose adaptability, society adjusts its expectations and less pressure is put on the older population. Picture it as a rainbow, which contains seven colours arching across the sky in parallel. The colour at the top of the rainbow is equivalent to pressure, with the bottom colour being equivalent to adaptability. It follows that the distance between the top and bottom colours is equivalent to stress. If we perceive the length of the rainbow as representing the human life span, then stress remains constant.'

The problem is, of course, that society no longer places only 'manageable' pressure on children. The stress factor of the equation is therefore becoming noticeably higher.

There is also a hereditary aspect to stress. Several US studies claim that one in 10 of us actually inherits a low stress tolerance or threshold, which means that 10 per cent of the population is already at a disadvantage. Most parents will have noticed that one or more of their children handle stress better than the others, and there can be a genetic basis to that.

Many people do not realise that stress also takes the form of environmental, leisure and even dietary factors. Indeed, anything that places a strain on the body can be considered to be a 'stressor', or pressure. Some of the less obvious ones include pollution (including noise pollution), inadequate sleep, a poor diet, additives in food and other substances, including cleaning products and toiletries, smoking and passive smoke, alcohol, electro-magnetic waves (*see* page 130), toxins in food and in the environment, insufficient exercise, poor fitness levels, and, of course, unhealthy leisure pursuits, such as watching too much television, playing for long stretches on games consoles or the computer.

A natural response

The stress response is normally described as a 'fight or flight' mechanism. In ancient times, it was crucial for humans to be able to deal effectively with threats to their safety, and our bodies are designed to do just that. In the presence of a perceived threat, which may, in the past, have been a bear approaching, or other danger to family or friends, the body begins to release adrenaline. Also known as epinephrine, adrenaline is the main stress hormone. It is produced by the adrenal glands, of which there are two, one above each kidney.

When a person is confronted with a stressful situation, levels of adrenaline in the blood increase by as much as 1,000 times within a minute. Adrenaline has a dramatic effect on the body. The heart speeds up and the arteries tighten to raise blood pressure. The liver immediately releases emergency stores of glucose into the bloodstream to give the body instant energy to fight or run. Digestion shuts down, because the energy necessary for this process is required elsewhere. The clotting capacity of the blood is also increased, in order to deal with any injury. The fight or flight from the scene would disperse the adrenaline, and levels would return to normal.

When I have exams, I feel that my stomach is all tight and I can't eat. I feel sick really. I think everyone feels that way because nobody eats very much lunch in exam time.
Lucy, 14

However, things are different in the modern world. Our bodies still respond in exactly the same way, but without the physical action to cause its dispersal, adrenaline continues to be released for prolonged periods of time. Sometimes the release is continuous, as we face stressful situations without any respite.

Think of this from a physical point of view: if our blood is programmed to clot more quickly when we are under stress – to prevent us bleeding to death, at the hands of a bear, for example – we are more susceptible to heart attack or strokes when under stress, particularly if the stressful situation continues. Because digestion is effectively shut down, even healthy meals cannot be properly digested, meaning that very little value is derived from the food we eat. It's not a healthy situation, particularly for children, whose bodies are still growing and maturing.

The stress response

The body responds in a variety of ways to stresses and the responses involve many body systems. The primary control mechanisms for the stress response are the *sympathetic* and *parasympathetic nervous systems*. The former is responsible for arousing the body into action; the latter for relaxing after the perceived stress or threat has disappeared.

The sympathetic nervous system is controlled by a neurotransmitter, or 'brain messenger', called *noradrenaline*, while the parasympathetic nervous system is governed mainly by a neurotransmitter called *acetylcholine*.

The adrenal glands control all this activity, producing the

three hormones adrenaline, noradrenaline and cortisol when the body is under stress. Cortisol (*see* page 59) acts as an anti-inflammatory agent, helping to deal with infection, while assisting other stress hormones to be more effective. It also helps to break down body fat stores, to turn them into energy for the muscles to use.

Noradrenaline creates a feeling of being in control and powerful. It's released by the adrenal gland to keep us motivated, energetic, concentrated and focused. When noradrenaline is in action, we feel great.

Adrenaline creates that panicky, heart-thumping feeling of being out of control and anxious, frightened or scared. You might experience this type of reaction if you are physically attacked, or enraged, or have a near-collision in your car.

When the *arousal stage*, also known as the *alarm stage*, has passed (which it does very quickly), the *resistance stage* is entered. Stressors do not immediately disappear, and the body has to be prepared to cope with them long after that initial 'fight or flight' response has worn off. During this stage, the amount of adrenaline in the blood decreases, and the other hormones swing into action to help the body to adapt to and deal with prolonged stress.

The final stage of the stress response is *exhaustion*, which occurs when the body no longer has the resources to deal with prolonged stress.

The first two stages of the stress response are designed to be short-lived and, essentially, life-saving. In today's society, we experience what amounts to chronic stress, which the body cannot deal with, even in the resistance stage. The time may come when we simply do not have sufficient resources available to deal with even mildly stressful situations. At this point, the body collapses and burns out. Illness is one result. Death is another.

Although this response occurs in both adults and children, children today are subjected to prolonged stress more than ever. Because they are likely to have fewer resources, and their bodies are not fully developed, the exhaustion or crisis stage is likely to occur sooner, with devastating results.

Hasn't there always been stress?

Stress is not a new concept. People have always had to contend with a multitude of demanding and even life-threatening circumstances, from plague, famine, poverty and persecution, to poor crops, flooding and early mortality. The difference is that most of the problems that faced our ancestors were not only expected and a normal part of day-to-day life, but many of them demanded a physical response, such as toiling on the land, building flood walls, hunting and farming for food and fleeing captors. These activities dispersed adrenaline and relieved its effects.

Over the years, we've demanded control over our environment. To a certain extent, we've managed to achieve it. We continue to have our share of physical stressors, such as flooding, but we expect them to be sorted out for us. We expect good health, regular meals, a reasonable place to live, money to pay for life's necessities, quality leisure activities and transportation to and from our place of work. When things go wrong, as they often do, we are less equipped to deal with them, largely because they are unexpected, and out of our control. The key word is control. We cope with daily life by controlling it – we vaccinate our children, save money in the bank, service our cars, pay our taxes, have insurance policies, pensions and a health service, and depend upon weather reports and forecasts. We like to think we are prepared for anything.

The fact is, however, that life cannot be controlled. However diligently we set ourselves up, we will inevitably face unexpected problems. Furthermore, most of the pressures in today's society are no longer physical. Many have a psychological or emotional basis, which do not allow for a physical release of adrenaline and tension. We live in a fast-paced society and face continuous change. The 20th century has seen the greatest technological advances of all time, moving us from horses and carriages to jet aircraft, from fountain pens to computers, from local markets to out-of-town superstores. Our lifestyle has become artificially accelerated.

Many of the threats we now face are personal, aimed at our security, our self-esteem, our role in society. A 'job for life' is no longer the norm. The financial arrangements we make to protect ourselves and to control our life often cause sacrifice and worry; we forego close family relationships in order to make enough money ultimately to buy some freedom from the rat-race, or to support a family. As they attempt to stay afloat, many working adults rarely see their children or even their partner. We sit in traffic jams, join long supermarket queues, wait for trains, all with the clock ticking. There is ever-increasing competition for material 'trophies'. We feel the need to look polished and slim, with an array of expensive accessories to look the part. We need to juggle the emotions that are normal aspects of humanity in order to keep all of the balls in the air. We have kids, jobs, households to run, and expectations.

All these psychological factors place an enormous strain on well-being, and few people enjoy the kind of emotional support they need to deal with them. Families have become increasingly isolated from the close-knit communities and extended families that were once the norm. It's not just an individual issue: adjusting to rapid and overwhelming change alters the nature of the human dynamic. Two-career households and single-parent families, the communications revolution and shifting moral values, have all had an impact on individuals and institutions world-wide.

It's easy to see why a small, seemingly innocuous setback can send someone over the edge. Furthermore, with no physical release from the constant pressures, adrenaline is left to play havoc with our bodies. And if you think most of these demands are relevant only to adults, think again. Children are under increasing pressure from all angles. It's important to understand what's expected of children today, and at increasingly younger ages.

Too much too young?

Imagine this scenario. Your seven-year-old is woken early to fit in a little piano practice before having a rushed breakfast and the inevitable battle over getting dressed and cleaning teeth. There's a last-minute scramble to collect together school bags and sports equipment, and to find the missing shoe. She's shoved into the car and has to listen to your moans of despair as the traffic builds up, making you even later. She sprints into school before the bell and sits quietly throughout the day, concentrating as required, behaving as expected, and working hard. The bell rings, but rather than relax into the expanse of evening ahead, she is shepherded into the car once again. Homework has to be done, clothes changed for ballet, and the endless sequence of activities is likely to involve a picnic dinner on the run, and falling behind schedule in an overscheduled day.

She finishes her reading in the car, while you concentrate on the road, and you return home just before bedtime. Not surprisingly, she objects to being sent straight to bed after her bath, but it's definitely past her bedtime and you've just realised that you have to collect your son from football practice. You give in to her pleas, and return 30 minutes later to find her watching television. Exhausted and fed up, you allow her to watch the end of her show, and she's rushed up to bed with no preamble, and no time for talk. You find a spelling test in her jumper pocket, and see that she's missed out five words that you'd practised only the night before.

You make a beeline for her room and lay down the law: no more television in the evenings until she gets her spelling words right. And has she practised her times tables today? You've become irritable because of the pressure on your time, and you are bound to have other elements of your life that are a source of stress. You sit down for a quick glass of wine and snap at your children when they make an unscheduled trip to the kitchen for a glass of water.

This scenario can be adjusted according to your child's age and interests, but the fact is that increasingly our children are victims of intensive scheduling and 'hyperparenting'. Every minute of their life is filled by activities and events, practices and practising, studying and school, and the inevitable travel in between it all. Mealtimes are rushed, eaten on the run or forgotten altogether. Bedtime runs late, television and games become the only way of letting off steam, and children are often subjected to a tirade of nagging, coercing, bribing, reminding and shouting to keep it all running to schedule. Most children do not have more than a few hours a week – if that – to play.

The most stressful thing in my life is traffic. *Simon, 7*

It's easy to see how school-aged children can be put under pressure by regular and constant demands, but babies and pre-schoolers are also at risk. Many parents fill the hours of even the smallest babies with enlightening and instructive activities, designed to stimulate their minds and develop their potential. Toddlers are entered into early-reading programmes, swimming lessons, music and gymnastics sessions, all designed to give them a leg-up when it comes to the real thing – school. And if they've got siblings, chances are they are spending a great deal of time in the car as well. The pressure to keep a family of children all heading in the right direction is exhausting for parents, and often comprises untenable schedules. But what is the effect on the children, whose lives are stripped of relaxation and learning through experience? The horrendous schedules of some small children may be fine preparation for the rat-race, but at what cost? Where is the time for play? For spontaneous experiment and experiences? For natural interaction with friends and the environment? Where can the natural exuberance of childhood be released if life is lived according to a carefully timetabled routine?

Studies show that children now play an average of one hour less per day than they did just three years ago, and spend a great deal more time accompanying parents on errands, attending outside activities and studying. *America's Children*, a study published in the year 2000, was based on data collected in 1997 and compared with findings made in the early 1980s. It found that children spent about eight hours more per week in child care, pre-school or school programmes, and three hours more per week doing household work, including shopping. Children also spent about three hours less per week in unstructured play and outdoor activities than in 1981. On average, children whose mothers worked outside the home tended to spend the most time in school and child care and the least time in free play.

I practise the piano for 20 minutes every day, I do sports for about an hour every day and I have an hour of homework. I don't have any time to play and I never get a chance to do whatever I want to do. My dad thinks that doing nothing is being lazy. *Christina, 6*

649
12

Less time spent eating is another indication of the way in which the work-family time crunch affects children, according to the researchers. In *America's Children*, it was found that children spent about one hour less per week eating in 1997 than in 1981. Altogether, free time – time left over after eating, sleeping, personal care, and attending school, pre-school or day care – decreased from 38 per cent to 30 per cent of a child's day. One-quarter of that free time was spent watching television (13 hours per week). Time spent studying increased by almost 50 per cent per week. Total study time averaged more than two hours per week for all children (the figure appears low because it includes pre-schoolers who don't study at all). The time children spent in organised sports more than doubled over the period to total more than five hours per week in 1997. Participation increased equally for girls and boys, but in 1997 boys spent twice as much time in sports activities as girls did.

This dramatic shift away from play and relaxation is just one of the reasons why children are under increasing pressure. There are many more.

CHAPTER TWO

Unwilling victims and unwitting perpetrators: The causes of stress in children

Very few parents could be accused of deliberately placing pressure on their children, or wanting anything other than the best for them. Therein lies the crux of the problem. We want to guarantee our children a rosy future, so we pull out all the stops to ensure that it happens. There are several issues involved.

Happiness

As probably the wealthiest and most financially secure generation in history, shouldn't we also be the happiest? We have jobs, homes, and lots of possessions. Isn't that what the technology race is all about? Comfort? Most of us have the money to buy far more than the basic necessities of life, and own what would once have been considered luxury possessions. But has this new wealth brought happiness? The answer is a simple no. Most research confirms that money is a key factor in happiness – at least until people have reached a certain level of affluence. Beyond that point, its importance may fall away, at different rates for different people. But other research shows a more worrying trend. In many countries it seems that increased wealth since the 1970s has led to a decline in the public's sense of overall well-being and happiness.

There are many reasons for this trend, but part of the problem is that our growing dependence on consumption brings with it some major social problems. We put time and energy into buying and consuming, and earning to buy and consume, which we might otherwise put into our families, neighbourhoods and communities.

According to a World Health Organisation report, 'About 50 per cent of the entire working population are unhappy in their jobs and as many as 90 per cent may be spending much of their time and energy in work that brings them no closer to their goals in life. About 75 per cent of those who consult psychiatrists are experiencing problems that can be traced to a lack of job satisfaction.'

Although there are significant variations between developed nations in relation to how happy they say they are, these variations are not explained by differences in wealth. The well-being of three of the richest countries – Germany, Japan and the USA – is less than that of many less wealthy developed nations, such as Ireland, Finland and Australia. Furthermore, surveys have consistently found little change over time, despite increases in wealth. The USA, for example, is much richer than it was in the mid-1900s, yet about the same numbers say they are happy today as then. Even more dramatically, although the Japanese real per capita income increased fivefold between 1958 and 1987, there was no change in the amount of reported well-being. Within developed nations, it appears that raising the income of all does not increase the happiness of all.

What does this have to do with parenting? A great deal. Parents who, generally speaking, experience unhappiness and a lack of contentment are determined to ensure that their children have the best possible chance of happiness. This manifests itself in several ways. Most adults have memories of being or feeling inadequate in childhood – a normal part of growing up. These memories become exaggerated and overemphasised because of widespread unhappiness. The argument is that if children are given every opportunity to be the best, and to succeed, they will never experience the rejection that could lead to later unhappiness. Children are encouraged in a number of ways – to take part in a wide range of activities, to succeed at school, to play instruments, to be model citizens – to give them every chance of a happy future. If they have a portfolio of talents and skills, surely they cannot fail to be happy?

No one can doubt the well-meaning intentions of parents, but the fact is that this kind of encouragement creates a great deal of stress. Children are neither physiologically nor emotionally ready to deal with the demands that are put upon them.

> If there was one thing I could do to make my life less stressful it would be not to do so many things. **Rachel, 11**

George Marsh, headmaster of Dulwich College Preparatory School in London, and chairman of the Incorporated Association of Preparatory Schools (IAPS), has noticed a marked trend in this type of activity over the years. He suggests that parents want their children to be involved in everything, in order to have chances that they themselves did not. A deep-seated insecurity or unrest can be eased by the thought that their children will never have to face the same sort of emotional unrest, as long as they are 'well prepared' for life.

Parental expectations

Alongside the issue of happiness lies another feature of modern parenting: a passion for excellence. This is undeniably affected by our society, which focuses so much on being the best, coming first, and winning. This is extended to children, who have little concept of balancing life's ups and downs. Childhood is a period of learning about the outside world, about experiencing defeat and coming to terms with strengths and weaknesses. The problem is that weaknesses are no longer acceptable. Given that there can only ever be one winner, there must be many children out there who experience massive disappointment, dejection, and feelings of failure and inadequacy – at a time when their self-esteem and personal identity are being established. Far from creating super-children, who will be able to handle anything that life throws at them, we are creating children who will have fundamental flaws in their emotional foundation. If they never succeed as children, they will never really have the confidence they need to try new things, to take risks, to believe in themselves, to make choices based on their own individual talents, skills and, yes, weaknesses.

While a certain amount of competition is essential in childhood – we do live in a competitive society, after all – the *amount* of *constant* competition is undermining and exhausting. A child can no longer feel proud of a single achievement – winning a running race, for example – she's expected to be brilliant at everything. And if she can't do it naturally, she will be cajoled, encouraged, tutored, coached and pushed until she improves. Chances are that she will still never be better than the children who have natural talents or affinities. If the only measure of success is being the best, what does that say to our children? The child who struggles with maths, improves her marks with lots of hard work, and still comes last in a class of 30 has effectively failed. Her personal achievement should be celebrated, not her place in the class, but in most cases it is not. If a boy beats 40 others to a place in the second team, his parents might assume he's no good because he didn't make the first. This kind of pressure is too much for most children to bear, and only part of what the modern child faces today.

I aim to win and be the best. When I don't win I get annoyed and frustrated. *Katie, 13*

The problem is that parents tend to encourage, often unwittingly, a frustration with not coming first. Too often, parents focus on 'failure' (a lack of excellence) as an indicator of long-term problems. If their child struggles academically, while others are apparently succeeding in all areas, they are concerned that they are producing a potential misfit who will never get a job. But even those lucky children who appear to excel at everything will encounter problems. Overachievers undoubtedly fail at something during their lifetime, and may be ill equipped to deal with it.

They may face burn-out, either academically or otherwise, and have to pull back from the constant competition and the stress that accompanies it.

Children are all individuals, with different patterns of development. Childhood excellence is no guarantee of future success, and parents must learn to accept weaknesses in their children, while celebrating their talents and individuality. Dulwich headmaster George Marsh describes a certain amount of jealousy among parents, who see other children achieving where their own sons do not. With the best intentions, they set out to ensure that their children are not left behind. He feels that parents often have to be reminded that happiness is much more important than success at everything.

Parents go to great lengths to give their children a competitive advantage – from baby swimming classes, infant music lessons and early reading programmes to extra-curricular tuition or coaching. (Some children are even signed up for a school while still in the womb, at a time when parents can have no idea of a child's personality or ability, or know whether the school will really be suitable.)

Seeking that competitive advantage can have a number of repercussions. Firstly, it can fill a child's timetable with activities at which he may never really be any good, or for which he may never really feel any passion. Overscheduling is a serious problem for today's children, and the focus on being the best is one of the driving forces behind it. Secondly, as George Marsh warns, a hothouse approach (which he has seen beginning as young as six) is often counterproductive. The apparent need for extra lessons shakes the child's self-confidence and, instead of enjoying success during conventional schooling, he becomes convinced that he is struggling. This tends to cause a dip, rather than an improvement, in performance.

Children should be accepted for who they are, in terms of both shortcomings and potential. Many parents and, therefore, children focus on the one area where they are not as good as their peers, rather than on their achievements. In the long term, this can cause serious problems in relation to self-belief, self-esteem and even self-awareness.

> Seventy-nine of the 80 children who completed my survey claimed that they weren't satisfied with their marks and wished they could do better. Every child cited parental pressure as one of the reasons why they wanted to do well.

Children are incredibly sensitive to parental approval, and will often pull out all the stops to ensure that they are performing according to expectation. The NSPCC poll (*see* page 11) showed that parental approval was highly regarded by 78 per cent of children. The vast majority are, it seems, performing with a view to achieving recognition from their parents. Given that excellence in every aspect of life is now the norm, this puts an intolerable pressure on young children who follow the lead of their parents.

Failure is a part of growing up, and learning from failure is often just as valuable as learning from success. More importantly, learning how to cope with failure is an important step in maturation, and a crucial aspect of stress management in children and adults. There will always be failure in life; if children are taught to avoid it, fight it, and disparage it, they will never be able to accept the things that will inevitably go wrong in life. What then?

Many – probably most – parents have a niggling feeling that their children are doing too much, and that their well-being is suffering as a result of their overscheduled lives. But few are prepared to take the risk that their son or daughter will miss out on a crucial activity or moment that may be their ticket to fame, excellence or happiness. It takes a brave parent to pull back from the kiddy rat-race, as they see all the other little girls and boys being marched off to activities designed to broaden their horizons. No parent knowingly overschedules or willingly harms their child; it's a trap, and it's difficult to escape. But knowing it's there can make a difference.

Living through children

If the majority of parents are dissatisfied with their life, and their work, they need to acquire feelings of happiness, success and achievement elsewhere. All too often, this falls on the shoulders of young children, who become the focus of their parents' mis-spent dreams. George Marsh concedes that there are many cases of parents living through their children, and suggests that every parent should ask him or herself why their child's success matters so much to them. There is a fine line between encouragement and support of children for the children's sake, and an over-whelming need for success that reflects well on parents.

Dr Robert Dato puts this well: 'Our accelerated rate of living adds to the pressure on children. They are no longer allowed to just be children any more. We treat them as small adults now. They have packed schedules, they must participate in everything, and they must achieve. For most children, parents reinforce this, and at the same time live vicariously through their children and parade their accomplishments before their friends as if they were their own.'

> My dad shouts a lot when I play football and always tells me how I could be better at everything. He makes me prac-tise lots when I wish I was playing with my friends. Sometimes when I am playing with my friends he tells me what I am doing wrong in football. He hurt his knee when he was young and couldn't be a football player. He wants me to be one now. I want to be one too but I think I am not good enough even when I try. And anyway, I like to do other things too. **James, 8**

When adults first become parents, their identities are often shifted; they become a 'mummy' or a 'daddy', rather than a high-flying career woman, or a top City lawyer. As part of that confusion of identities, parents often feel that their child's success and achieve-ment (or lack of it) are reflections of their own status in society. The other dads on the football pitch may not know how indispensable you are at work, but they'll certainly know if your child scores three own goals. As your child is an extension of you, this sort of public 'failure' doesn't sit well – and it gives you another reason to strive for excellence in your child. If we have a stumbling academician on our hands, we feel that we have failed. If we have a 'naughty' or 'disruptive' child, we are concerned that the outside world will consider us to be inadequate parents. Such neuroses are common, largely because of the type of society in which we live. But it extends to and affects our children greatly.

Children are led to believe that success and excellence are the hallmarks of a happy future; unsurprisingly, they experience enormous pressure en route.

Parents under pressure

Most adults admit to suffering from stress, and parenting certainly increases the burden. According to a UK survey of 5,000 women, 93 per cent of working mothers find it difficult to juggle a career with family life. Many of those questioned said they were overworked, underpaid and at 'breaking point' from stress, causing them to shout at their children. Working mothers feel they are damaging their children emotionally and putting their own health at risk by working. Three out of four believe that career stress is causing their health to suffer.

The vast majority of parents feel under pressure, and studies show that this affects their children dramatically.

I don't really see my dad because he has to work so hard. When we do things together at the weekends he gets cross and tired and my mum says to leave him alone. Sometimes they fight. **Chloe, 5**

Modern parents are caught in a difficult position. Children can be enormously demanding, particularly when they have a whirlwind of activities that require transportation, equipment, payment and time. Furthermore, over-stressed children are much more likely to require emotional imput that parents simply cannot dredge up and sustain, especially when they feel exhausted and undermined themselves. The majority feel great concern for their children's well-being, and every individual child requires different input and levels of understanding. Children do not come with an instruction manual, and every year brings different challenges. And where parents associate themselves so intimately with their children's achievements, the pressure to 'succeed' as a parent is heightened, placing further pressure on parents, and affecting the family dynamic.

Parental stress has many implications. Stressed parents are much more likely to take out their problems on their children. The saintly mother who can face a long working day, then cope calmly and energetically with demanding children at bedtime, is in the minority. Our resources are not endless. If we are emotionally exhausted throughout the day, it can be too hard to find the patience and the time to parent the way we would like to.

The compensation culture

Feeling that we are inadequate parents in any way encourages us to 'make up for it' in other ways, often through material goods. Guilt is assuaged by giving our children the best things in life, whether we can afford it or not.

According to the research group Mintel, overworked parents tend to lavish their children with expensive designer clothes to compensate for their busy and stressful lives. Working mothers in particular feel so guilty about not spending enough time with their families that they spend less on clothes for themselves, in order to have the money to dress their children in top brand names. Others, according to the research, use their children as a fashion accessory, as a means of displaying their own personal wealth; their offspring often 'stand out in the playground'. The study, based on interviews with 2,000 people, found that in the last five years spending on children's clothes in the UK had increased by 34 per cent in real terms, to £6 billion. This was expected to rise in the next five years to £6.8 billion.

And it's not just clothes. Computers, games consoles, televisions, CDs and new sports equipment are all used in the same way. This increase in materialism affects our children, both now and in the future. First, they develop a need for and interest in material goods, which they begin to associate with affection and love. The focus can become obsessive; children require more and more to satisfy them, and to reassure themselves that they are important and loved. Second, it creates a scenario of instant gratification; children have only to demand, and they receive. They fail to learn the important lessons of patience, of financial management, and of working hard for something (which brings with it a sense of achievement). They are led to understand that things are quickly and easily replaced, so they do not learn to care properly for them. They are in a 'competition' with their friends, and feel inadequate and upset when they do not have all the stuff that their friends have.

I mostly get all the clothes and CDs that I want, and if I bug my parents for a long time they usually get me anything. I feel like I am more cool when I have lots of things that my friends have. When my friends have other things that I want, I feel a bit annoyed. **Thomas, 10**

Such a situation is undoubtedly stressful. Every child who answered my questionnaire felt that their life would be improved in some way, and that they would feel 'cooler', if they had more of the things that their friends had. In a perfect example of consumerism run wild, children have begun to associate well-being with possessions – exactly the same problem that plagues many adults in today's society. What will be the long-term effects?

Too little time

Hard-working parents undoubtedly have little time to spend with their children, and this in itself is stressful. Some parents have less than an hour a day to spare. Rosanne Musgrave, head of Blackheath High School in South London, and a former president of the Girls' Schools Association, describes it as 'a sad outcome' of modern life. She has seen parents try to compensate by showering children with material goods, or cramming activities into what was mistakenly viewed as 'quality time'. The result was an 'impoverished' upbringing that could be as damaging to pupils as the effects of poverty of the conventional kind.

> My mum is the only mum I know who sits down and talks to me and my friends at dinner. Most of the mums talk on the telephone or get cross when we are too noisy. None of the mums except my mum eats dinner with children because they have to wait until later. *Luke, 7*

Children require parents for more than material purposes. Without the regular, patient guidance of a loving parent, a child may feel out of control and emotionally unstable. New experiences, concerns, fears and every other aspect of growing up can no longer be sorted out over the dinner table, on a family outing, or during a long bedtime chat. Children often need to unwind before being able to spill out the day's woes; many need to be encouraged to express their emotions, and this takes time. If there is no time available, they will learn to shut it all away. My survey showed that 73 of 80 children felt it was easier to 'pretend that everything was all right' rather than sharing a problem.

Bottling up emotions is an extremely dangerous scenario, and one of the most powerful sources of stress. Children need to learn to manage conflicting emotions and problems by expressing them and then coming up with a solution. If they pretend that everything is all right, they will ultimately begin to take a step back from reality. It is a parent's job to provide guidance, love, understanding, nurturing and advice on the path through life, and to be an unbiased listening ear. If a child never has the opportunity to express his concerns, either because he is being ferried from activity to activity with no chance to stop and contemplate, or because he simply doesn't spend time with his parents, he will feel stressed by even the most basic aspects of growing up – from peer pressure, identity and relationships to school marks and performance.

What are we teaching our children about relationships if we ourselves are unable to forge them at home? Children who are busy from morning to night simply don't have time to interact with family and peers. This interaction is essential for the renewal of spirit, the expression of problems and hopes, and the basis of relationships that will sustain them through periods where they simply cannot adapt alone. The bottom line is that too many children are alone too often. In this accelerated society, people are too busy to stop and simply *be*.

I don't really have anybody to talk to about things that worry me. My mum asks a lot of questions but I don't think she really listens to the answers, and she sometimes gets angry when I tell her the truth. I think that she really doesn't want to have any more problems because she has enough of her own. *Katja, 14*

Many very good parents are shocked when they realise how little time they spend with their children in an average week. Work it out. How often do you chat, laugh, share and plan with your child? How often do you get a chance to listen properly, with nothing else on your mind? Parents can't be blamed for the situation but they need to be aware that it exists. Children need parents, and they are receiving less of the nurturing care they need than ever.

This isn't just another dig at working mothers; at-home mothers are often just as busy. Amid the hectic run of school deliveries, activities, homework, instrument practice and running a household, there is often very little useful interaction. In fact, research shows that working parents often devote more time to their children than their non-working counterparts. This is partly because of guilt, but also because the day-to-day running of their children's lives is turned over to someone else, such as a nanny; this leaves them free to concentrate on the children themselves.

I don't really talk to my parents about important things. They talk about school work and my test results, and want to know how the other guys in my class are doing. When they talk they just want me to listen. They don't really care what I have to say. I don't think they are bad parents. I just think they don't really know me and they wish I was a better person at a lot of things. *Ben, 15*

How much time do we spend with our children?

- In the UK, research funded by Powergen found that six out of 10 parents do not have time to read to their children before bed. Dr Aric Sigman, the psychologist who ran the study, questioned 84 parents with 150 children, to compare reading patterns between generations. While almost three-quarters recalled being read to regularly when they were young, only 40 per cent of their children heard a story most nights of the week. Other researchers have said that a culture of long working hours destroys parents' relationships with their children, making it difficult for them to talk to them or monitor their homework. One common complaint from children is that their parents – especially dads – fall asleep themselves before they have finished reading a story.

- Only one in five households enjoys a meal together once a day, and a quarter said they eat together only once a month. A survey of 1,000 households by the Food Foundation, the UK's healthy-eating group, found that only 15 per cent sat down together every day, although a later study, published in April 2001, showed that more than 80 per cent of parents felt that family dinners were a vital part of home life. More than a third thought that the dinner table provided the only opportunity to discover what their children were thinking. Despite this, only 75 per cent of the sampled group, in a survey carried out by the Consumer

Analysis Group, on behalf of Paxo, managed a family meal once a week. Studies show that eating with our children is important. A large federal study of American teenagers found a strong association between regular family meals and academic success, psychological adjustment, and lower rates of alcohol use, drug use, early sexual behaviour, and suicidal risk.

- Sandra L. Hofferth, author of *Changes in American Children's Time, 1981–1997*, found that over the past couple of decades, household conversations have declined by 100 per cent!

- In a UK 2000 national poll, 21 per cent of teenagers rated 'not having enough time together with parents' as their top concern.

- According to the US National Longitudinal Survey of Adolescent Health, children who reported strong family ties were somewhat less likely to be involved in interpersonal violence than teens who did not report close family ties. Having a parent present at key times during the day – breakfast, after school, dinner, and bedtime – was linked to lower levels of violence.

The particular pressures of childhood and adolescence

So, children's lives tend to be overscheduled, but there are other factors that add to the pressure placed upon them. Some of these are societal – in particular, the breakdown of the family; others are caused by well-meaning authorities, such as educational institutions, which create intensely pressurised situations for children.

It is important to remember that childhood and adolescence are inherently stressful, quite apart from the pressure of the modern lifestyle. Childhood is a time of change and learning, of

seeking to find a place in the world, of learning to forge relationships, to deal with peers and peer pressures, and to cope with
issues such as bullying, of establishing moral beliefs and of
coming to terms with a changing body. At the same time as the
hormones rush madly around their body, children may change
schools, or go through a bereavement or the loss of a parent.
Every parent will remember the insecurities, the cringing feelings
of embarrassment, the faux pas, the lack of confidence in certain
situations that characterise childhood and adolescence. We recall
first crushes, the overwhelming need for approval from parents
and peers, the trauma of falling out with best friends, even in the
nursery years. We remember coveting the newest boots or jeans,
experiencing sibling rivalry, and battling with parents to be
allowed to express our own ideas and individuality.

None of this has changed. Children still experience the same
emotions and undergo the same stages of development. The difference is that an increasing number of other factors affect their
well-being and their ability to adapt to stress. Chapter 8 examines some of the common and natural forms of stress in a child's
life, such as bullying, peer pressure, competition, jealousy, divorce
and sibling rivalry, and looks at ways of dealing with these situations. Some of the other reasons why children are under
increasing pressure are explored below.

Education

Every child that I surveyed found school stressful. Some of the
children were only five years old. A number of issues relate to
eduction, and most are associated with the current trend for excellence. League tables between countries and schools put teachers
and the education system under increasing pressure to perform.
Unsurprisingly, this pressure is passed down to the children themselves, who face a battery of exams and tests at increasingly
younger ages.

In the year 2000, parental concern in the UK forced the education and the then employment secretary, David Blunkett, to
offer to review the testing of seven-year-olds, in light of the fact
that they appear to suffer from unacceptable levels of stress.

Caroline Wigmore, the national president of the Professional Association of Teachers in the UK, said recently that the stringent testing requirements mean that youngsters are treated 'like products on a conveyor belt'. School staff report increased stress among pupils. Half the teachers in a recent survey had seen entire classes suffer mass anxiety or panic attacks caused by testing and exams.

This complex situation is driven partly by parental and societal demand for success, and partly by a genuine need to improve national standards. The latter is intended to benefit every child, but the way in which it is being approached is open to criticism. No child should be pressured to perform for anyone other than himself. In other words, school standings in league tables, and working for parental approval, leave a child not only susceptible to failure, but also likely to fail. This intense focus on academic achievement undoubtedly affects the way children approach their work, and the emphasis that is placed upon it.

Starting school early

The 'headstart' approach to learning has been widely encouraged, and there is some evidence that capable children will benefit from early stimulation. However, this policy is not appropriate for a wide range of children with differing abilities. Shoving children into a system too young does much more than rob them of freedom; it increases pressure to perform at an age when many children are simply unable to adapt. They are forced to learn time-management skills, self-control, high standards of behaviour and concentration, and cope with teamwork, continual change, testing and competition. These are all skills that should be developed across a much longer period of time, and at a gradual pace, in line with a child's maturation and development.

Starting school early is encouraged by educational authorities, and it has also spawned a secondary issue, which has to do with parental insecurities. Once again, no parent wants their child to be 'left behind', which is why they arrange so much extra work and activities. There is a huge amount of competition between parents, and between children. Results are regularly and publicly posted, which means that children who may not fare well academically are constantly reminded of their inferiority. This often serves to undermine self-confidence and pride in personal achievement.

Dulwich headmaster George Marsh recently abandoned the practice of posting exam results, which inspired an unhealthy level of competition between the parents, who genuinely could not understand why their children were anything less than the best. Instead, his school has chosen to adopt a policy of encouraging personal and individual success, focusing on meeting personal goals rather than achieving a particular rank in the class.

Why start children so early? The example of countries such as Denmark proves that children can do perfectly well starting school as late as seven years old. We have research that tells us that good schools can improve pupils' performance a little, but not much, because academic ability is largely shaped by psychosocial factors. We have research that tells us that streaming doesn't improve grades and dampens children's morale. We have research that tells us that a child's mind develops through music and free play. We have research that tells us that humans underperform when they are stressed. What is the need to start it all so early? It's a question that needs to be answered, and a pattern that needs to be changed.

> I started school when I was two and a half, and I have been going every day since. I feel like I need a break sometimes because I think I've spent too much of my childhood learning. *Freddie, 15*

SATs

Standard achievement testing was first established to monitor the overall standards of children at different ages, ostensibly to find areas of weakness within the educational system and in individual schools. It is just one more way of evaluating individual and collective performance, and many children are under pressure to perform to ensure a school's league standing. Parents also use SATs as a benchmark of their child's overall ability, and his long-term potential.

The Institute of Education in the UK has recently resolved to undertake what is thought to be the first nationwide study of stress in schoolchildren. A preliminary survey commissioned by the BBC revealed alarming levels of stress in seven-year-olds who took national tests in the year 2000. Teachers reported pupils in tears, feeling sick and tired, and refusing to work. Other symptoms included stuttering, tantrums, sulks and psychosomatic illness. Six out of 10 said that there was no doubt that stress was generated by the Key Stage One standard assessment tests (SATs). One in five of those believed that stress levels were 'very high'. The children most likely to suffer the highest stress were those who were not tested by their normal classroom teacher.

All of the teachers who reported highly stressed pupils said the children were also under pressure from their parents. Alan Jensen, a senior educational psychologist at the Institute of Education who specialises in stress and stress management, described the findings as 'alarming'. 'I thought there would be a few tears and a tiny proportion of other symptoms,' he said, 'but here we had children not wanting to come to school. What are we doing for these youngsters at six and seven years old? What is it all about and how can we prepare children better?'

It's not surprising that parents are concerned about results. Too much emphasis is placed on individual grades at increasingly younger ages. SATs have become a focus for parents who are already concerned about their children's performance. Parents' meetings are organised to warn of oncoming tests; it has been alleged that SATs predictions are raised artificially year on year to satisfy national education watchdogs (regardless of the fact that results vary according to pupil intake and staff changes); there is rivalry between some teachers for best SATs scores, following announcements about performance-related pay; extra coaching is used to improve statistics; classwork, sometimes a year early, consists mainly of SATs papers, and priority is given to English, maths and science; and scores are benchmarked against test levels. Dr Robert Dato claims that standard testing has produced a generation of 'cheats', in which grades are artificially raised to satisfy parents and educational authorities. He says, 'Grade inflation is rampant in both public schools and at the university level. Now this feeds into the wish of parents to have superior children, and the narcissistic wish of children to be perceived as more powerful than they really are.'

I feel stressed by my exams because I know that I will be in trouble if I get a bad result. Bad results mean that you don't get into good schools and you can't go to university and get a good job. That means you'll be poor for ever.
Joseph, 9

In this fearful climate, many parents worry about their children's grades. Publishers have cottoned on to their concerns, offering literally hundreds of preparation workbooks to encourage children to put in extra study time. If parents and teachers are frightened and stressed, what impact does that have on children? The answer is fairly clear, when even five-year-olds show concern about their academic progress.

Homework

In the USA, eight-year-olds regularly have at least an hour of homework daily, plus 20 to 30 minutes of mandatory reading. The situation is similar in the UK and Canada.

Many studies have looked at the need for, and efficacy of, homework. The majority have come to the same conclusions. Children who do only occasional homework appear to perform better than children whose time is regularly absorbed by an extension of classwork. Homework is not necessarily detrimental, but it does add to a child's stress load. Time that should be spent in free play (*see* page 47) is used up by activities that require concentration and application. Homework is assigned to children increasingly early in their school life, even though many educational researchers say that homework in primary and even elementary school has almost no effect on a child's achievement.

Homework also presents another opportunity for parents to control – and even criticise – their children's academic efforts. Parents often think that they are giving their children a tactical advantage by closely supervising assignments, usually to ensure that their children get the best possible grades. As assignments become increasingly complex, parents find that a huge chunk of the 'quality time' they could be spending with their children is devoted to battling over homework.

According to Rivka Polatnick, a senior researcher at the Center for Working Families at the University of California, Berkeley, 'For many families, this means a choice between homework battles or a "solution" of almost doing it themselves, just because they want to get it over with.' That pattern of intervention can continue long past primary school, robbing teenagers of the opportunity to develop maturity and independence. Polatnick claims that students who've never learned to make their own choices can feel lost and confused when they go on to further education.

George Marsh, headmaster of Dulwich College Preparatory School, defends the institution of homework. He does concede, however, that the standard of work often improves miraculously when it is done at home; clearly, parents are intervening more than is necessary or even healthy. (There is a class issue here; according to studies, middle-class children are significantly more likely to report having done homework or reading together with a parent in the last week.)

Marsh believes that homework offers an opportunity for children to be creative, to enhance their vocabulary, to use the skills they have learned, in a less time-pressured context. Learning how to research and to work independently is vital. Homework also encourages parents to share time with their children. But he is adamant that its value must not be overstressed. At his school, weekly homework has been cut by an hour and 30 minutes over the past few years; he's open to the idea of reducing it still further, if there is evidence that it is putting too much pressure on growing minds. He feels that one of the most important aspects of homework is reading, which enhances vocabulary, encourages good, relaxing habits, and allows children to learn through pleasure and by example. In his view, children should be encouraged to work hard at home for a short period of time and then, as a reward for that work, given freedom to relax and simply to be.

Homework may give parents the chance to share time with their children, but is it 'quality time'? Unfortunately, many parents also use homework to push children harder. In some ways, it's the only control they have over the academic performance of their offspring.

The time I spend with my parents is really only when I am doing my homework. They get cross with me if I don't do it when they want me to, and then I get cross so we end up fighting. They don't think I do my homework well enough and they check it all the time and make me change it. Sometimes I have to write things out lots of times before they think it's all right. I find this stressful because my marks are good at school and my homework is as good as anybody else's. They say that I have to be the best if I want to get into the top stream. **Jamie, 10**

Societal pressures

No parent can be blamed for feeling pressure in the current climate. We all want the best for our children, but we all lack time, so the majority of us do our parenting by going along with what everyone else is doing. It's easy to justify overscheduling, unreasonable expectations and the drive for success if every other parent you know is doing the same. Behind the parenting issues, societal factors are afoot. It all adds up to a potentially unbearable load on today's children, and on the whole question of parenting.

Growing up too soon

One of the side-effects of the modern get-it-now society is the fact that children have been drawn in on the act. No longer content to wait until the appropriate age for certain activities, clothing, possessions and levels of freedom, today's children expect to be (and are) treated as miniature adults, complete with miniature

versions of everything adult. With this comes inevitable responsibility and a need for acquisition; the majority of children are
too young and immature to deal with either of these.

Learning the art of patience is an important part of childhood.
Childhood and adolescence are marked by other rites of passage
– such as understanding the rewards of a job well done, a lesson
learned and a privilege earned – which should be experienced at
appropriate stages through the years. Children find it difficult to
wait for the moment when their power is increased. When they're
six, they can't wait to be seven; when they're 10, they can't wait
to go to 'big school'; when they're 16, they can't wait to get their
driving licence, have some freedom, and go out alone with friends.
This sort of impatience is normal, and even healthy, but children
need to learn to wait for each of the stages, and to feel a sense
of pride as they reach them.

Today, everything is pushed on more quickly. Children go to
school younger, and learn to read earlier. Sport at weekends is
organised with 'adult' equipment, and some sports teams even
go on overseas tours. Children have CD players and all the latest
CDs; they wear mini-Calvin Klein and Paul Smith; they have
mobile telephones and their own computers. Advertising encourages them to look and be seductive and cool; young girls dress
in the same style as their heroines – usually pop stars – many of
whom are scantily dressed and turning a buck by being overtly
sexy. The inevitable question is, 'What next?' How can a child
who has already toured Europe with his football team be satisfied with playing for his school? How can a child who is bom-
barded with sexual messages through the media be content to
hold hands at a school dance?

The pressure on children to become more grown up more
quickly tends also to suit our modern style of parenting. If we
treat our children as if they were older, dress them as if they were
older, and push them on to achieve things at an increasingly early
age, we can justifiably expect 'adult' behaviour.

There are several other problems with the 'adultification' of
childhood. The first is the boredom factor. Many children now
complain of being bored, largely because there is very little to
look forward to in terms of personal goals. They have 'been there,

done it'. They travel, they eat out, they wear designer clothes, and have all the trappings that matter. They perform in ambitious school productions, take part in international sports events, surf the internet and set up email accounts on their own, have their pocket money paid into their own bank account, and use their considerable purchasing power to get whatever it is they need.

When children are exposed to an increasing number of experiences at an early age, they become bored with routine, average activities. They require greater stimulation and excitement to keep them satisfied. What fun can be had in the park with your parents, when you are used to watching satellite TV in your room with your mates? How boring a day trip to the seaside will seem after a two-week holiday in Florida. Who wants to watch a 'U'-rated film, when you've seen an adult-rated movie with your friends?

Once children become accustomed to a steady diet of stimulation, it's very difficult to turn back the clock. This is stressful in itself; the need for constant stimulation indicates a need to keep adrenaline flowing. It can only be detrimental to the emotional and physical health of our generation. Many adults find it hard to switch off on holiday, and seek out extreme sports and other risky activities to satisfy their growing need for stimulation. If children have done it all by the age of 12, what effect will it have on their ability to relax?

I find it hard to relax in the holidays and I feel bored. My mother arranges lots of activities for me but they are usually boring. *Louise, 10*

This adult-style lifestyle is an assault on young and impressionable bodies and minds. Stress becomes a factor because of the emotional and physical demands that it involves. What's more, many children are being left to make the transition from child to adult on their own. Many children come home to an empty house, and have to organise their own time structure and make their own meals. Most are allowed to choose their own entertainment, and this often means that they are subjected to conflicting messages on a regular basis. A vast industry has built up around consumption by children, and an ever-increasing amount of advertising is directed at them. Advertisers use the media, primarily television, to convince children that they need a whole host of possessions in order to reach the status of 'cool', and to be happy.

Television also provides children with experiences of violence, sexuality, broken relationships, and inappropriate mentors. Even children who are at home with parents during the day and after school have unhealthy pressures placed upon them by the various media, including television. Children in the USA spend an average of 38 hours a week exposed to media outside of school; by the time they reach the age of about 11, the average child will have witnessed more than 100,000 acts of violence on TV. Children may be exposed to as many as five violent acts per hour during prime time and an average of 26 violent acts per hour during Saturday morning children's programmes. And that's just violence.

There is a similar problem with sexual imagery, with teenage starlets being paraded regularly in the media in sexy, adult clothing. Sexual precocity is evident increasingly early, and teenage pregnancy is on the increase in the Western world. If children have seen it all on-screen, or heard it all in the lyrics of a pop song, what's to stop them trying it out for themselves? Why should they bother waiting?

Ignoring or disregarding the vital sequential steps in a child's development can have serious consequences. Children are confronted with decisions to make before they have the necessary emotional or psychological tools; they are entrusted with obligations, possessions and responsibility that make them feel more independent and adult, but which are ultimately too much to bear. Children need to be parented and allowed and encouraged to be children. Parents are not always to blame for the situation, but they must take charge and become involved. This way, their children can learn something along the fast lane to adulthood, and avoid the stress that comes with it.

My grandpa gave me a stress smartie and I squeeze it. But sometimes when I am under pressure I just scream. When I am with my friends I control my emotions by trying to keep the tears in. *Lily, 9*

Leisure activities

When children are constantly stimulated, they require constant stimulation. When their hours are filled by activities, they need a busy schedule to keep them occupied. When they do have a little time to spare, it tends to revolve around artificial stimulation: loud music, games consoles, computers and television.

There is nothing wrong with any of these activities – in moderation – but when they become the sole way that a child 'relaxes' and 'recharges', there is a problem. None of these activities will do anything to reduce stress in the short or long term. They also take the place of healthy activities, such as unsupervised play, exercise and quiet reading, thinking or simply daydreaming. They also disrupt sleep, which adds to the stress load (*see* page 118).

In the UK, children spent more than five times as long watching television as they do playing outdoors, and over half of all 7 to 10-year-olds have a TV in their bedroom (and that number increases to 74 per cent for older children). According to a *Radio Times* View of the Nation survey (2001), 67 per cent of parents use TV as a babysitter. Given the long hours spent at school, doing homework and being involved in extra-curricular activities, there is little time left for the kind of activities that every child requires to be emotionally and physically healthy. And with the increased load, these activities are even more important for emotional health.

Does your child really have time for positive interactions, and for personal growth? Have you allowed the stresses and technological advances of modern life to overwhelm the significance of your family? Many households are built not around *interactions*, but around *distractions*, such as the television, the video, the CD player and the computer.

Families and parents are there to guide children through life, to support them through decisions, to love them unconditionally, to teach them what's right and wrong and to establish the basis for interactions and relationships that they will have as adults. If that interaction does not exist, if children are encouraged or even allowed to choose distractions in their place, their stress load will be enormously increased. In the longer term, they'll be facing life alone, or turning to an artificial support such as alcohol in order to deal with it.

Dr Robert Dato is concerned about the choices our children make to relax: 'Let there be no mistake, television, loud music, video games, etc., are not relaxing to children, even though they rationalise this, to the unbridled glee of greedy producers and "artists". Physiologically, these all stimulate already overburdened nervous systems. For instance, the reason "boom boxes" are so popular among children is that so much conflict is going on inside the heads of kids that only loud music will drown out and suppress the horrors in their minds. Psychologically, these activities promote mind pollution.'

Mostly when I feel stressed I listen to my music in my bedroom with the headphones on. My parents hate the music I listen to because there is swearing, but it makes me feel better to listen to it. *Patricia, 12*

THE IMPORTANCE OF PLAY

Play is an essential component of healthy development in children, providing an opportunity for children to develop motor, cognitive, perceptual and social skills. It encourages creativity, imagination and self-sufficiency. In play children discover, solve problems, dramatise fears and, most importantly, enjoy themselves. It also allows children to make choices: for quiet or boisterous games, for a relaxing dawdle or a good sprint around the park. It puts children in control of their entertainment and their environment. They are in charge of their emotional health, because they can do what they feel like doing, what their mind and body say they should be doing. Play can involve interacting with friends, or going it alone.

The fact is that children have far less leisure time than they once had. And, having lost confidence in our ability to rely on the family and the household for entertainment, we fill their days with a multitude of 'improving' activities.

What does this have to do with stress? If children are not relaxing in the true sense of the word (*see* page 134), their stress levels are not being reduced at any stage of the day. They are actually increased by the constant stimulation.

I don't have time to play because I have to do my homework and go to ballet and swimming and practise my recorder and do boring things with my mum and dad. The thing that would make me less stressed would be no homework and more fun. **Kate, 7**

Broken families

The life of many single-parent family set-ups is anything but fractured, but there are undoubtedly implications for children in broken families, who lose a parent or siblings through divorce. The trauma that can ensue is stressful for all involved.

Broken families are not necessarily dysfunctional, but the family members involved often do not have the same network of close, loving carers on which to rely. Divorce or death are not always at the root of this problem; today, extended families are often separated by hundreds of miles. Children grow up without regular contact with grandparents, cousins, aunts and uncles, all of whom can, at times, play an important role in development and, of course, stress relief. With parental expectations being so high, children often feel less than confident about relating negative information to their parents. In this case, other family members can provide an outlet and advice without recrimination and with unconditional acceptance and love. Children today have one less avenue down which they can turn.

The effect of divorce on children should not be underestimated. Even if a child appears to take it in his stride, he may have deep-seated concerns and worries that are never really expressed. It is particularly damaging when parents continue their battle post-divorce. Studies have shown that staying in the same community and school post-divorce is less disruptive for children. Unfortunately, families often have to move. Frequently, too, there's less money to live on, and the children have to adjust to a different lifestyle.

The post-divorce stress load clearly relates to more than the simple, immediate loss of a parent. Children may also feel that they have to be more self-reliant, to take the pressure off an unhappy home life, or an upset parent. Their basic security system becomes flawed, and one of the bricks of their emotional foundation is effectively shifted. It's also common for children to feel guilty, particularly if they have heard parents arguing about them at any time. They may also feel angry, frightened, and worried that they will be abandoned by or 'divorced from' their parents.

We live in an uncertain world, where around one-third of marriages end in divorce. Over the last 30 years, the annual divorce rate has increased in the UK from about 50,000 to more than 100,000. A 2000 study by the Family Policy Studies Centre paints a picture of the traditional family in decline, with fewer people marrying and more divorcing, more step-families, more cohabitation, more single mothers, fewer children and more older people. According to the centre's director, Ceridwen Roberts, 'Family life in Britain is undergoing unprecedented change. Marriage and partnerships are much more fragile than they were and more people are living on their own.'

The family is a child's stable environment that allows growth, self-understanding, comfort and love. It's not surprising that many children feel unsettled and under pressure, when the very basis of their life could change at any given moment. They will find it difficult to learn the trust that is necessary for self-acceptance, friendship, successful relationships and security – all of which are necessary for maturation into a young adult who can react to, interact with and adapt to the surrounding world.

It is certainly worth considering the implications of absent or arguing parents on a child's psyche – and on his stress levels. In Chapter 8, we'll look at some of the ways to help children through divorce.

As for children who are bereaved, Dr Richard Harrington argues in the *Journal of the Royal Society of Medicine* that there is little evidence that such children suffer mental health or behavioural problems. He believes that children who witness their parents separating or divorcing are much more likely to develop depression than those who experience the death of a parent.

I feel stressed when my parents fight because they might get divorced. When they fight I be really quiet and hope they don't notice me. All of my friends' parents fight too and some of them don't live together any more. *Lucy, 7*

Violence

Clearly, increased violence on television, in song lyrics and in computer games can increase the stress load on children. But what about the violence that many children from 'good' families are now accustomed to seeing, hearing about and witnessing on a daily basis? Children live in a society where acts of violence are the norm. While very few children actually experience murders and shootings in their school (although these seem to be on the increase), their awareness of them is likely to increase fear, and stress. If the once-safe sanctuary of school holds the possibility of danger, feelings of fear become more common in youngsters, who can have little idea of their own risk.

This type of violence can be one of the causes of post-traumatic stress disorder in children, but it can also add to the stress load of an ordinary child living an ordinary life.

On a more direct level, more than half of all British schoolchildren have been bullied, according to a report by the charity Young Voices, and Oxford University in the UK. The evidence of the children, aged between 13 and 19, from rural and inner-city schools, is alarming. One in 10 reported severe bullying, including physical violence. Many felt they could not tell anyone what was happening to them; their treatment by other children had sent them into a spiral of depression and misery. Many went on to become bullies themselves in a desperate attempt to deal with feelings of powerlessness.

> The NSPCC calculates that 40 per cent of abuse on children is committed by other children, and the true scale is much deeper than that, because not all children report violence.

Bullying in childhood has also been linked to a number of problems in adulthood, including alcohol abuse, violence against children, marital breakdown and psychiatric disorder. A 12-year-old bully is three times as likely as other pupils to have a criminal conviction by the age of 24.

The torment is so severe that many victims told the Young Voices researchers that they had attempted to take their own lives. Suicide among adolescents has risen in the past decade, and now attempts among under-14s seem to be going up too. According to Professor Keith Hawton of the Centre for Suicide Research in Oxford, girls largely account for the increase in non-fatal overdoses and self-inflicted injuries. They outnumber boys by at least six to one. Psychologists believe that the concept of death can now develop very early in stressed children, at around seven or eight years of age.

Although the average child may not be in contact with such violence, they live in a society where it occurs. In itself, this has the potential to blight childhood. According to reports in Scottish newspapers, for example, children as young as eight have been attacked in the street and robbed of their latest toys and accessories (in particular, scooters, mobile phones and designer clothing). In most cases, the children were either attacked physically, abused verbally or threatened.

The BBC's survey of 3,000 young people in England found that one in four had been robbed and four out of five knew someone who had been robbed.

One of the reasons why we aren't allowed to bring our mobile phones to school is because we might get mugged. I know lots of guys who have been beat up for their mobile phones. *David, 10*

Other factors

Every aspect of a child's lifestyle has the ability to enhance or detract from his health. Stress isn't always a physical response to an emotional situation, or even to an external pressure. In fact, anything that places a strain on the body can be considered 'stressful'. Many aspects of daily life in the 21st century have an impact – some stressors are less obvious and more insidious than others, but they all take their toll and add to the possibility of overload.

Environment

Every chemical with which your child comes into contact has to be dealt with – or 'detoxified' – by the body. If your child uses drugs to control eczema or asthma, for example, they place a strain on the body. When your child walks to school, or sits in a pushchair on the way to the shops, he breathes in carbon monoxide that poisons his body. Scented shampoos and soaps, cleaning products, perfumes, radiation from televisions, computers, mobile telephones, electricity masts, pollution, smoke and even ordinary household dirt and dust have to be dealt with by your child's body on a daily basis.

All of these environmental factors are stressors, putting pressure on growing bodies. Noise pollution, which has recently been shown to raise blood pressure in children, is another. Many children choose loud music, television and noisy computer games as their leisure activity, so it's not surprising that sustained periods of stress are the result.

Children also ingest chemicals in food. These not only put a strain on the body, robbing it of key nutrients, but can also actually impair the way the mind and body work, putting it under tremendous strain during a period of intense growth and development.

All these factors can be considered to be stressors because they have a negative effect on the body. It is forced to make a series of rapid physiological changes, called 'adaptive responses', which deal with threatening or demanding situations.

Diet

Chapter 5 looks at the positive effects of a healthy diet, but what about the negative effects? What does diet have to do with stress?

An unhealthy diet has the potential to undermine even the most emotionally secure child, largely because nutrition has such a dramatic effect on emotional health. A diet based around 'junk' and 'fast food' puts a child's body under pressure; energy that should be directed towards living, growing, learning and developing is diverted to detoxifying, processing and struggling to find sufficient nutrients.

There's another factor at work here. The average 21st-century child's diet is extremely high in sugar, a refined carbohydrate that causes a sudden energy boost and a subsequent fall. The effects of refined carbohydrates are most obvious at birthday parties – when cakes, biscuits and sweets cause children to become manically energetic. A short time later, it all falls apart as their blood-sugar levels slump. This process can cause mood swings, irritability, temper tantrums, lethargy and tears. If you think these sound surprisingly like the symptoms of stress, you're right.

Blood sugar and stress are strongly related. When blood sugar drops, adrenaline (the stress hormone) kicks in, and brings all the symptoms of stress, including feelings of being out of control, emotional and irritable. When blood-sugar levels are stable, there are no such surges of adrenaline.

Children are often tearful and tired as they come out of school because of low blood sugar. They are hungry and need more fuel to raise blood-sugar levels. If their lunch was based around refined carbohydrates (such as white bread, biscuits, sweets, jellies and soft drinks), their post-school slump will be worse than that of children whose lunch included fruit, wholegrain breads or pastas, vegetables and fresh juices. It's easy to offer a quick pick-me-up in the form of a sweet or a chocolate bar. The symptoms will improve instantly, but you'll have showdown time well before dinner, as the child's levels slump again.

Furthermore, an unhealthy diet can cause a child to be less capable of managing stress. Refined foods are, for example, stripped of B vitamins, which are necessary for the health of the nervous system. Other nutrients, such as those that maintain a healthy immune system, tend to be low in the average child's diet, which means that children become run-down and more susceptible to small setbacks.

Diet really does matter. A good diet is one of the key ways to help children to overcome stress; poor diet is one of the main reasons why children may appear to be suffering from so much more stress today.

Sleep

Sleep is just as important as diet, but it is often considered low on the scale of essential activities. In our 24/7 society, you can do virtually anything around the clock, from getting a haircut to shopping for groceries. Children are part of this culture, too, and it's difficult to explain to them the importance of sleep when the whole family stays up into the early hours. Sleep is important for children if they are to manage stress, and a lack of sleep is also one of the key causes of stress.

Even occasional sleeping problems can make daily life feel more stressful or cause a reduction in productivity. A survey in the USA showed that children who get enough sleep report a better ability to concentrate, accomplish required tasks and handle minor irritations. In contrast, those with a higher 'sleep deficit' (regularly getting less than required) showed impairment of ability to perform tasks involving memory, learning, logical reasoning and mathematical calculation. They also found relationships at home and with friends more difficult. Childhood is a period of intense learning and physical and emotional development, and it is crucial that children have all the resources at their disposal.

I sleep about six hours a night. I try to get to sleep earlier but I can't so I read, watch TV or play with things in my bedroom. Usually my mum and dad are asleep before I am.
Lara, 11

Professor Jim Horne, who runs the Sleep Research Laboratory at Loughborough University in the UK, feels that sleep deprivation in children affects the brain. The fact that sleep is vital for the cerebrum is clearly demonstrated by sleep-loss studies. Whereas most of the body can physically relax and recover in wakefulness, to levels similar to those of sleep, the cerebrum cannot. Even when the eyes are closed and the mind is blank, the waking brain remains in a state of high activity and quiet readiness. He says that the cerebral (brain) metabolic rate is particularly high in three- to eight-year-old children, which suggests that this organ may be in need of even greater recovery during sleep at this time.

Adolescents may be particularly affected by a lack of sleep. A recent study showed that when the body does not get enough sleep, even over one night, a 'sleep debt' begins to build. This debt increases, until it is 'paid off' by a sufficiently long period of sleep. In general, pre-adolescent children may be getting enough sleep, particularly if parents help to protect sleep times. Older adolescents, however, are staying up later, rising earlier and incurring sleep debts that may never be 'repaid'. A US study indicates that adolescents commonly experience 'microsleeps, attention lapses, decreased reaction times, impaired divergent thinking skills, impaired mental functioning, low mood, and a higher rate of accidents and injuries'. Sleep continues to be a critical issue in emotional and intellectual development throughout the teen years. (For more on problems associated with adolescents, *see* page 123.)

Many of these symptoms indicate and create high stress levels, and cause children to feel that they are unable to manage. Lack of sleep, or poor sleep, also puts a strain on the body, which is forced to function without the necessary renewal and repair that sleep has to offer.

Exercise

The importance of exercise cannot be overstated, and Chapter 5 looks at the positive benefits of exercise in relation to stress. Children who have inadequate exercise are missing out on an important way of letting off steam, and releasing the adrenaline that builds up in the course of the day. Children are forced to sit for long periods of time at a desk, concentrating and 'behaving' well. Even pre-school children are often carted from activity to activity without any time to expend physical energy. Not only does a lack of exercise increase stress levels by disrupting normal, healthy sleep (*see above*), but it also causes dips in concentration, focus and even brain function, making normal school work more difficult and demanding.

How widespread is the problem in the Western world?

- A UK study of 1,000 children confirms that half of girls and a third of boys do not even do the equivalent of a 10-minute brisk walk once a week.

- Less than half of Britain's children do 30 minutes of exercise a day – the minimum recommended by the government to keep fit and healthy. A survey by Norwich Union Healthcare showed that only one in eight children takes one hour of exercise a day (the ideal), although most say that they enjoy sport at school.

- 60 per cent of Canadian youngsters do not meet the average fitness standards for their age group.

- Since 1977, three-quarters of schools in the USA have either terminated the role of physical education teachers or reassigned them to other classes. Consequently, most children receive only one or two physical education classes a week.

- Around half of US children do not engage in regular physical activity.

Immunisation

This may sound like an odd one out, particularly in light of the fact that it is designed to prevent serious illness, but immunisation undoubtedly puts a strain on young bodies, leaving them more susceptible to stress. In other words, immunisation is a physical stressor. For a full explanation of the potential dangers of immunisation, *see* my book *Commonsense Healthcare for Children* (Piatkus, 2001). If a child is already under stress, or suffering from a chronic illness that may already be placing a strain on the body, it's worth considering whether they should be immunised.

Every aspect of your child's lifestyle has the ability to enhance or detract from his health; even the more insidious stressors, such as noise and constant contact with chemical cleansers, for example, take their toll and add to the possibility of overload. Physical overload is as much a factor in a child's overall wellbeing and ability to respond to stress and emotional or psychological overload. In Chapter 5 we'll look at what children really need to cope with stress and 21st-century life. Before that, however, we will look at the effects of stress on the body. Is it really cause for concern? The facts are nothing short of staggering.

CHAPTER THREE

Overburdened: The effects of stress in children

Most adults can list at least one or two symptoms of stress – the result of the stress response (*see* Chapter 1) – from which they have suffered. In the short term, adrenaline causes the body literally to shut down as it prepares for fight or flight. This is the reason why we lose concentration, why we feel irritable, why we suffer from digestive problems and high blood pressure. And with adrenaline surging through our bodies, we experience tension, headaches, shakiness, tearfulness, anger and even fear.

Although many of the symptoms are physical, even emotional stress has a profound effect on the workings of the body. The mind-body relationship is now firmly established, above and beyond our knowledge of the hormones that are secreted during periods of stress. An argument with a loved one, or falling out with a best friend at school, can be as physically detrimental as long hours working at a computer, or facing exams. When children are under pressure, they respond in exactly the same way as adults.

ADRENAL GLANDS
The adrenal glands, which sit on top of the kidneys, are responsible for pumping out adrenaline in response to stress or when blood-sugar levels are low, but they do much more than this.

The glands are made up of two parts, the medulla and the cortex. The medulla produces adrenaline, while the cortex, which is stimulated by hormones from the pituitary gland, produces three kinds of hormones that are absolutely crucial for growth and physical development: cortisol, aldosterone and the sex hormones, oestrogen and testosterone.

Cortisol helps to control fat, protein and carbohydrate metabolism. In turn it helps energy production, thyroid hormone production and the strength of the immune system. Cortisol is produced at different levels during the day – ideally, highest in the morning when you are ready for the day ahead and lowest at night when you are going to bed. This rhythm is as important as the amount of cortisol that the adrenals are producing.

When a child is under stress, the normal rhythm of the stress hormones, particularly cortisol, can be upset. This can affect his body in many ways. If a child has low energy levels and finds it difficult to get up in the morning, for example, this can be due to an abnormal adrenal rhythm.

If stress continues for any length of time, the adrenal glands increase their output of cortisol. Although this rise seems to be essential for survival, continued stress and cortisol levels that are persistently high are harmful to health. Any stimulus that increases secretion of cortisol is described as a stressor.

If too much cortisol is produced, the efficiency of the immune system is reduced, making the body more prone to infection and inflammation, and, according to some research, cancers, auto-immune conditions, ageing and arthritis. Cortisol also increases blood-glucose levels, which may lead to the development of diabetes (*see* page 66). It prepares the organs of the body to be more sensitive to the action of nor-adrenaline and adrenaline, and suppresses the inflammatory response.

Emotional factors

In the short term, stress is related to a variety of different problems affecting children. First, it makes it more difficult for them to forge and sustain relationships. Childhood is a time of great self-consciousness, indecision, peer pressure and a growing understanding of the nature of friendship, love and acceptance. When children are stressed, these experiences are heightened, and children become overly sensitive to normal feelings and emotions.

It's interesting to note that children now feel acutely concerned and stressed by relationships. Professor Stephen Palmer, from London's City University, who led a study into the stress in children, says, 'Children often reported that they felt stressed by difficulties in forming good relationships with their peers. They had trouble making friends or felt excluded from groups that they wanted to be part of. That was said to be very stressful.'

It's a double-edged sword. Not only are relationships a source of stress, but any problems are enhanced by the chronic levels of stress experienced by children. Stress affects relationships with family and friends. Many adults have experienced periods when stress has threatened to drive them over the edge, causing them to shout at or lose patience with their children, partners or friends.

Adults can often rationalise the feelings, and take steps to control the symptoms of stress. A child, however, may have no idea why he or she feels so gloomy, irritable, tearful or powerless. My survey showed that children often feel out of control, and cope by shutting themselves away. Stress makes it difficult to form relationships, or to feel loving and cheerful. When children are under pressure, they often exhibit what is described as 'naughty', 'disruptive', 'emotional' or 'irritable' behaviour. It's difficult for others to respond kindly and lovingly in the face of such negativity, and this has an impact on emotional well-being as well as on physical health.

The thing that makes me most angry is when my friends think bad things about me. **Scott, 8**

Some interesting links have been made recently in relation to emotional stress and physical health. For example, young girls with close relationships with their fathers may enter puberty later than girls with distant or non-existent links. Good mother-daughter relationships may also delay the onset of sexual maturity, according to a report in the *Journal of Personality and Social Psychology*. A research team from the Vanderbilt University in Nashville, Tennessee, found that the 'quality of fathers' investment' was the most important factor in their study of development. Bruce Ellis, who led the research, followed the progress of 173 girls for eight years, starting before they entered education. He found that where fathers were observed to be more affectionate with their daughters, and spent more time caring for them before they reached school, the girls tended to enter puberty later than those who had poorer relationships.

The team was baffled by the exact reason for this delay, but Mr Ellis speculates that it may be related to stress, or lack of it: 'It may be the particular kind of stress associated with either low levels of positive family relationships, a lack of paternal investment, or both, that provokes earlier puberty.' It seems that lower levels of parental involvement, and a lack of time spent developing a positive family dynamic, can have a surprisingly dramatic effect on physical health.

Furthermore, according to research supported by the National Institute of Child Health and Human Development in the USA, children whose parents reported doing the most activities with them tended to have the highest scores on an applied maths test. The researchers found that parents who had a warm relationship with their children – who hugged them often, and told them they loved them and were proud of them – reported that their children were happier, less withdrawn, and had fewer behaviour problems than others. Although around two-thirds of parents reported behaving warmly towards their children, including joking or playing together several times a week, the nature of the relationship appears to change as children age and spend more time with peers. Almost 80 per cent of parents of pre-schoolers reported high levels of warmth in their relationships, compared with only 57 per cent of parents of school-age children.

It's not surprising that a warm family relationship encourages a sense of well-being. It's equally clear that an erratic relationship, or one in which both children and adults are stressed, is less likely to be a source of stress relief. In fact, in many cases, it can add to levels of anxiety, particularly when children are subjected to deep-rooted insecurity.

The most stressful thing in my life is fighting with my brother and having a massive fight with my parents. We fight all the time because everybody is stressed and angry all the time. *Kylie, 11*

In the short term, stress can cause enormous problems with emotional health. Children learn to recognise symptoms and know that they are associated with feeling unhappy, unwell, nervous or frightened. Several potential scenarios can result from this. In the first instance, children can literally become phobic or intensely preoccupied by events that they know are stressful. For example, if a child faces a difficult test when he's seven, and experiences a host of debilitating symptoms, he'll learn to dread tests. The feelings and symptoms of stress will be exacerbated and exaggerated with each ensuing test.

Secondly, if stressed children find it difficult to cope with relationships at home or at school, and experience distress, they can literally 'opt out'. This means choosing not to commit or to put themselves in a position where it matters so much. Normal emotions are heightened under stress and, rather than experience paranoia, distress, anger or loss of control, many children will resolve simply never to put themselves in that situation again. This is a short-term problem with long-term ramifications.

Thirdly, stressed children may give up more easily, learning never to push themselves to a point where they experience unpleasant symptoms. They risk never experiencing the joy and sense of achievement that comes with mastering something, and adapting successfully to the normal stresses of day-to-day life. They may also become fearful, and reluctant to try new experiences. Taking risks is a part of life, and every child needs to learn to make rational decisions based on his or her abilities. If children learn at a young age to avoid anything that leads to unpleasant feelings, they'll never understand that it's possible to overcome those feelings, and to succeed.

> **I** don't like to try new things because I hate it when people look at me and think that I am rubbish. *Luke, 6*

At the opposite end of the scale are children who become literally addicted to stress. Like many adults, they love the feeling of adrenaline surging through their body, which can, for some people, provide a 'buzz' and a sensation of power. While this quality can often be controlled and even harnessed in adulthood, in children it can manifest itself as manic behaviour, a 'what next?' mentality and easy boredom. It also leads to a cycle of a superficial 'high' and then a 'crash', with children swinging from feeling fantastic to being dangerously low.

Physical effects

Pressure can have other physical effects, which can affect the way a child grows, develops and even learns.

Immunity

A child's immune system can be compromised if he is under stress, even in the short term. Stress will prevent it working efficiently. Not only will he be more prone to infections, he will find it difficult to fight them off if he does become ill, and infections may linger for weeks or even months. Stress has been implicated in flare-ups of arthritis and asthma, and the urinary tract can also be affected. A natural balance of friendly and unfriendly organisms normally co-exists in the body's digestive and urinary systems. Constant anxiety can destroy this immunological balance, leading to an excessive growth of harmful bacteria and infection. One study showed that when students who are approaching exams are given a small wound, the damage takes up to four days longer than normal to heal.

A child's immune system is immature, and children are much more susceptible to illness than adults. It's a normal and healthy part of the maturation process. However, if a child is chronically or even frequently ill, he'll never build up the resources he needs to become and stay healthy. His sleep patterns are likely to be disrupted, he'll find it more difficult to concentrate at school, and he will feel 'different' from his peers, which is extremely unsettling for a growing child. What's more, he'll be more likely to miss school, which will affect his overall education, relationships with friends, and, ultimately, his self-esteem.

Asthma

Experts have found that chronically stressed children are far more likely to have asthma attacks than children who are less stressed. Research carried out at the University of Helsinki in Finland, and published in the *Lancet* medical journal, shows that the link between a stressful life and wheeziness could result from damage to the immune system. Even the children of excessively anxious parents have been found to be more likely to develop asthma.

For 18 months, the researchers followed a group of 90 child asthma patients in Glasgow, aged between six and 13, noting when they had attacks, and finding out about the stressful events in their lives. Stressors included poor housing, having a parent or relative with a chronic mental or physical illness, the death of a grandparent, family break-ups or being bullied at school. The effect of a single 'severe event' was delayed, but there was more than one and a half times the normal risk of an asthma attack in the following four weeks. When a 'severe event' affected a child who was also considered to be suffering from ongoing stress, the risk rose sharply. These children were almost three times more likely to have asthma attacks. (All the risks were even worse for girls, and for those who had had three or more attacks within the previous six months.)

According to the researchers, 'Stress may well be a major factor in increasing susceptibility to viral infections. These studies make a strong case for psychosocial stress increasing the risk of somatic diseases, particularly those that result from the weakening of the body's natural defence mechanisms.'

Brain function

One important line of research has focused on brain systems that control stress hormones such as cortisol. In an emergency, cortisol and other stress hormones help the body make energy available to enable an effective response, temporarily suppress the immune response, and sharpen attention. However, a number of studies conducted in people with depression indicate that excess cortisol released over a long time may have negative consequences for health. Excess cortisol may cause shrinking of the hippocampus, a brain structure required for the formation of certain types of memory. This is a serious worry for children, both in the short and long term.

Blood-sugar levels

Stress plays havoc with blood-sugar levels, which can cause both 'hyperactive' symptoms, and the inevitable slump, with its familiar symptoms of tearfulness, fatigue, temper tantrums, bad mood and lack of concentration. It is obviously unhealthy for children to be at the mercy of these types of mood swings, and it also affects their ability to interact, concentrate and learn.

Dr Marilyn Glenville, author of a number of bestselling books on health, suggests that perhaps stress should be looked at more closely as a cause of hyperactivity. Because of the link between blood sugar and adrenaline, and because hyperactive children exhibit so many symptoms of blood-sugar imbalance, perhaps the problem has been addressed from the wrong angle. Rather than 'depressing' children with the drug Ritalin, whose use is becoming increasingly common, Dr Glenville feels we should instead be looking at the stressors in children's life. Some children may be particularly sensitive or susceptible to stress (*see* page 14), which could affect their ability to concentrate, and their self-control.

Many experts now believe that 'attention deficit disorder' (the most recent term for hyperactivity) is nothing more than a buzz term for the late 20th century. The fact that children are hyperactive or have difficulty concentrating is probably due more to the fact that Western diets are so poor, children are forced at an increasingly early age to sit still in a classroom or nursery with large numbers of other children, they watch too much television, get inadequate sleep and get little or no exercise. All these factors are stressors, putting undue pressure on the body. If the same restrictions were placed on an adult, the same negative effects could be expected.

Alarmingly, numerous studies show that teachers believe that most of their students have deficits, disorders or problems. In one study, 57 per cent of boys and 42 per cent of girls were deemed 'overactive'. In another study of boys, 30 per cent were called 'overactive', 46 per cent 'disruptive', 43 per cent had a 'short' attention span. Is stress playing a part here?

Diabetes mellitus

The onset of this type of diabetes is now increasingly common in childhood, but is it a long- or short-term effect of stress in children? It is certainly related to the problems associated with blood sugar. There is now a huge increase in Type II diabetes in children; this type is also known as mature onset diabetes, or MOD, and normally strikes in middle age. According to Dr Glenville, 'Although diet obviously has a lot to do with it, there is also a strong relationship with stress. It's a bit of a chicken-and-egg situation. Is stress making children eat more junk food, or are cravings for sweet foods caused by the effects of adrenaline in the body?'

Over 90 per cent of diabetics have Type II diabetes, and the increase is certainly a product of our modern world. It's now been linked with stress, as well as poor eating habits, and these may well be the reasons why it is being seen in children to such a degree.

Headaches

This is a triple-whammy. Headaches are not only caused by tension, but also by the effects of adrenaline and by low blood sugar, all of which are associated with stress. They can also be the result of an inadequate level of B vitamins, which is also associated with stress. The body requires more B vitamins during stressful situations but, paradoxically, it is also able to absorb far less, as the digestive system effectively shuts down during periods of stress. Headaches can be debilitating and lead to loss of concentration, an overreliance on painkillers and cause children to miss school and other, more relaxing activities. If a child has frequent headaches, stress is very likely to be at least one of the causes.

Digestive problems

Diarrhoea, nausea and vomiting are all common side-effects of stress, as digestion is disrupted through the stress response. More seriously, chronic problems such as irritable bowel syndrome (IBS) and colitis are on the increase in childhood.

IBS is a digestive disorder that causes abdominal pain, bloating, gas or wind, diarrhoea, and constipation – or a combination of these problems. It is caused by a problem in how the intestines, or bowels, work, and it affects people of all ages, including children. People with IBS tend to have an overly sensitive intestine that suffers muscle spasms in response to food, gas or wind, and, notably, stress. In children, IBS tends to be either diarrhoea-predominant or pain-predominant. Diarrhoea-predominant IBS is most common in under-threes, while pain-predominant IBS mainly affects children over five. In younger children the pain tends to occur around the navel area, and in older children, in the lower left part of the abdomen.

The pain is crampy and gets worse with eating, and better after passing stools or wind. In addition to the above symptoms, children with IBS may also have headache, nausea, or mucus in the stool. Weight loss may occur if a child eats less in an attempt to avoid pain. Some children first develop symptoms after a stressful event, such as teething, a bout of flu, school problems, or difficulties at home. While stress does not *cause* IBS, it can trigger symptoms. The increased stress load of the average child may be one of the main reasons why the condition is on the increase.

Any digestive symptoms, whether serious or transient, should be taken seriously. A child's nutritional status will suffer if his digestion is impaired, and this will affect his growth and ability to perform. School days missed through illness put a child at a social and academic disadvantage, and symptoms can be enormously embarrassing, adding to the stress load. No child wants to feel different from his peers, and most children feel embarrassed by abnormal bowel movements, or the possibility of an 'accident'. Furthermore, the pain and discomfort associated with most digestive conditions reduces quality of life to such an extent that every area suffers.

Digestive problems are becoming more common, and it is vital to be alert to the long-term ramifications for children who, as a result of stress, cannot eat normally or live a normal life.

Malnutrition or sub-nutrition

It seems unlikely that children in the Western world, with such a plentiful food supply, could be malnourished, but studies show that this is indeed the case. In fact, the Western diet is often very poor, particularly in children, and this can lead to malnourishment. Stress is another culprit. In combination with a poor diet, stress can cause serious health problems relating to nutrition.

A 1995 study in the UK revealed that only 50 per cent of children under the age of five eat any fruit, and the same number eat only peas and carrots (and potatoes), if they eat any vegetables at all. This problem was highlighted again in a 2001 study. In the USA, only 9 per cent of children aged from six to 11 eat the recommended five-a-day of fruits and vegetables. In a study of 1,800 New York children, 15 per cent ate no vegetables and 20 per cent ate no fruit. This is doubly alarming when stress is taken into consideration, since part of the stress response involves a shutting down, or slowing, of the digestive process. Any nutrition available is probably not absorbed, and the few nutrients that do make their way into the average child may never be used.

Does nutrition have a major impact on children's health? This is a complex subject; my book *Commonsense Healthcare for Children* (*see* Further reading) gives a clear picture of the risks and the options. A number of basic facts need to be considered:

- It is estimated that 3–4 per cent of children in primary school have severe iron-deficiency anaemia. In the 18-month to two-and-a-half-year bracket, the number increases to one in eight toddlers. Many more children probably have mild forms of iron deficiency. In many cases, low blood-iron levels translate to poor school performance. Studies link low iron levels with decreased attention and concentration, irritability, low IQ tests (especially in vocabulary), perceptual difficulties, and low achievement. Iron deficiency is one of the most common problems affecting children in the developing world; it's extraordinary that it should be on the increase in some of the world's wealthiest nations.

- Recent research provides compelling evidence that undernutrition during any period of childhood can have detrimental effects on the cognitive development of children and their productivity as adults. When a child eats poorly, he does not develop at a normal rate, and some fail to develop normally at all.

- Children who are deficient in just one or two key nutrients can show symptoms that will affect their development and their school work. For example, a shortage of B vitamins can translate as fatigue, listlessness, moodiness and even attention problems. The B vitamins are crucial to the development of a healthy nervous system, and long-term deficiency (even mild deficiency) can lead to depression and neurological problems, among other things. A shortage of vitamin C can result in an impaired immune system, constipation and bleeding gums. A low calcium intake will affect bones and teeth, and cause muscle cramping and poor growth.

Allergies

Allergies relate to immunity and to problems with nutrient absorption, both of which are related to stress. Many food allergies have been linked to a deficiency of digestive enzymes, which could be a direct result of inadequate digestion caused by stress.

The incidence of allergy-related conditions in children, including food allergies, have increased dramatically in the past decade. A recent survey of 3,000 children aged six and seven found that 23 per cent of them had suffered from asthma at some point in their life; when a similar study was carried out in 1992, the figure was 13 per cent. The survey, by Dr Mohammad Shamssain and colleagues at the University of Sunderland, also found that 28 per cent of children coughed at night – a symptom of asthma – compared with 16 per cent in the earlier study. The UK has one of the highest incidences of asthma in the world; indeed, its incidence in the UK has increased 30 times over the last 30 years! The severity of the illness has also become worse. There's no doubt that stress has played a role in this.

Eczema, also on the increase, is believed to be related to digestive problems, which are affected by the stress response.

ADRENAL EXHAUSTION

When they are placed under constant pressure, the adrenal glands can become exhausted and fail to perform properly. This has numerous implications; the most serious is an inability to release the correct hormones in the correct amounts. Adrenal fatigue can affect sexuality, self-esteem, energy levels and an overall ability to cope. In the end, the body reaches a state known as 'burn-out'.

Stress hormones not only produce the stress reaction, they also help us to tolerate prolonged stress. But stress uses them up, and the supply is limited. If there are inadequate nutrients in the body to make replacement supplies (a common side-effect of prolonged stress), or if we use them more quickly than we make them (always the case in periods of prolonged stress), they simply run dry. This condition is known as adrenal exhaustion, and involves a decreased stress tolerance, which means that we are often unable to cope with even mildly stressful situations. Blood-sugar levels are also reduced, with less energy going to the brain and other muscles in the body, resulting in chronic, debilitating fatigue.

Menstrual problems

This may seem an obscure reference in relation to children, but in the long term stress may have serious ramifications. PMS (pre-menstrual syndrome), which blights the life of so many women, is now associated with stress levels. Part of this has to do with diet and blood-sugar levels (*see* page 65), which means that women feel under increased stress in the lead-up to their period, but there is also a direct correlation between stress and PMS symptoms. The symptoms can be anything from uncomfortable to seriously debilitating.

Stress affects hormones in dramatic ways. According to Dr Marilyn Glenville, stress has a direct effect on the reproductive system. She says, 'Women going through a bereavement or other kind of trauma, for instance, can stop having periods. Furthermore, the hormone prolactin can also be released when we are under stress and this hormone is known to aggravate breast tenderness and may also be connected with depression.' She also points out that the adrenal glands are responsible for producing the sex hormones oestrogen and testosterone, in addition to those produced by the ovaries. This can not only delay the onset of periods – a stress factor for young girls yearning to be like their peers – but it may also cause long-term problems with fertility. If the adrenal glands are effectively 'worn out' (*see* above), they will not be able to produce the hormones necessary for ovulation. Later in life, around menopause, the adrenal glands take over from the ovaries, producing oestrogen that can protect against osteoporosis.

All parents have a responsibility for their children's future health, however distant that future may seem. If our own children are unable to have their own children because of stress they experienced in childhood, we will have a lot to answer for in years to come.

I don't really have anyone to talk to when I feel stressed and angry and sad so I listen to loud music and pretend that everything is all right. **Jamie, 9**

On his questionnaire, Jamie said that he regularly suffered from the following: headaches, stomach upsets, trouble getting up in the morning, irritability, being worried about things, tearfulness, difficulty concentrating, feeling out of control, eczema and asthma.

Strokes

Stress causes the blood to clot more quickly, causing a dramatic rise in the possibility of a stroke. This problem has always been associated with late adulthood, partly because of the risk factors involved – high blood pressure, a poor diet, being overweight, high cholesterol and inadequate exercise are clearly indicated in stroke, as is stress. The risk for women increases as they approach menopause, and continues to increase thereafter, probably because of the loss of the natural hormone oestrogen.

Is it too improbable that stroke could affect our children? Many children have a poor diet, and poor leisure habits. Because of increased stress load, children are at the mercy of adrenaline, which raises blood pressure; the increased pressure on the heart causes it to enlarge and weaken over time. When combined with obesity, smoking (also on the increase in teens), high cholesterol or diabetes, stroke risk increases several times. Type II diabetes is on the increase in children. And if stress is playing havoc with hormones, what is the effect?

It may sound a tenuous link, but a Louisiana study showed many American three-year-olds with fatty deposits in their aortas, and one in six teenagers with a coronary artery blocked. So, perhaps stroke in children does not seem so unlikely. Althoug᠁ stress is only one part of the equation, given the now-established link between stress and heart disease, we have a potentially dangerous scenario on our hands. A new study published in 2001 showed that up to 1,000 children under the age of 16 in the UK have had a stroke. That number is even greater in the USA. While the cause has not yet been confirmed, the link with stress cannot be ruled out.

Liver damage

Like every other system in the body, the liver is under pressure in stressful conditions. The liver is the detoxifying organ of the body, responsible for clearing out the toxins to which our children are in contact. These come in the form of environmental toxins (*see* page 52), food additives and preservatives, and every other substance to which they come into contact. Although the liver has the ability to renew itself, it can, however, become less efficient and eventually fail. Stress causes the liver to produce glycogen to keep blood-sugar levels steady. The high incidence of diabetes in children is, perhaps, one indication that liver exhaustion is occurring in today's children. (*See* substance abuse, below)

Eating disorders

Eating disorders – most commonly, anorexia, bulimia and compulsive overeating – are responsible for the highest number of deaths from psychiatric illness. The Eating Disorders Association estimates that about 165,000 people in the UK have an eating disorder, with 10 per cent dying as a result; experts believe that these figures are conservative. At one time, eating disorders were thought to affect primarily pre-teen and teenage girls in upper socio-economic groups. However, according to the latest statistics, eating disorders are increasingly apparent in younger children and boys, across all socio-economic groups.

Feeling inadequate, perfectionism, a need for control and a desire to please and to gain approval are all symptoms of stress disorder, where children feel under pressure to perform, achieve

...sure is as much societal as it is a natural
...p; and it's exacerbated by parental pressure. As
...ders and poor self-image are on the increase, and now
... positively with stress, it's important to keep an eye out for
...cll-tale signs (*see* page 241).

> **I**f I could change one thing about myself, I would want to be thinner. *Kathryn, 8*

Substance abuse/dependence

Children are becoming more reliant on caffeine (*see* page 113), alcohol, nicotine and drugs in much the same way as adults are. Children who are under pressure are more likely to use alcohol and drugs because these substances can momentarily allow them to 'forget' about problems, and seem to offer a perfect 'fix'. Like adults, young people need a form of instant relaxation or release. As more and more adults turn to alcohol, so do children. Children are enormously impressionable, learning from the adults around them. If they consistently see alcohol or other 'fixes' being used for relaxation, and as a leisure activity, they are likely to adopt the same habits. In fact, these substances can make a child feel worse.

The health risks of alcohol abuse, for example, are worrying enough. It puts pressure on a child's liver, which is already working overtime dealing with the effects of stress. Long-term use of alcohol – even on a binge-drinking basis – can cause heart disease, and damage to the brain, liver, pancreas, digestive system and central nervous system. Alcohol also causes metabolic damage to every cell in the body and depresses the immune system. It overstimulates the adrenal glands, and the effect on blood-sugar levels and brain chemistry is significant.

> **I** drink about five cans of Coke every day. When I don't have Coke I get headaches. My mum says that I am addicted to Coke. *Harry, 11*

Quite apart from the physical effects, alcohol can also increase feelings of paranoia and being out of control, and anxiety and depression. Alcohol also interferes with our perception of reality and our ability to make good decisions. This is problematic for adults, but it's even worse for adolescents and children, who have less experience in problem-solving and decision-making.

Dr Robert Dato feels that one of the most worrying health problems related to children is drug dependency: 'These are the problems that cut short the lives of children before they even have a proper conceptualisation of stress and a valid way of managing stress.' Abuse of substances of any nature are worrying in both the short and long term, and their increased use by children at younger and younger ages indicates a clear problem with stress load.

Initial results from the largest survey of adolescents ever undertaken in the USA indicate that a feeling of personal connection to family and school plays a crucial role in protecting young people from cigarette, alcohol, and marijuana use, as well as violence, suicide, and early sexual activity. The National Longitudinal Study of Adolescent Health found that adolescents who reported a 'connectedness' to their parents were the least likely to engage in behaviours that endangered their health. These young people felt close to their parents, believed that their parents and family members cared about them, and were satisfied with their family relationships. To a lesser extent, teens were less likely to engage in risky behaviour if their parents were present at key times during the day, and shared activities with them.

Contrary to common assumptions, the study found that parents – not just peers – play a central role for their children *throughout* adolescence. The findings offer parents guidance on what works in protecting their children from harm. The researchers suggest that parents who wish to help their children avoid risky behaviours should spend time with, talk with, be available to, and set high standards for them, and send clear messages about what to do and what not to do.

THE SCALE OF THE PROBLEM

- British children are among the heaviest under-age drinkers in Europe, according to research that compared drinking levels among children in 29 countries, including America and Canada. The research also found that British youths consistently came ahead of most of their European counterparts. In most places, drinking among 11-year-olds was almost non-existent. Yet England was behind only Greece and Israel, with 14 per cent of boys and 9 per cent of girls experimenting with alcohol at least once a week. Around 9 per cent of 11-year-old boys and a quarter of 13-year-olds in England said they had been drunk at least twice in their lives. The study was carried out on behalf of the World Health Organisation.

- Children as young as 12 are drinking the equivalent of 15 measures of whisky at a session, according to a study on 'designer drinks' and young people.

- Girls aged 11 to 15 are increasingly becoming smokers, according to the UK Office for National Statistics. Their survey showed that girl smokers outnumbered boys in nearly every age group and 33 per cent of girls were regulars by the age of 15 compared with 28 per cent of boys.

- Children from wealthy, middle-class backgrounds and aged as young as 11 are as likely to take drugs as those in socially deprived areas, according to research. A study found that 10 per cent of 11-year-olds had taken illegal drugs, with cannabis cited as the most commonly abused substance. Previous research has also shown that teenagers from 'stable' backgrounds at private or grammar schools comprise the fastest-growing sector of the drug-taking population.

I've never been drunk but some of my friends get drunk. They drink beers and shandies and wine. Most of them got sick, but they said it was fun until they were sick. *Klara, 12*

Depression

Some children are genetically more predisposed to stress as they have lower levels of serotonin, a major neurotransmitter that has a calming effect on behaviour and feelings. Under pressure, such children are more likely to become anxious and depressed. It's another double-edged sword: some children are more susceptible to the effects of stress, and we now know that stress can cause anxiety and depression. Depression and anxiety are alarmingly rife in children. In the UK, experts suggest that it probably affects one in every 200 children under 12 years old and two to three in every 100 teenagers. These figures represent cases of clinical depression – depression that is diagnosed and treated as a medical condition. For many children, feelings of depression, even those that last for weeks or months, may remain untreated because of a lack of awareness.

According to the Young Minds Parent Information Service in the UK, children are more at risk of becoming depressed if they are under a lot of stress, have no one with whom to share their worries, and lack practical support. Past events, such as the death of a parent in childhood, or being abused or neglected as a child, can also increase the risk of depression.

Seventy-two of the 80 children I surveyed said that they regularly felt depressed. One seven-year-old boy described depression as 'feeling rubbish and sad all the time so that you just want the whole family and school and world to go away for ever'.

One of the reasons why children may be at risk from depression is that they undertake so little regular exercise. Physical activity not only lifts mood and encourages the release of endorphins (the 'feel-good' hormones), but it also disperses adrenaline, which can cause problems otherwise. Diet, also linked with stress, can have an effect. A third factor – sleep – is also associated with both depression and stress. Stress causes disrupted sleep patterns, and depression is a common side-effect of sleep deprivation.

Depression is dangerous for a number of reasons. Children who are depressed are much more likely to exhibit patterns of depression and anxiety as adults. Depression causes a serious disruption in learning, forming relationships, undertaking activities and communicating with others. Depression is covered in more detail in Chapter 3, but it's worth noting here how the condition can affect a child's life. Symptoms include the following:

- Becoming withdrawn – avoiding friends, family and regular activities.

- Feeling guilty or bad, being self-critical and self-blaming.

- Feeling unhappy, miserable and lonely a lot of the time.

- Feeling hopeless and wanting to die.

- Difficulty concentrating.

- Neglecting personal appearance.

- Difficulty getting off to sleep, or waking very early.

- Tiredness and lack of energy.

- Frequent minor health problems such as headaches or stomach aches.

Many of these symptoms are shared with stress, and are part of the same syndrome.

Suicide

Parents of healthy, lively children will probably be shocked to see this included, but the end result of overstress can be suicide – and victims come from all types of family. One of the most commonly cited reasons for suicide attempts among children and teens is stress, whether it is caused by exams, bullying, family difficulties or peer problems. Suicide is a common feature of depression, which is now linked so closely with stress.

Stress often becomes too much for children to bear. Rather than let down other people, including parents, or face any further disappointment, discomfort, struggle or emotional turmoil, they choose an option that is guaranteed either to end it all, or to draw attention to their problem in the blind hope of getting help.

Suicide among adolescents has risen in the past decade, and now attempts among under-14s seem to be going up too. According to Professor Keith Hawton of the Centre for Suicide Research in Oxford, girls largely account for the increase in non-fatal overdoses and self-inflicted injuries. They outnumber boys by at least six to one. In most cases, these children are sending out the simple message: 'I feel so bad I could die.'

Consider this: every day in the USA, 20 children or youths commit suicide. There's something very wrong going on if *children* do not want to go on living, if they feel intolerable pressure and have nowhere to turn. While some depression leading to suicide is undoubtedly biological or inherent, many cases are related in some way to pressure and stress, or the victim's perception of pressure.

In the UK, a survey by Young Minds found that more than half of all teenagers questioned had been bullied, and that many had contemplated suicide as a way to escape the torment. It seems that some children now see suicide as a viable escape route – a way of getting away from what they perceive to be an intolerable situation. Stress exacerbates an inability to cope, and placing too much pressure on children may actually contribute to a signing of their death warrant.

*   *   *

You may have been shocked by the effects of stress outlined so starkly here. Some parents may even dismiss the statements out of hand, as being alarmist. With busy lives to organise, children seemingly happy at school and progressing, it's easy (and sometimes even necessary) to paper over the cracks – those niggling feelings that children are not having the childhood they deserve and need. The chances are that your child is stressed, whether or not he or she appears to be adapting, and his or her physical and emotional health will undoubtedly be affected. But how can you recognise signs of stress in children, and how can you help lighten the load?

CHAPTER FOUR

Could this be my child?

U ndoubtedly, stress can have unhealthy and dangerous effects, but many parents will, quite rightly, deny that their children are anything other than stimulated by their busy lives. And some will be correct in thinking this. Not *all* stress is unhealthy.

In fact, stress can be stimulating and life-enhancing. It can provide the drive, the initiative, the energy and the motivation to see a job through. If you need to rise to the challenge of a deadline, for example, stress hormones keep you active, alert and focused; in fact, the challenge often inspires our best work. Children experience much the same response to a healthy level of activity – many children enjoy school because of the buzz of competition, the variety of activities, and the thrill of interaction. In this case, the stress they face is positive, and hopefully balanced by a healthy dose of relaxation later. These children are experiencing stress that is within their personal threshold, and it lifts them from boredom and feelings of isolation to being effective at meeting a challenge.

Stressful situations also teach children important skills, such as decision-making, time management and self-control; how to find solutions, cope with failure, develop people skills, and understand the need for relaxation; and the art of compromise. Properly learned, these essential lessons will help children to adapt to the rigours and pace of the modern world.

But everyone has a threshold – the point at which stress becomes unhealthy. For children, the threshold can be reached when one more activity is added to an already busy day, or when they are streamed into a more challenging academic class. It can result from falling out with friends, failing to make a coveted sports team, or being bullied at school. Most parents may never know exactly what sends their child 'over the edge' but, once the negative effects of stress set in, it's often difficult to reverse the pattern. Because the physical and emotional impact of stress is so dramatic, a child's behaviour, approach to life, attitude, moods and health can change, literally overnight. When *un*healthy stress is experienced, the entire body responds in a negative fashion: stimulation becomes overload; effective work becomes inefficient; irritability, anxiety and even depression set in; it all ends in the inevitable burn-out.

Children are enormously resilient and often appear to be coping when they are not. They are very adept at bottling things up, in order to maintain the status quo, and this makes it difficult for parents to know when things are going badly wrong. Just past their threshold, on the way down, they can appear moodier, or find it more difficult to get up in the morning, but these are insipid symptoms. The majority of parents will acknowledge the approach of exhaustion, but fail to link it to stress.

A fairly clear indicator that stress has become negative is a child's behaviour around bedtime, and at the beginning of holidays. If they find it difficult to unwind at bedtime, become irritable and moody, and find it impossible to settle down, chances are their stress load is too high. At the beginning of the holidays, a child may become ill, slightly manic and unable to unwind, or 'crash' for days on end, demanding stimulation and claiming boredom. Often accompanied by emotional behaviour or mood swings, this type of reaction indicates that the child has been 'living on adrenaline' to see him through. If either of these symptoms is the norm, your child is stressed, and you'll need to make some changes to restore their health and well-being.

Different ages, different responses

Children exhibit different patterns of stress-related symptoms at different ages, and it's worth learning what to expect at each stage.

Babies

Can babies really be stressed? The answer is yes. Babies are susceptible to the same physical, emotional and environmental stressors as older children and adults, with little or no way to communicate their distress. A change in routine, weaning, teething, a new carer, stressed parents, bullying by a sibling and lack of physical comfort, among other things, can all cause a baby to become stressed. Most babies respond by showing erratic sleep patterns, constant crying or withdrawal, chronic, niggling but unserious illnesses, such as colds, 'demanding' behaviour or irrational fear at being left alone, for example. If your baby develops what amounts to a different 'personality' or pattern in his daily life (and if he's not ill), it's worth considering whether stress is at the root.

BABIES AND STRESS

Psychiatrists have reported that there may be a physical basis linking stressed babies to personality disorders in adulthood. Babies who are made to sleep alone or are not picked up and comforted enough may grow up being susceptible to post-traumatic stress disorder and personality problems, according to Dr Michael Commons of the Harvard Medical School, and colleagues.

The idea that babies need physical contact is not new – that is why they are no longer swaddled in tight blankets and left to cry for hours. But researchers speaking at the annual meeting of the American Association for the Advancement of Science said they were starting to find evidence of physical changes in the brain caused by stress in infancy. 'Parents in most cultures have infants sleep with them,' Dr Commons says, 'As an infant, sleeping by yourself is very stressful. We can see this because infants cry.'

Scientists have also found levels of the stress hormone cortisol to be much higher in crying babies. Commons suggests that constant stimulation by cortisol in infancy causes physical changes in the brain. 'This makes you more prone to the effects of stress, more prone to illness, including mental illness and makes it harder to recover from illness,' Commons says. 'These are real changes and they don't go away.'

Commons and his team undertook research with Kenyans, people of Mayan descent and residents of Boston, and found a startling difference between upbringing and stress resilience. In the West, children are encouraged to be self-sufficient and face danger alone. 'They don't have the emotional resources to seek comfort and consoling and the experience becomes unspeakable,' he says.

Other cultures teach infants to stay close and look to others for emotional and physical support. 'The infants sleep touching the parents,' he says. 'They are carried around touching the parent or some family member.' Commons theorises that such constant support keeps down levels of cortisol, and helps the cortical structures in the brain develop better. He notes that illnesses such as PTSD and phobias, on the rise in industrialised countries, barely exist in more primitive societies. His advice? Use the power of touch.

Pre-school children

This is a difficult age to assess because toddlers and very young children are naturally and inherently curious, erratic, develop mentally unique and, most importantly, are unable to verbalise emotions.

There are, however, a number of things to watch out for, these are listed overleaf. Remember that every child is different, and a change in behaviour could indicate illness, or just a simple phase of development, involving some anxiety or rebellion.

- irritability;

- anxiety;

- uncontrollable crying;

- trembling with fear;

- eating problems;

- sleeping problems;

- regression to infantile behaviour, such as bedwetting, sucking a thumb (after they've given up), wanting to wear nappies, or drink from a bottle;

- uncontrollable anger;

- loss of control that frightens them;

- fear of being alone or without a parent;

- withdrawal;

- biting;

- sensitivity to sudden or loud noises;

- inexplicable sadness;

- aggression;

- nightmares; or

- suddenly becoming prone to accidents.

Primary school children

Once again, it's normal for children at this stage to exhibit a wide range of behaviours, including tantrums when things don't go their own way, aggression when they are angry and do not have the maturity to cope with conflicting emotions, persistent questioning, whining, a healthy fear of new experiences, loss of concentration, nightmares and the normal complaints about friends, siblings, discipline and school.

These responses are all normal, and part of development. Children are coming into contact with a wider and more frightening world, and they are bound to have worries and fears. They are also leaving behind the comfort of having a parent or carer by their side almost constantly, and probably a favourite blanket or stuffed toy as well. At school, they begin to master simple and then more complex tasks, which involve reasoning and logical thinking. A huge range of skills are developed, and for the first time they may experience peer competition and a need for intense concentration, while becoming more self-aware and conscious of differences, performance and achievement.

Doubts, normal fears, questions and feelings of inferiority are to be expected during this period. Watch out, however, for the following:

- withdrawal;

- feeling unloved;

- distrust;

- showing a constant fear or dislike of school;

- failing to establish friendships, or withdrawing from regular friends;

- difficulty in expressing feelings;

- chronic worrying;

- a need to know exactly what the future holds;

- headaches or stomach aches;

- trouble sleeping;

- trouble unwinding;

- loss of appetite;

- frequent urination;

- regressive behaviours;

- constant aggression and/or outbursts;

- becoming prone to accidents; or

- worsening reports from school.

Adolescents

Adolescence is a period of great physical and emotional change; we enter as children and emerge as adults. The course of adolescence is necessarily bumpy, with many rebellions, cries for independence, experiments and periods of self-definition. Self-image becomes increasingly (and almost obsessively) important, as do appearance, peer relationships and status. This period is also characterised by great physical development, complete with skin problems, growing pains, weight issues and the onset of puberty, in which hormones often win the battle for self-control. Sexuality becomes an issue, and this can be at once confusing and elating for adolescents.

Expect some irresponsibility, disturbances in sleep and behaviours, rebellion, arguments, sulking, agitation and selfishness during adolescence. Although some of these may be linked to the stress of growing up, they are normal and not usually cause for concern.

Some children sail through the transition from childhood to adulthood. This may have something to do with genes, conditioning and stress tolerance; furthermore, children with a strong family background, good relationships, high self-esteem and a strong self-respect will normally find it easier than others to cope with the pressures of adolescence. A wide variation of behaviour can be expected from adolescents, but every parent needs to look out for *sudden* changes in behaviour, personality, temperament, levels of activity and approach to life.

If the following symptoms are a common feature of your adolescent's everyday life, he or she is more than likely to be under too much pressure:

- long-term and seemingly inexplicable anger;

- feelings of disillusionment;

- lack of self-esteem;

- lack of self-respect;

- extreme behaviours, such as committing crimes, overt rebellion, complete lack of respect for authority and figures of authority;

- drug abuse;

- depression;

- truancy or refusing to go to school;

- distrust; or

- a marked change in grades at school.

Assessing your child

It's extremely important to remember that children behave differently throughout the course of their development; their behaviour, approach to life and even happiness will go through different phases, good and bad. It's also important to remember that children do not go through life with a map. Constant guidance, reassurance, interaction and experiences with adults are needed along the way, to keep them on track and to ensure that they develop into happy, healthy adults.

It's crucial to keep an eye out for significant changes during every developmental stage, but niggling and more insidious changes may also indicate a problem. Not all health and emotional problems caused by stress are clear-cut, and it's easy to overlook a series of smaller issues and health problems that form a clear picture of a child under stress.

In today's society, we deal with health problems with a variety of drugs and other quick-fix solutions. A child with a headache is given a teaspoon of paracetamol, and put to bed. For a tummy ache, there are dozens of antacid, anti-nausea or anti-diarrhoea treatments. Furthermore, if a child has trouble getting up in the morning, we put him to bed earlier, or threaten to take TV off the menu if he doesn't start getting up on time. We also tend to blame emotional symptoms on poor behaviour ('she's so ratty at the moment'; 'she's a complete nuisance these days'), rather than looking for the cause.

Looking for causes rather than cures is crucial in recognising and dealing with stress in children. We need to look at the whole child, rather than the individual symptoms. Many children suffer regularly from a multitude of symptoms associated with stress. It's not that parents knowingly ignore these symptoms – most parents are quick to offer comfort and treatment when a child is out of sorts – but this does not get to the crux of the problem. Until a link is made between the various physical and emotional symptoms, and a clear picture of a child's overall health and well-being is available, it is impossible to assess whether or not the child is under too much pressure.

Emotional health or happiness cannot be defined in a way that applies to all children. Some children are naturally exuberant, and others find contentment in quieter pursuits. Some children whistle and sing in the morning, others prefer to curl up with a good book, or to daydream. It's important not to try to create a lively bubbling child from an introspective dreamer, but you must look out for signs that all is not well.

A stressed child will not be emotionally healthy, no matter how well he seems to be coping with day-to-day life. The following checklist will help you to assess the emotional health of a particular child. It isn't a test, but provides a basis for understanding signs of emotional ill-health, which can have an impact on your child's life in so many ways.

How is my child's emotional health?

Answer the following questions honestly:

Can my child tell me how he is feeling? (This doesn't mean he can come out with a pat 'I am sad', or 'I am happy' in response to questions, and it doesn't mean that he volunteers information upon request. It means that he can express his feelings – at bedtime, in a quiet moment, or in the throes of an argument – without being prodded.) ☐

Does my child exhibit signs of stress (*see above*)? ☐

Does my child seem listless or withdrawn on a regular basis? ☐

Does my child laugh less than he used to? ☐

Does my child smile or show delight easily? ☐

Does my child become frustrated easily, and want to give up? ☐

Does my child push himself too hard, to be the best, the top of the class, the best player on the pitch, or the winner of the prize? ☐

Is my child reluctant to take on new challenges or activities that he would normally enjoy? ☐

Does my child become extremely upset if criticised or corrected? ☐

Does my child put himself down regularly? ☐

Is my child overly critical of others? ☐

Does my child try to hard to please people (teachers, friends, family members)? ☐

Is my child clingy? ☐

Does my child suffer from inexplicable fears, or is he afraid to face new situations? ☐

Does my child need continual approval? ☐

Does my child boast? ☐

Is my child aggressive or attention-seeking? ☐

Is my child impatient and unappreciative? ☐

Does my child suffer from a series of low-grade infections, abdominal pains or headaches that cannot be explained, but appear regularly? ☐

If you answered 'yes' to the first question, and 'no' to all the others, you have a supremely balanced child who is clearly not under stress to any adverse degree, and is obviously coping well with his lifestyle, commitments, relationships and sense of self. Chances are, however, that you will have a mixture of 'yes' and 'no' answers.

Your aim is to ensure that your child is emotionally balanced, so that he feels good about himself, feels confident in new situations, doesn't feel a need to be the best or to get the most, is patient and, above all, likes himself. No child will ever be perfect, and everyone has times when they experience a dip in confidence, have feelings of low self-worth, lose their temper and lash out, and even become depressed. Like physical health, emotional health can be up and down. However, in the same way that you can take steps to boost your child's immune system, you can boost your child's emotional health (see Chapter 6).

Could it be stress?

Emotional health is a reflection of overall resilience. Let's take the assessment a step further, and fine-tune the questions to deal with stress-related issues.

Answer the questions honestly, placing a tick beside those that apply:

My child:

Physical Symptoms

Has unexplained physical symptoms that occur frequently or even constantly, such as headaches, tummy aches, limb or joint pains. ☐

Suffers from regular constipation or diarrhoea. ☐

Feels faint, or is subject to fainting. ☐

Suffers from indigestion. ☐

Suffers from palpitations. ☐

Has skin problems. ☐

Has sweating or clammy hands. ☐

Seems to pick up every infection going round. ☐

Takes a long time to reach top form after being ill. ☐

Always seems tired. ☐

Finds it difficult to get out of bed in the morning. ☐

Has a poor appetite. ☐

Is unusually hungry or obsessive about food. ☐

Suffers sleep disturbances, such as nightmares, night waking or night terrors. ☐

Finds it difficult to fall asleep at bedtime. ☐

Falls asleep during the day. ☐

Clenches his fist or jaws. ☐

Grinds his teeth (awake or asleep). ☐

Relies on stimulants, such as fizzy drinks, sweets and chocolate, to keep going. ☐

Emotional/Behavioural Symptoms

Has mood swings. ☐

Shows a lack of concentration on a regular basis. ☐

Won't settle down to tasks or focus on short-term projects. ☐

Is *overly* sociable, reluctant to spend any time alone. ☐

Is unsociable, preferring to be alone as often as possible. ☐

Seems manically energetic at times, and then crashes. ☐

Seems nervous, fidgety or unable to sit still (not relevant to under-fives!). ☐

Is often irritable. ☐

Becomes angry easily. ☐

Cries easily. ☐

Loses patience easily. ☐

Suffers from temper tantrums (not relevant to under-twos). ☐

Is highly competitive. ☐

Shirks any competitive activity. ☐

Spends free time with 'distractions', such as games consoles, loud music, computers or television. ☐

Becomes aggressive without warning or explanation. ☐

Reverts to childlike behaviour, such as sucking a thumb, bedwetting, clinginess. ☐

Is reluctant to talk about problems. ☐

Seems anxious, apprehensive or frightened. ☐

Is often ashamed or embarrassed. ☐

Suffers from occasional or chronic depression, or generally feeling low. ☐

Feels helpless, out of control. ☐

Daydreams more often. ☐

Becomes obsessive about people, interests or activities. ☐

Has mentioned suicidal thoughts. ☐

Worries a lot. ☐

Is accident prone. ☐

Manages time poorly and often panics. ☐

Withdraws from supportive relationships. ☐

Is too busy to relax. ☐

If you have more than five ticks, your child is exhibiting symptoms of stress overload. For ways of reducing that load, and encouraging optimum health and well-being, *see* Chapter 6. In the meantime, however, remember that stress comes in many forms, including those with an environmental basis. Certain aspects of your child's lifestyle may be overloading his system, adding to the stress burden, and perhaps making him more susceptible to stress.

Is my child's system under pressure?

If the honest answer to even one of the questions below is 'yes', your child's system is under pressure. While two or three of these lifestyle factors will not have a dramatic impact on your child's health and ability to cope with stress, any more than that will certainly have an effect. In the first instance, he will have fewer natural resources to cope with stress; in the second, his system will be under the sort of pressure that exacerbates stress and increases the number and severity of the symptoms. While many of the questions may seem curious inclusions (for example, the vast majority of households use cleaning products!), the point is that all of these elements place your child's body under pressure.

Food and Drink

Does your child eat junk food more than once a week? ☐

Does the bulk or your child's diet consist of processed foods or refined products, such as white bread and pasta? ☐

Does your child drink fizzy drinks or any sweetened drinks (such as squash) on a regular basis? ☐

Is the majority of the fruits, vegetables, meat, milk or grains you serve not organic (*see* page 110)? ☐

Does your child crave sweet foods? ☐

Lifestyle

Is your child under any stress (such as exams, parental divorce, changing schools, playing competitive sports)? ☐

Is your child in contact with cigarette smoke, either at home, at friends' homes, or at a carer's? ☐

Does your child smoke, or drink any alcohol? ☐

Do you live in an area with high levels of air pollution? ☐

Do you use non-natural household cleaning products? ☐

Does your child use a mobile phone, or watch a lot of television? ☐

Physical Symptoms/Medication

Does your child have asthma or eczema, or suffer from frequent skin rashes or hives? ☐

Does your child take medication regularly? ☐

Has your child had frequent prescriptions of antibiotics? ☐

Is your child overweight? ☐

Does your child seem tired, but have difficulty sleeping? ☐

Does your child suffer from frequent constipation? ☐

Does your child have mood swings, linked to blood sugar (after school, before breakfast or after sports, for example)? ☐

The number of 'yes' answers indicates the toxicity of your child's lifestyle, which has a direct impact on the stress response.

The parent effect

Children do not live in isolation; the majority cohabit with siblings and parents, and their relationship with their parents can affect the amount of stress under which they are placed, and their ability to cope. The other issue is the whole family dynamic. The following questionnaires are designed to work out how healthy your home life is, and to see whether your child has the safety net he needs, not only to stay within healthy levels of stress, but also to establish habits and patterns of behaviour that will allow him to manage through childhood and into adulthood.

Life is stressful. The majority of parents are under considerable stress and that stress certainly affects children, creating an environment of negative energy. (Don't dismiss this as New Age ideology! Children consistently behave less well when their parents are least able to cope. Their sensitive antennae pick up negative vibes and they respond in kind.) The pressure on parents also makes them less well equipped to deal with their children in an effective, affectionate and positive way.

Interaction is crucial to the development of healthy coping skills, both now and in the future. If you are too much under pressure to spend time with your child, sharing what he needs to share, allowing him to verbalise his emotions, he'll find it difficult to counterbalance the stress of daily life by letting off steam, relaxing, relating, making guided decisions and, ultimately, feeling loved and important.

The Dato Stress Inventory

Dr Robert Dato has kindly allowed me to reproduce his 'Stress Inventory', which is designed to work out your personal stress equation. In other words, to find out whether your Adaptability (A) is higher than the Pressure (P) you face. Remember: Stress = P − A.

The Dato Stress Inventory is a stress assessment and evaluation instrument designed for adult use. The DSI is comprised of the Personal Symptoms Profile, the Personal Needs Profile, and the Personal Skills Profile. The accuracy of your scores will depend on your comprehension of the profile items, and your honesty in responding. Follow the inventory procedures and guidelines to score and interpret the DSI (see Appendix II).

If you have no time to fill in the inventory, you are probably too busy. If you don't have time to stop and assess, chances are that the right priorities are not being made in your family. In order for a family to function well, every member must be emotionally and physically healthy, and that involves taking the time to ensure that individual needs are being met.

Stress has various effects on children, and the list of symptoms for older children can be adapted to relate to parents as well as children. See how you score. Add the following questions:

Do you drink too much alcohol or coffee? ☐

Is your work performance reduced? ☐

Are you smoking more? ☐

Are you comfort eating or have you lost your appetite? ☐

Do you suffer from thrush or cystitis? ☐

Do you experience intrusive thoughts or images? ☐

Do you find it difficult to juggle family and work life? ☐

Do you find it difficult to keep all the balls in the air? ☐

Look honestly at your score. If you are under pressure, your family dynamic will be affected, as will your children's stress levels. Studies show that children of stressed parents not only adapt less well to stress in adulthood, but fail to learn important skills, such as interaction, relaxation and problem-solving.

In order to be able to adapt to stress, children need guidance, interaction, friendship, love, discipline, understanding, and a healthy example to follow. These are the cornerstones of emotional well-being, and all take time, patience, understanding and evaluation on the part of parents. If you are too busy to give your children the time they need, too pressured to show the required patience and interaction, or too stressed to be affectionate and loving, your child will have difficulty managing the demands of the modern world. If your child's stress is related to your own stress levels, you need to think about ways of making things easier for your busy family; *see* Chapter 7 for some ideas.

In this modern world, it's easy for even the most devoted of parents to forget what parenting is for. Children are often treated as little adults, and parents tend to gauge their success in that role – and as a person – by the achievements and failures of their children. Think about what you want for your child, and the expectations you hold. When your child 'fails', how do you feel? Similarly, how do you feel when your child succeeds? Are you affected by competition and jealousy between your children's friends' parents?

A parenting self-assessment

To identify areas where you may be placing too much pressure on your children, and where your aspirations for their future may have gone off course, answer the following questions. Although it's not easy to question your own motives, when you feel that you're doing everything in your power for the good of your children, be as honest as you can. Certain factors may be in place – unhealthy expectations, or a need for achievement – that are not actually related to your children's well-being. This isn't a test or a quiz; it merely poses questions that every parent needs to consider. There is no 'right' or 'wrong' answer. These questions are set out to make you think about why your child might be under pressure in the home environment.

- Do you feel that you expect too much of your child?

- Do you have high, clear expectations, without being overly rigid?

- Why do you want your child to succeed?

- Do you mind when your child fails? If so, do you mind because it has affected him/her in a negative way, or because it is somehow a poor reflection upon you?

- Is it important that your children have the things their friends have? If so, why?

- Do you encourage individual goals in your children, or do you expect excellence in all activities?

- Do you spend a lot of money on material goods for your child? If so, why?

- Do you have dreams or aspirations that weren't fulfilled in your own life? What are they, and could you possibly be trying to relive them again through your children?

- Do you spend time alone with your child every day, not including time spent over homework? If not, why?

- Do you judge your child before knowing the full facts, or do you give him/her time to explain?

- Do you feel that you cope well with stress?

- Do you feel that you recognise signs of stress in your child and take steps to change things in a more positive direction?

- If your child announced that he/she wanted to give up an activity that you believe is important, such as a sport, an instrument, a subject at school, would you consider it? If not, why not?

- What do you ultimately want for your child in life?

Assessing your family

A positive family environment, in which children learn the lessons of life in a carefree, loving atmosphere, is one of the keys to helping children meet the demands of life. Children from a nurturing family environment develop a range of coping strategies and become more resilient. Resiliency is the ability to bounce back from stress and crisis. Your child's stress threshold can actually be raised and maintained by a positive home life.

If even one family member is unhappy, under stress or failing to cope, the entire family dynamic will be altered. All family members need to be considered, and their rights respected.

> Fifty-nine of the 80 children I surveyed said that they didn't 'laugh a lot'.

The primary function of the family is the optimum development of each member. The meeting of the reasonable and basic needs of each family member is the cornerstone of individual fulfilment. This responsibility needs to be shared out and, as children grow older, they need to be encouraged to take on more responsibility for meeting their own needs. The way that parents meet their own needs and children's needs forms the model that the children will adopt later on in meeting these needs themselves.

The more family members interact with one another, the greater the cohesiveness and the closeness within the family. According to the old saying, 'the family who prays together stays together'. But it takes more than one type of interaction these days to create bonds between family members. Listening, helping, interests, hobbies, sharing, humour and playing are all important.

The essential ingredient in any happy family is unconditional love. Erich Fromm once wrote that 'unconditional love corresponds to one of the deepest longings, not only of the child, but of every human being'. In today's chaotic world, where time is at a premium, the foundation stone of unconditional love can ensure a happy family relationship, allowing all family members to benefit and grow.

Do you sometimes feel you don't have as many things as your friends?

No. I have a loving family and friends and that's what counts. *Lily, 11*

How healthy is your family?

Does everyone in the family have an equal voice and recognition? ☐

Do you feel that your family members respect one another, and you? ☐

Do all family members take pride in the others' achievements? ☐

Do you have a family system for recognising achievement? ☐

Do you eat together as a family at least three times a week? ☐

Do you share family activities at least three times a week? ☐

Does every family member have time to be alone? ☐

Does every family member have separate interests, activities and hobbies, with time allowed to undertake them? ☐

Does your family watch less than three hours of television a week? ☐

Does everyone in the family have responsibilities? ☐

Is your family environment calm and loving? ☐

Do all family members cope well with stress? ☐

Does your family laugh a lot? ☐

Does your child feel comfortable bringing friends home to play or visit? ☐

Do leisure activities play an important role in family life? ☐

Does your family have extended family members in close, regular contact? ☐

Is everyone in good physical health? ☐

If you can answer 'yes' to all these questions, your child is likely to have a perfect family atmosphere. The object of this exercise is, however, to find areas of weakness. Think about why you may have answered 'no' to any of the questions. All these elements add up to a happy family life, which will affect the way your child grows, learns, views the world and, ultimately, copes with stress, both now and in the future.

Building on self-assessment

Working out whether or not your child is genuinely stressed, and why, is vital to a family's well-being. Awareness is the key to making changes. Once you have considered your child's individual needs, your own needs and your impact on your child's well-being, and the effect of the family environment, you'll be in a much better position to make changes. Every child is unique and has a different point at which he 'peaks', when fun, energy and stimulation become lethargy, poor concentration and stress.

To establish which areas of your child's life are too stressful you will, first and foremost, have to communicate with your child. Ask him directly what he finds stressful. You might be surprised by the results. Often a child's perception of events and life in general are different from what we expect. It may not be an accurate reflection of reality, but it's the *perception* that matters. If your child perceives something to be stressful then, for him, it is. It may be something seemingly innocuous, such as being rushed at breakfast, or it may be something serious, like bullying or concern about parental harmony.

With that knowledge in hand, go on to assess things from an external point of view. Take into consideration the following:

- your expectations;

- the motivation behind your expectations;

- overscheduling;

- the time your child spends with you;

- the time your child spends with other family members;

- time allowed to play and be free;

- diet;

- environmental factors;

- the way in which your child chooses to relax;

- overall health;

- the stress load of every family member.

This should provide a clear picture of your child's lifestyle, and help to pinpoint areas where changes can be made.

It would be ridiculous to suggest that perfect family harmony, with equally content family members, can ever be achieved and sustained. But you can take certain steps to look after your child's well-being, and the well-being of every family member, yourself included. That way, you can ensure that your children meet the challenges of life with enthusiasm, adapt to the ups and downs that they will inevitably face, and have the best possible chance of a healthy, happy, successful future.

PART TWO

Breaking the Cycle

It might sound a paradoxical thing to say – for surely never has a generation of children occupied more sheer hours of parental time – but the truth is that we neglected you. We allowed you a charade of trivial freedoms in order to avoid making those impositions on you that are in the end both the training ground and proving ground for true independence. We pronounced you strong when you were still weak in order to avoid the struggles with you that would have fed your true strength. We proclaimed you sound when you were foolish in order to avoid taking part in the long, slow, slogging effort that is the only route to genuine maturity of mind and feeling. Thus, it was no small anomaly of your growing up that while you were the most indulged generation, you were also in many ways the most abandoned to your own meagre devices by those into whose safe-keeping you had been given.

MIDGE DECTER, *Liberal Parents/Radical Children*, 1975

CHAPTER FIVE

What children really need

There are a number of reasons why childhood stress is increasing. If they are to manage their stress, children need security, tolerance, encouragement, approval and, above all, time and love. These are the foundations upon which a child's emotional health is built, and which ultimately establish his ability to adapt to stress.

A knowledge of the elements of a healthy childhood, from both a physical and an emotional point of view, is vital for parents.

A healthy diet

Good nutrition can do more than change your child's life; it can even save it. If that sounds like an exaggeration, consider the fact that almost all cancers are linked in some way to nutrition, as are heart disease and dysfunction of the immune system. Fertility, mental prowess, weight, the health of our bones and teeth, and allergies, are all related to what we eat. An unhealthy diet can undoubtedly have an adverse effect on a child's body. What do children actually need?

Families in the Western world have adopted a peculiar Anglo-American diet, with an emphasis on speed and ease of preparation. The most bizarre aspect of this trend is that a new product has arisen: 'children's food'. Children no longer eat what adults eat, nor do we expect them to. If parents feel the occasional pang of guilt when they look at their child's diet of chicken nuggets, chips, pizza, burgers and crisps, they are swiftly reassured by the fact that everyone is doing it, and that the supermarket shelves are laden with the stuff.

The upshot of this new trend is that the majority of children are eating a diet that is seriously low in nutrients, and this can affect their health on every level, both now and in the future.

Children who live on spaghetti hoops and the odd glass of milk may look perfectly healthy, but their diet matters enormously. They are growing and developing more quickly than at any other time in their life. Everything they eat contributes to that growth and development, and lays the foundation for their future, and for the future of their own children. It affects their emotions, their ability to concentrate, to ward off illness, to play sports, to grow and to develop into happy, healthy adults with a successful outlook.

Furthermore, stress in children under pressure can play havoc with both digestion and the uptake of nutrients, as well as robbing the body of key nutrients that your child needs to grow and, ultimately, to cope. It's also the cause of a wide range of health problems, all of which require additional nutrients for successful recovery.

If your child is in optimum physical health, he will be more likely to deal successfully with stress. The mind-body relationship is incredibly strong, and when children feel unwell, their emotional status is also affected. You can see this in action in the days before an illness sets in – your child will often become tearful, irritable or lethargic. His behaviour and emotions are affected by his physical health, which is just one reason why it's essential that he has everything he needs to ensure and maintain good health.

Improving the diet of our children

Given that digestion often suffers under stress, the food your child eats needs to contains the best possible combination of nutrients.

At the very least you need to be confident that what your child is eating is contributing to health and growth, rather than detracting from it. Clearly, our children's diet needs to be improved; replacing processed foods with natural, unrefined alternatives, and offering more fruits and vegetables, wholegrain foods, pulses, lean meats and low-fat dairy produce will make a dramatic difference to their overall health.

Artificial chemicals, in the form of additives, preservatives and flavours, all put a strain on the body, particularly the liver, which is so crucial for the stress response. What's more, these chemicals are a form of environmental stress, which will raise your child's stress load, even if other aspects of life are going well.

The next step is to offer supplements to balance some of the unhealthy aspects of a child's diet, and to reverse some of the damage caused by poor eating habits. Despite their parents' best efforts to provide good, nutritious meals, many children are faddy eaters, putting themselves at an increased risk of vitamin and mineral deficiency. Every child past the stage of breastfeeding needs a good multivitamin and mineral tablet.

Aim to include the following in your child's diet:

- Lots of healthy protein, including very lean meats, fish, poultry, cheese, yoghurt, nuts, soya products (including tofu), pulses such as lentils, and seeds (three to five servings a day).

- Plenty of fruit and vegetables and their juices. Anything goes. Remember, the more colourful the vegetable, the more nutritious it tends to be (five to seven servings a day).

- Lots of carbohydrates for energy. Anything wholegrain or unrefined, including pasta, bread, brown rice, grains (such as rye, barley, corn, buckwheat), pulses, potatoes and wholegrain, sugar-free cereals (four to nine servings a day).

- As much fluid as your child can drink. Water is the most important. Between 500 and 2000ml is recommended, depending on age and weather.

- Fibre-rich foods, to help encourage digestion and optimum uptake of nutrients from the food eaten.

- Lots of nutritious snacks. Keeping blood-sugar levels stable throughout the day will help your child to cope with stressful situations more efficiently, and lower the stress response significantly. Eating little and often is the key to keeping levels stable, but try to make sure that your child gets at least three good, healthy main meals every day as well. Healthy snacks include fruit, vegetables, low-sugar live yoghurts, wholemeal toast, nuts, seeds, rice cakes, cheese, sugarless cereals, plain popcorn, hummus and breadsticks.

In addition, try to achieve the following:

- Eat organic when you can. There is still considerable debate about whether or not it is more nutritious, but there is no doubt that it is lower in chemicals that place strain on your child's system.

- Cut down on sweets, crisps, soft drinks and fast or 'junk' foods of any nature. These not only tend to take the place of healthier alternatives in our children's diet but they are also a key source of damaging chemicals and 'anti-nutrients'.

- Watch the sugar! Given that stress causes the immune system to become less effective, it's important to take steps to ensure that it is being boosted in every other possible way. Sugar is one of the worst culprits in terms of immunity (*see* box on page 111).

- Make sure your child does not skip meals; this can send blood-sugar levels plummeting, and adrenaline soaring. A huge number of people miss meals because of the frantic pace of their life; in a recent survey, supermarket chain Sainsbury found that nearly 70 per cent of people regularly miss at least one meal a day.

A healthy diet need not mean monotonous, tasteless meals. Experiment with herbs and spices, and try out new recipes to tempt your child. Get them involved in choosing menus and preparing food. Let them know why you are eating what you are, and how it will make them feel better, do better on the sports field, or get over those constant colds. And don't worry about occasional slips. Life would be joyless without the occasional treat. As long as your child's diet is 80 per cent healthy, you can do what you like with the other 20 per cent!

WHY CUT OUT SUGAR?

Sugar is linked with a variety of different health problems, most of which are implicated in the stress response.

- Sugar has a strong depressive effect on the immune system. According to a 1997 study, as little as six teaspoons a day can reduce the immune response by 25 per cent. Most common foods – particularly those geared towards children – contain a substantial amount of sugar, much of it hidden within the ingredients, which can have a dramatic effect on our children's health.

- Sugar causes blood sugar to rise dramatically, followed by a dramatic slump, which causes tearfulness, fatigue, temper tantrums, low mood and lack of concentration. Blood sugar is linked to stress (*see* pages 53–54), and keeping levels stable can help your child to cope better with potential stressors.

- Foods high in sugars are also often high in saturated fats (biscuits, chocolate bars, cakes, pastries, for example), which can lead to weight gain, heart disease and even diabetes. These are now known side-effects of stress, so it's important that you reduce the risk factors wherever possible.

- Most importantly, the extra calories of sugars often displace more nourishing food in the diet. Diets high in sugar are often also high in fat and low in fibre. If children fill up on sugary foods, they are likely to be at risk of vitamin and mineral deficiency.

Do children need supplements?

Even a balanced diet may be lacking in essential vitamins, minerals or trace elements because of the way in which the foods were produced. There is evidence that intensive farming robs soil of its nutrient content, which means that food produced in this way is lower in minerals than it should be, and processing, refining and cooking all cause further nutrient loss.

Perhaps more importantly, our modern, overscheduled lives may cause our bodies to require extra nutrients. Pollution, noise, stress, food additives and many other factors combine to put stress on the body. Stress of any kind – whether emotional or physical – increases our need, and our children's need, for nutrients.

Every child will benefit from essential fatty acids (EFAs), now dangerously deficient in most diets. Try flaxseed oil (dribbled on foods or whizzed in the blender with orange juice), which is high in crucial omega-3 oils. Essential fatty acids are converted into substances that keep the blood thin, lower blood pressure, decrease inflammation, improve the function of the nervous and immune systems, help insulin to work, affect vision, co-ordination and mood, encourage healthy metabolism and maintain the balance of water in the body. There's also exciting new research showing that it can affect a child's behaviour and ability to learn. Evening primrose oil, pumpkin seed oil and borage oil are also good sources of EFAs. A shortage of EFAs has been linked to stress: a deficiency exacerbates symptoms and makes it harder to cope with stressors, while stress itself sets up conditions in which your child's body actually requires more.

If your child has recurrent infections (colds, coughs and ear infections), make sure that he has extra vitamin C, which helps to boost the immune system. Constant, low-grade infections are a sign of stress, and an indication that the immune system is not functioning optimally. Many experts recommend extra vitamin C as a matter of course, to help ward off illness. Between 100 and 1,000mg is appropriate, depending on the child's age. A two-year-old, for example, might have an extra 100mg. If there is any diarrhoea after taking the tablets, reduce the dose by half.

With iron-deficiency anaemia on the increase, it may be necessary to supplement iron. Most good vitamin and mineral tablets contain iron.

Stress reduces many nutrients in the body, particularly the B vitamins. If your child is experiencing stress of any kind, it's a good idea to increase his intake of this vitamin. B vitamins work together, so don't try supplementing any one at a time, unless recommended by a nutritionist. A good multivitamin or mineral tablet should provide adequate B vitamins, but for children over the age of six, 10 to 25mg a day is an acceptable level at which to supplement.

Children who are unable to eat or drink dairy produce because of allergies, or simply because they don't like them, should be able to get enough calcium from vegetable and fruit sources. However, really picky eaters may need calcium supplements.

All children need antioxidants, which help to reduce the onset of degenerative diseases, and which are now known to have cancer-preventing qualities. The main antioxidants are vitamins A, C and E, and the minerals zinc and selenium. Make sure these appear in your child's multivitamin, or look for antioxidant tablets prepared specially for children. Ultimately, the antioxidants are the nutrients that will help to repair some of the damage done by emotional, physical and environmental stress.

Zinc is crucial for children under pressure. It's needed for cell repair, efficient digestion, immune function and emotional health. What's more, zinc is required for the production of the adrenal hormones, which means that what little your child gets in his diet will probably be zapped up by the stress response. About a third of all children do not get even the minimum suggested amount of zinc. Try a supplement of around 10 to 15mg per day.

CUT THE CAFFEINE

A new study shows that caffeine increases stress levels. Although the findings are based on adult consumption, mainly in the form of coffee, it's important to consider these findings in relation to children. Many children drink a great deal of colas, tea and even coffee, and caffeine is also found in chocolate, 'energy drinks', headache medication and painkillers. Not only are children's bodies smaller, but their immature systems also cope less well with the effects of caffeine.

Researchers from Birmingham University's Dental School found that one in eight teenagers in the UK now consumes more than 22 cans of cola every week, and three-quarters of all children drink it regularly. There are two issues here: one is that children are choosing unhealthy pick-me-ups in an attempt to cope with feelings of fatigue and loss of concentration caused by stress, but it's also a habit that compounds the stress response. Caffeine overstimulates the adrenal glands, which might appear to help stress levels, but in the long term will reduce your child's ability to cope with pressure. Even a moderate amount of caffeine raises levels of the stress hormones, adrenaline and cortisol, to levels higher than those normally produced during a stress reaction. Caffeine also prevents the absorption of some essential nutrients, particularly zinc and B vitamins.

According to research, drinking four or five cups of coffee a day makes the body act as if it is under constant stress. Combined with other stressors, it can increase blood pressure significantly, leading to an increased risk of long-term heart disease. A study of 72 regular coffee drinkers by researchers at the Duke University Medical Center in the USA found that they produced high levels of adrenaline and noradrenaline hormones. According to Professor James Lane, who took part in the research, 'Moderate caffeine consumption makes a person react like he or she is having a very stressful day. If you combine the effects of real stress with the artificial boost in stress hormones that comes from caffeine, then you have compounded the effects considerably.'

Henry, aged 10, claims to have a good diet. He eats one veg-etable every day, no fruit, and 'only a few sweets and crisps'. He says he drinks a lot of 'juice' (later identified as Ribena) and fizzy drinks only on the weekend. He has pasta or pizza almost every night of the week, and chips for lunch at school. He eats no meat other than chicken nuggets and ham, and dislikes yoghurt, cheese and milk. His breakfast normally con-sists of chocolate-covered cereal or white toast with choco-late spread. Henry suffers from regular headaches, pains in his tummy, difficulty getting to sleep and panic attacks. He was surprised to hear that his diet might be part of the cause.

Exercise

Exercise is all too scarce in the modern child's lifestyle. Not only is it crucial for overall health, but it dramatically affects well-being. Given the number of health risks associated with stress, it's even more important to counterbalance the ill-effects by encouraging children to take part in activities to strengthen body and mind, and to increase their resilience. For example, the risk of stress causing heart disease can be cut in half by ensuring that children get adequate exercise. While heart disease in our chil-dren may not be an issue for present contemplation, there is evi-dence that it is present in very young children (*see* page 72); apparently, the likelihood of heart attack or stroke at a young age is dramatically increased.

Let's look at some of the effects of exercise:

- Exercise strengthens the cardiovascular system and increases heart mass. This reduces the risk of heart disease, the number-one killer of both men and women in the Western world. It also reduces blood pressure.

- Exercise reduces stress. One study in particular claims that regu-lar exercise can reduce it dramatically. During periods of high stress, those who reported exercising less frequently had 37 per cent more physical symptoms than their counterparts who exercised more often. Exercise works by using up the adrenaline that is created by stress and stressful situations. It also creates endorphins, the 'feel-good' hormones that improve mood, motivation and even tolerance to pain and other stimuli.

- Exercise is good for the brain. Aerobic exercise helps to increase the number of brain chemicals called neurotransmitters, so that messages can be carried more quickly over brain cells. This increases mental flexibility and agility over longer periods of time. Furthermore, regular exercise increases the supply of oxygenated blood to the brain, which can improve concentration, alertness and intellectual capacity. All of these are diminished in periods of stress.

- Regular exercise can promote better sleeping habits. Many children are simply not tired at the end of the day; bedtime is later and later, and sleep is disrupted.

- Several studies show that children who exercise regularly are more apt to do so when they become adults. Parents have a role to help children establish healthy long-term habits.

- A study published in *Medicine and Science in Exercise and Sports* reported that exercise can affect growth in a number of ways. Children whose activity levels fall far beneath their biological requirements may not achieve optimum development and growth. Furthermore, it has been shown that physical activity naturally stimulates the release of growth hormones into the circulation, and that the healing process of wounds and recovery from health conditions is significantly faster in children who exercise regularly.

- Preliminary evidence suggests that exercise helps to increase insulin sensitivity and resistance to diabetes. Stress and diabetes are also linked (*see* page 66).

- Exercise is clearly linked with self-esteem and mental attitude. The resultant improved muscle strength, gains in aerobic fitness, feelings of control over their environment and positive feedback from friends can make children feel better about themselves.

What do children need?

According to the first comprehensive set of exercise guidelines issued by the American National Association for Sport and Physical Education, children should be active for at least 60 minutes a day, and ideally for much longer.

Fitting it in

- First, assess your schedule. If time is a problem, you may need to book 'fun' appointments for your children, to ensure that they are getting playtime. Given some freedom and a little open space, most children will get plenty of exercise with little prompting from their parents.

- Make sure that your children get fun time every day. Allow time for turning them out into the garden, or making a visit to the local park, playground or gymnasium every day after school.

- Don't rely on structured activities too much. While these are undoubtedly good for fitness levels, they can mean a lot of waiting around and are less useful for releasing built-up energy. Sometimes children just need to run and play, left to their own devices (*see* page 47) and without strict supervision.

- Do try *some* organised sports. Children need to have a taste of all types of activities before they can decide what they like best. Don't be concerned if your child is not a natural athlete, and never criticise or suggesting quitting, particularly if your child enjoys a sport. Team sports teach many things above and beyond fitness and reducing stress levels, and children benefit from group activity. Many children who begin a sport in child-hood will carry on the hobby in later life, so it's important to find something that they enjoy and will want to practise regularly.

- If walking to school or the local playgroup is impossible, park further away than usual and walk part of the way. Consider organising a 'walking bus', which involves children walking to school in a large group, accompanied by a 'driver' (a parent volunteer at the front of the bus) and a 'conductor' (at the back of the bus). The bus stops at pre-arranged points to collect other children, who join the queue. This scheme has met with a great deal of success in the UK, where children involved are given advice and information on road safety, and high-visibility bibs to wear.

- If it's manageable, consider accompanying older children to school on bikes. Enrol them in a cycling proficiency programme first, to learn the basics of road safety, signalling and skills. Invest in a good helmet and a high-visibility bib.

Whatever you choose, make a decision to commit to it. Adults are often wary of the term 'exercise', which conjures up visions of enforced routines at school, or hours on a treadmill trying to lose unwanted weight. The word holds no such associations for children; ensure that it never does. If they start off being active, they'll be more likely to continue that way. Instil the idea early on that exercise is fun and sociable, makes you feel better and is a natural, normal part of life.

I do lots of exercise because we do it at school on Fridays. I also have a swimming lesson. Mostly I play on my Play-station, watch TV or lie on my bed when I don't have to do homework. **Joe, 11**

Sleep

The importance of sleep for children in relation to stress cannot be overexaggerated (*see also* Chapter 2). Children of all ages need sleep, and lots of it, in order to grow, develop, interact, learn and adapt to their environment. A sleep deficit will exacerbate feelings of being out of control – in fact, all of the emotional symptoms of stress – but it will also compromise immunity and the efficiency of your child's body.

Sleep is crucially important in childhood and adolescence, and there are very few children who do not need to get at least the average required hours. Your child may not fit the norm exactly – very active children and children who are under intense pressure will have higher sleep requirements – but it's helpful to have an idea of what to expect, and what to aim for. If you find your child is getting dramatically less or more than required, you may need to assess why.

Aim to set bedtime at a point at which your child falls asleep and stays asleep until he wakes naturally. If he has trouble waking in the morning, move bedtime to half an hour earlier.

Stress has a significant effect on sleep patterns, and most children have real trouble waking in the morning as a result. Not only do they need more sleep, but they also need to reduce their stress load. Notice how difficult it is to wake your child during the school term, and how early they rise at weekends and holidays! In a stress-free environment, children sleep better, perform better, waken naturally, and have energy and enthusiasm to face life.

Average required hours of sleep

Age	Number of hours
New-borns	16 to 18
3 to 6 months	15
6 to 12 months	14 to 15
1 to 2 years	14
3 to 6 years	10 to 12
7 to 9 years	8 to 10
10 to 11 years	8 to 9.5
11 to 18 years	9 plus

I can't get to sleep at night because I am not tired. I also can't get up in the morning because I am too tired. I am supposed to be in bed at 9 every night but I usually listen to music in my room until about midnight or something.
Joshua, 9

Establishing routines

The key to successful sleep habits for children of all ages is a sound pre-sleep routine that is followed on a daily basis. Many parents adopt a good routine with their babies, and have little trouble throughout childhood. Others are careful about routine in infancy, but let it slide when toddlers and older children begin to assert their own ideas about bedtime. It is much easier to impose a regime when children are younger than it is to introduce something new later on.

The importance of routine cannot be overstated. Children feel secure when they know their boundaries and what to expect. If the rules and routines change repeatedly, they feel unsettled and will be more likely to create a pre-bedtime fuss, or wake in the night. Setting up your life in a series of ordered events may seem tedious and monotonous, but all family members will benefit from a carefully designed routine. Your child will sleep better, with less disruption. You will avoid distressing and exhausting bedtime battles, and you will have time on your own and get a good night's sleep. Children who have slept well are less irritable throughout the day and perform better at school.

No child benefits from being allowed free rein to set their own bedtime. Every one of us needs good, nurturing sleep in order to perform well at whatever age. Putting a good routine in action can help everyone in the family to unwind and fall asleep at an appropriate time.

I find it hardest to concentrate at school in the morning because I am tired. I feel better after lunch but the best after dinner when I don't have to do anything. *Lizzie, 12*

Toddlers

If you haven't already got a routine in place, it's not too late to start one. You may find that an existing routine needs to be altered slightly to take into account a later or earlier bedtime, or a later than expected arrival home from work. One of the most important things to remember about a bedtime routine is that it needs to be calm. It can be difficult for parents who have been away from their children all day to avoid boisterous play, but the excitement of seeing a parent again, coupled with some rough and tumble, tickling or chasing, can make it impossible for a child to settle down to sleep.

Some of the bedtime routine may have to be undertaken before you get home – by a nanny or other carer – and you'll need to make sure that they are aware of the best sequence of events to settle your child. The beauty of a routine is that anyone should be able to put it in place. If all of the sleep associations are in place – a warm bath, some time spent talking, a story or a puzzle and maybe a warm drink – your child will be less likely to make a fuss, even if you are not there.

If you or your partner do return home later, keep things low-key. Settle down with a story and a drink, or even just a little chat. Play some soft music, and take time to relax yourself. As your child gets older, he'll learn to welcome this peaceful period and you'll be much more likely to build up a good rapport if he knows that he always has this time allotted to him. This can be quiet time – a time for praise, gentle activities and comfort. If you are stressed or tired after work, try not to let it show, and never use this time to air disagreements or inflict discipline. It's certainly acceptable to talk things through – perhaps your toddler had a bad day at nursery, or wouldn't eat his dinner – but keep things calm. If you are too enthusiastic, excited or angry, he will react in kind. No child will sleep well is he is anxious or overexcited.

Try to make an evening bath part of the daily routine. Although your child might not need one every night, a bath can have the positive psychological effect of 'washing away' the stresses and strains of the day. Younger children may splash and become excited, but they will feel warm and relaxed when you have dried them off and put on their pyjamas. A drop or two of tea tree oil and lavender oil will relax the child, and boost immunity – and will work wonders for fending off nits when the child reaches school age. A daily bath also instils good hygiene habits in children, and can teach them how to wash and dry themselves properly.

Older children

As children get older, there are more demands on their time – homework, extra-curricular activities, exercise and play – and many more distractions. Routines are important not only to ensure that they fit everything in easily and comfortably, but also to allow your child to get the sleep he needs. Even older children find comfort and security in routines, and when a good routine is in place, they'll learn the valuable skill of planning their own time.

If you've had a routine in place since babyhood, keep it in place and adjust it according to your child's needs. Most children will benefit from some quiet playtime, a relaxing bath, a chat and a story. As your child gets older, they may like to choose the story and read to you. Some children enjoy listening to a story tape at night; as long as it's not too long or exciting, this can be a good way of lulling them to sleep. Bedtime reading is seriously under-rated.

If you haven't set up a routine before, try to do so now. Begin the wind-down from dinner-time. You may need to put some new rules in place, but try to make it look like a series of lifestyle changes for the whole family, rather than a rigid new routine for the child or children, which is sure to be greeted with horror.

My mum and dad don't read stories to me because they don't have time. Sometimes my brother reads me a story at bedtime but mostly I just listen to tapes. **Jack, 5**

It's a good idea to get homework and other necessaries out of the way before dinner, unless you eat very early. Like adults, children need time to unwind before bed and if they are struggling with or resisting homework, it's bound to have its effect on their sleep. After dinner, give them a period of time in which to choose a favourite activity, but set a time limit and if necessary set up a 'star chart' to ensure that it is maintained. If your child is used to watching television for several hours every night and you suggest a one-hour slot instead, you'll have to use some positive encouragement to implement the changes successfully.

After 'free' time, work your way towards bath-time, and then play a quiet game or work on a puzzle together. You can listen to music, perhaps, or just chat. As long as the activity is quiet, anything goes. This may sound idealistic in a family with more than one child, but if you ensure that everyone has their free time at the same time, and each party knows what happens next, you'll find that things do slip into place. Reading together or letting your child read to you before bedtime is a good way to end the day, especially if you can arrange to do it in their bedroom. Older children can be given time to read alone or listen to a story tape before lights out.

I watch TV for about two hours before bed. I only get nightmares if I watch something scary. I don't read because I don't like it. I don't really talk to anyone at bedtime because we are all watching TV or my parents are out. My dad only reads the newspaper when he's home anyhow. **James, 9**

Adolescents

The sleeping habits of adolescents have become a matter for serious concern. It is vital for teenagers to get enough restful sleep, but activities out of the house in the evenings, and a great deal of homework, can push bedtime later and later. Routines may be a little harder to put into place, and to adhere to.

If your child is a good sleeper, and has no trouble getting into bed and falling asleep at a reasonable hour, you don't need to worry. If, however, your child gets a second wind around midnight and stays glued to the computer or television long after he should be in bed, it is in everyone's interests to get a routine in place. If you do not already have one, encourage your teenager to set his own bedtime routine. Propose that he spends some time every night doing his own thing, and some time with you, or with the family, after dinner. Make sure he gets homework done early, to avoid winding himself up and finding it difficult to get to sleep. Suggest a bath or shower and a short reading session before bed every night. It's usually possible to reason with an adolescent, and you can use the same ploys that you use with exercise or nutrition – that is, make it relevant to their lives. If you point out that sleep deprivation will affect athletic or academic performance, or even make them irritable with family and friends the next day, they may take this into consideration.

TELEVISION AND SLEEP DON'T MIX

A study from Hasbro Children's Hospital and Brown University in Rhode Island said that doctors should be aware of the potential negative impact of television viewing at bedtime and recommended that parents be questioned about their children's television-viewing habits as part of general screening for sleep disorders. Researchers surveyed the parents of 495 children aged five to 10 to assess sleep behaviour and TV-viewing habits. They found increased daily TV viewing and increased viewing at bedtime were associated with sleep disturbance, especially when children had a TV in their bedroom (*see* page 46).

According to the report, sleep characteristics most often affected included bedtime resistance, sleep onset delay, anxiety and shortened sleep duration. The researchers suggested that children might be overstimulated, disturbed or frightened by the content of programmes, particularly those containing violence. However, they also suggested children might sleep better if they were taking more exercise rather than watching television.

What's the answer? Make sure that television is not part of the bedtime routine. At least an hour should elapse between watching television and going to bed to encourage optimum sleep. If your child has a favourite programme that comes on at a later hour, tape it and play it back at a more appropriate time.

I don't get enough sleep because my mum makes me do extra work and my brothers annoy me. Sometimes I cry because I feel so tired and I just want to be alone but I know I have to work hard to get into a good school. *Kay, 11*

What can you do about adolescent sleep problems?

- Keep an eye on activity levels. If a teen is playing sports every day after school, practising an instrument, has a part-time job or takes part in too many clubs, you may need to encourage him to drop something. Many adolescents enjoy being busy and they are much less likely to be drawn off the rails if they are kept occupied. However, if it's disrupting sleep, you'll need to make changes. Stick to a reasonable schedule that allows time for homework, fun and adequate rest.

- Make sure your adolescent is part of the family routine – eating regularly, enjoying some free time and going to bed at an appropriate time. If his bedtime is running later and later, strike a deal and let him choose a more appropriate bedtime. Explain the importance of sleep in relation to academic and sports performance, and if he's struggling with moodiness mention the idea that sleep has now been linked with mood swings. Reward his efforts.

- Keep an eye on his diet. If he's drinking coffee or a lot of cola in the evenings, he'll find it difficult to get to sleep and his sleep may be disrupted. Sources of caffeine should be avoided from noon, if possible. Point out that alcohol can also disrupt sleep.

- Intense studying or computer games before bed can be over-stimulating.

- Avoid arguing with an adolescent just before bedtime; it might make him feel stressed, under pressure and less able to sleep.

- Keep the television and the lights off when trying to go to sleep, and open the blinds or curtains as soon as the morning alarm goes. This can help to create a more acceptable sleep/wake cycle.

- Don't discourage weekend lie-ins, but limit them to no more than two or three hours later than the usual wakening time, or the body clock will be disrupted.

Environment

Your child's environment – the atmosphere in which he grows and is nurtured into adulthood – should place as few demands as possible on his growing body. Many of the toxins with which your child comes into contact in daily life are now considered to be stressors – a form of environmental stress. Everything your child eats, drinks and breathes contributes to his overall state of health. But a child's home environment is just as important, having a profound effect on his physical and emotional health.

There are many actions you can take to make your child's environment positive and healthy, from choosing household chemicals that will have the least impact on your child's body, to ensuring that the general atmosphere is conducive to happiness and well-being.

Many parents who have children with allergies will understand the concept of an allergen-free home, which involves taking steps to remove substances that can trigger a reaction in susceptible children. In fact, all children will benefit from such an approach, whether they suffer from obvious allergies or not. Anything that triggers a reaction in a susceptible child may also put a strain on the body of a healthy child. All these substances need to be dealt with by the body, using energy that could be better used in the context of overall health and coping with stress.

Cut the chemicals

Consider the products you are using in your home. A recent report called *Multiple Chemical Sensitivity Recognition*, published by the British Society for Allergy, Environmental and Nutritional Medicine, urged the government to tighten the regulation of chemical use, including stricter controls on the authorisation of new chemicals, and the removal of persistent chemicals from food. The authors found that exposure to chemicals can not only cause allergies and fatigue in susceptible people, but can also lead to a condition called 'multiple chemical sensitivity', or a severe allergy to the chemicals in everyday products.

Research published by the European Chemicals Bureau shows that only 14 per cent of the most commonly used chemicals have a full set of basic safety data publicly available. In other words, we do not know the long-term effects of the majority of chemicals that we use on a daily basis.

What can you do?

- Solvent-based paints, varnishes, cleaning fluids and sprays, glues and chemical treatments all have the potential to cause a reaction in a child's sensitive skin or airways, and they need to be dealt with by the body whenever there is contact. Buy emulsion-free paints and other DIY products from specialist suppliers.

- Throw out the majority of your cleaning products, and replace them with environmentally friendly products, which use the least noxious chemicals and pose the least threat to health. Don't be misled into believing that your house will only be really clean if you use special antibacterial products; this is a fallacy, and they can actually do more harm than good. Old-fashioned soap and water, or soda crystals and water, are your best bet. If you have young children and are concerned about contact with bugs, use plain bleach.

- The healthiest carpets are hessian-backed and not treated with pesticides (such as permethrin or mitin FF), which can give off a vapour and soak through to the surface, affecting your children's skin and health.

- By law, all washing-up liquids are biodegradable. Choose a brand that is unscented, or naturally scented, and use it in place of most household detergents. If you are concerned about bacteria, use a drop of two of essential oils, such as lemon, tea tree and lavender, in the washing-up bowl.

- Naturally bleach white clothes by hanging them out in the sunlight, or add soda crystals to your wash. Bicarbonate of soda can remove many stains, as can soap and water and a little elbow grease. A mild bleach solution is not dangerous occasionally, but put clothes through another wash cycle before your child wears them.

- For personal hygiene, soap and water are the best options, although young children need nothing more than water, with a drop of a gentle essential oil, such as lavender. A little olive oil can soften a child's skin. Choose a mild, unscented shampoo and conditioner (again, environmentally friendly, or one of the new organic products).

- Consider the effects of household pollution, particularly carbon monoxide, an invisible, colourless and odourless poisonous gas to which we are all exposed in varying degrees on a daily basis. Carbon monoxide progressively starves the body of oxygen, and victims may develop headaches, dizziness or fatigue and weakness, and may have a flushed face. Children are particularly vulnerable to carbon monoxide poisoning because their bodies are not able to detoxify as effectively as adults'.

- Living around a smoker adds an inestimable load to a child's stress burden. Smoke contains more than 2,000 different toxic chemicals and passive smoke is a serious source of pollution, although the exact extent of the damage it causes is not yet completely clear. It will have an impact upon your child's health, no matter how scrupulous you are about opening windows and avoiding smoking in their presence.

CUTTING INDOOR POLLUTION

- Cut down on indoor air pollution and improve the quality of the air in your home by increasing the ventilation. Make sure that windows are opened and rooms aired on a daily basis, even if only for a few minutes. Cross-ventilation is important. Open a window on the opposite side of the room to the door. If you can't seem to get a flow of air going, consider a ceiling fan. Make sure all heating or cooking appliances that use gas, oil, coal or wood are well vented.

- Don't smoke.

- Use natural material for furniture. Many artificial products can let off toxic gases. Foam-filled furniture and carpet backings are common culprits.

- Turn off electrical appliances when not in use.

- Invest in some houseplants, which absorb toxic fumes from the air. Peace lilies and spider plants are particularly good, and can also absorb EM radiation and tobacco smoke. Keep a plant by the television, the computer, the microwave oven, and in hallways. Some people claim that plants should not be kept in bedrooms, as they remove oxygen at night, but their environmental benefits will outweigh this disadvantage.

- An electrical ioniser emits negative irons to help clear the air of dust, smoke and some allergens. Ions are positively and negatively charged molecules. A healthy balance of positive and negative ions promotes a feeling of calm and well-being. Central heating, electrical appliances, synthetic fabrics, pollution and dust all deplete levels of negative ions, which can contribute to headaches, irritability and general malaise.

The downside of technology

Electromagnetic fields

All parents need to be aware of the dangers of too much technology. Electromagnetic fields exist in most households, derived from extra-low-frequency AC electrical wiring and appliances. Some children and adults seem to be sensitive to their effects, while others are not, but everyone seems to be affected to some degree. The appliances at the centre of the storm include microwave ovens, electric blankets, televisions, computers and (not electric) mobile telephones.

With new research appearing on an almost daily basis, there is increasing controversy about the possible health risks from the radiation in these EM fields. If there is *any* risk, however, surely parents need to be made aware of the situation?

The facts are as follows:

- A number of studies have reported higher childhood leukaemia in homes in which the EM fields were higher than average. Another showed that high appliance use leads to strong EM fields that are associated with an increased risk of cancers in all children.

- Using a VDU screen has been linked to miscarriage and birth defects, and televisions are much the same as VDUs.

- Another study suggests that EM fields may reduce the production of melatonin, a hormone that maintains the normal daily rhythms of the body, including the sleep and wake cycle. Reduced levels of melatonin are associated with depression.

Mobile telephones are also the subject of intense controversy, and conflicting studies. In their relatively short history, they have been blamed for causing all manner of ills, including cancer, headaches, memory loss, high blood pressure and strokes. A recent study suggests that the microwaves generated by mobile phones may damage the ability of white blood cells to fight off infection and disease. White blood cells, known as lymphocytes, were taken from a donor, kept alive with nutrients and exposed to different electric fields. After 7.5 hours, just 13 per cent of the cells exposed to mobile phone radiation remained intact and able to function, compared with 70 per cent of cells exposed only to the natural EM field produced by the human body. The authors of the study claim that the body's immune system is partially controlled by EM fields emitted by the body. Their conclusion is that the radiation emitted by mobile phones damages the body's own EM fields, and undermines the proper functioning of the immune system.

Another study showed that the rate of death from brain cancer among people who held mobile phones close to their head was higher than those who used phones away from their head. Confusingly, more recent research has shown that hands-free headsets increase the damage caused by radiation even further.

What's the answer?

It's easy to be overcautious and suggest that children be banned from anything emitting EM radiation, but that would not be practical in the modern world. Parents should, however, keep an eye on research, and take in any new safety guidelines. Research is often contradictory, so decisions need to be made based on the best information available. If there is any indication that an appliance is linked in any way with adverse reactions, it pays to take note.

It is clear that the strength of an EM field is rapidly diminished when there is more distance between the source and the child. Rather than ban everything electrical, you might prefer to consider the following:

- Most televisions emit very low levels of ionising radiation. If you have an old set, think about replacing it with a low-radiation version.

- Ensure that children sit at least 2m/6ft away from a television set; if they are playing a game on a computer, using a remote controller allows them to sit well back.

- Limit the number of hours that your child spends in front of the television. Obviously, increased exposure means increased EM radiation.

- Don't use electric blankets on the bed while your child is sleeping. Warm the bed by all means, but turn it off and remove it before your child goes to bed.

- Turn off electrical appliances when not in use.

- Discourage your child from standing in front of a microwave oven when it is in use.

- If your child spends a lot of time in front of computer (for school work or playing games), make sure he takes frequent breaks. Consider one of the new screens that can help to reduce radiation. Incidentally, to prevent RSI (repetitive strain injury), ensure that your child is sitting above the keyboard, and the VDU screen is set at eye level or above.

Lighten the load

The home environment can greatly influence a child's ability to absorb vital energy into his system and thus directly affect his well-being and quality of life.

Natural light is necessary for health on all levels. For example, the endocrine system, which is governed by the pituitary and pineal glands, requires light in order to function properly. These glands control the release of hormones into the body, which are closely linked to moods and emotions. The endocrine system is put under enormous pressure when a child is stressed, and a simple way to balance this is to increase your child's exposure to natural light.

No form of artificial lighting can match the healing effect of natural sunlight. Try to ensure that you get as much natural light as possible into your house:

- Keep windows clean and check that they all open, to let in the air.

- Design curtains or blinds to allow the maximum amount of natural light into the room.

- Draw curtains back as far as possible and keep blinds up during the day.

- Move away any plants or objects which obstruct light coming into your home.

- Use mirrors opposite windows in rooms with low light levels.

- Use low-energy lighting or full-spectrum lights where possible, as a good alternative to the real thing.

- If possible, create skylights or a sunroom where you can enjoy the benefits of sunlight.

- Most importantly, make sure your child spends time outside every day, so that he gets the chance to absorb the energy of as much natural light as possible. (Remember to apply sunscreen and get him to wear a hat if the sun is strong.)

Leisure

The average child gets very little quality leisure time, and activities traditionally associated with leisure are now the focus of intense competition, performance and parental expectations, all squeezed into a highly organised schedule.

Leisure time and levels of stress are inversely proportional – the less leisure, the more stress. Stress-reduction experts ask patients to fill in a chart to see what their work/leisure ratio looks like. They are asked to think of their life (excluding sleep time) in the four compartments of work, family, community and self, and then to assess what percentage of their time and energy in an average week goes into each part. There is no 'normal' range but there is cause for concern when 'work' is over 60 per cent and/or when 'self' is less than 10 per cent. Everyone needs time to meet their own needs (self-care, self-nurturing, and so on); when that is neglected, trouble usually follows. Self-directed activities can include exercise or recreation, relaxation, socialising, entertainment and hobbies.

What percentage of leisure time do your children have in relation to planned activities, school, homework, instrument practice and other obligations? How many of their activities are genuinely relaxing and fulfilling? What activities actually add to their stress load? Parents must establish or encourage a healthy leisure/work ratio if children are to manage stress successfully.

Parents also need to ask themselves about the *quality* of their children's leisure time. If a day filled with activities ends with two hours in front of the television, your child will not actually be relaxing or gaining anything fulfilling or satisfying from his leisure time. The same goes for games consoles and computers, many of which artificially stimulate the senses and create a reaction similar to the stress response.

Over the past couple of decades, passive, spectator leisure (not counting television, but including watching sports) has increased by 30 minutes per week to over three hours. One of the main reasons why this has happened is that children are so exhausted and stressed by their lives that they can summon very little energy to do little more than flop.

George Marsh, headmaster of Dulwich College Preparatory School in London, agrees that children have an inadequate amount of quality relaxation and leisure time. His school has an inordinately bustling atmosphere, with a wide variety of different activities from which to choose after school and in the lunch break, but he feels that this approach is healthier in the long run than leaving all of the organising to parents. At his school, the children are empowered to choose their leisure activities. They can choose to be busy or to relax; they can relax in groups, or choose to be alone. While parents can try to direct choices from the sidelines, ultimately it is the children who decide what they want to do and when. This way, they are not put under too much pressure.

Parents need to listen to their children, he says, and to watch for subtle shifts in personality or attitude indicating that there is a problem. From George Marsh's viewpoint, busy parents often continue their hectic schedules at home, timetabling everything and creating a whirlwind of activity that allows no breathing space for children. Far from relaxing with their children, they increase the pressure, and set habits that children will learn to emulate in later life. He also feels that interaction is an important part of relaxation and leisure, and too many children receive little or none of this on a regular basis.

Stress and relaxation are opposite sides of a coin, and each is required to counterbalance the other. The problem with today's children is that they are actively discouraged from being 'lazy', 'lying about' or not making the best use of their time. Because they are continually under pressure, they will actually find it difficult to unwind and relax. Living on adrenaline, they choose exciting activities that stimulate them and blot out any concerns or worries that they would rather not address. Once again, slumping in front of the television might require little effort, and appear restful, but true relaxation and rest involve contemplation, peace, reflection, interaction, exuberance, play and an opportunity to let off steam in the process of having fun. While many of these factors may seem contradictory, your child's choice of relaxation will reflect what he needs. He may want a quiet daydream in the corner or a rollicking good pillow fight with his dad. Whatever the case, let your child choose. As long as it doesn't involve more competition, take up too much of his free time, or involve distraction-leisure activities only, any way your child chooses to relax will be right for him.

Five minutes' peace

In every day, your child should also have some time alone with no distractions, and no noise. This probably sounds idealistic in a busy household, but you can aim for a sense of quiet by establishing periods when radios, televisions and everything else are unavailable. Noise is a stressor and an environmental pollutant, and everyone needs respite. Time alone, and in peace, gives children a chance to reflect, to plan and to think. Children cannot make reasoned decisions or become self-aware if they are never given a moment to stop and contemplate. You child may choose to read, to draw, to daydream or even chat quietly with a family member. If there are many distractions in your household, your child is unlikely to remember important thoughts and worries in the general chaos, and is also less likely to communicate. It's amazing what comes out when the world is turned off. Give your child a sanctuary where he will feel free to form thoughts and express them.

Giving children an outlet

Today's children are expected to adhere to parental and societal expectations from a much earlier age. They attend school earlier, their lives are packed with activities, and there is much less time for play and relaxation. Not surprisingly, this can cause an enormous amount of stress in a child, and it can be reflected in his overall health, well-being and behaviour.

We offer little opportunity for children to be children. They are expected to conform to an ideal – not making a fuss, not interrupting, concentrating at school, on the sports field, on their homework, eating their dinner and getting dressed without a murmur, bathing quietly, and going to bed, where they are expected to fall asleep immediately, and sleep through the night.

At what point are children offered an outlet to express emotion, to unload tension, to let off steam, to be children, to show their natural energy and spirit?

Many parents complain that their children are so good at school but a 'complete nightmare' in the home environment. Such children have learned appropriate behaviour for the school environment and have probably worked very hard at keeping their emotions and enthusiasm in check for an entire school day. In the comfort of their own home, they are able to let down their defences and let out all that energy that has been suppressed all day. And that is how it should be! A child's home should be the place where he can be himself without expectations, judgement or punishment.

Naughty or rebellious behaviour at home is not always appropriate, but you must allow some leeway. If your child comes home in a state every day, he needs an outlet and it is up to you to provide it. Organise some fun exercise. Throw him out in the garden to run and explore. Laugh, tell jokes, wrestle, play, relax – anything that lets the energy flow. The rigid routine of school should not be followed by an equally rigid routine at home. Certainly, a household routine will help your child to feel secure, but that routine needs to include time for fun, high spirits, laughter, shouting, cheering, crying or just lying about. If your child is exhibiting signs of stress, he does not have an appropriate outlet, and you will need to create one.

Children need space and freedom to be themselves and it is unreasonable to expect adult behaviour and self-control from a child. If they have learned appropriate behaviour in certain situations, you've done a good job. The rest of the time, you need to modify your expectations accordingly.

Furthermore, don't be too harsh about their choice of entertainment. If they choose to lie on the floor reading a comic for an hour, don't be tempted to rush them into something more challenging, educational or 'fulfilling'. Every child will have an 'ideal' relaxing activity. Find out what your child needs in order to relax and do your best to provide it. Sometimes, all they need is some *un*scheduled time.

Emotional support

Remember, what children need most from their parents is unconditional love and acceptance, which gives them the courage and strength to explore, take risks, challenge, attempt and achieve the things they want in life. In what way do you offer emotional support for your child? Do you accept the good with the bad, the failure with the success? If your approach to parenting focuses too heavily on judging your child, discipline, behaviour, achievement, performance and fulfilling expectations, your child will not have the support he needs to deal with stressful situations. Furthermore, he will not have the communication channel he needs to express concerns, will not learn from failure, and, ultimately, will not be in a position of knowing that there is someone, somewhere, who will love him no matter what he does.

A child who lives with encouragement and appreciation becomes confident. If his main relationships are with people who are patient and undemanding, he will feel secure enough to try new things without a fear of failure. He will not be afraid of failing to live up to expectations, and he will be encouraged to celebrate his own achievements and success in attaining personal goals. These will make him stronger and more resilient to peer pressure, to life's ups and downs, and to all the knocks along the way. If a child feels good about himself, and is supported in that belief, he will meet challenges with vigour and enthusiasm. Most importantly, he will be happy.

The importance of praise

Praise is essential for well-being and for self-esteem, both of which create the emotional foundation your child needs to be happy and fulfilled. Most children are extremely busy, and rushed through daily activities. There is little time to stop and appraise or, indeed, to praise. Achievements tend to be praised rather than effort, and this can be daunting for children who need encouragement in order to succeed. Good marks are applauded, as are results on the sports pitch, passing a music exam, making a team, for example, while all the effort that goes into these successes passes largely unnoticed. Children develop an unhealthy focus on winning and succeeding, rather than simply doing their best. Given the nature of the stress that already exists in their lives, this creates an extremely unhealthy balance. They see that the winner takes all, while the ones who tried their best, and reached their own personal goals, are disregarded.

How often do you praise your child and really mean it? You may be lavish with praise, but has it become meaningless? Praise has to be heartfelt to be effective. Lots of 'lovely, darling, aren't you clever?'s and 'you've done so well's throughout the day will make your child feel good initially, but eventually become irrelevant.

Not only does praise have to be directed, but it also needs to be genuine and believable. If a child fails an exam, and you still go on and on about how clever he is, he'll know you are being duplicitous. If you choose, however, to praise his effort and point out how much he has improved since the last test, he'll not only learn to respect your comments, but will also feel good about his own personal achievement. This is an important part of living life in the fast lane. If children learn to recognise and celebrate the milestones along the path to adulthood they will, as adults, have a much healthier self-image and the confidence to cope when things don't go according to plan.

Try to fit as much praise as possible into your child's day, but make sure it is relevant to your child's effort, and to his potential. From morning to night, notice and dwell on the good things about your child's behaviour, his actions, his personality, his efforts and his views. Children are notoriously inconsistent, and often only half-finish tasks. Praise the parts that he completes, the things he has remembered, and help him to see that he's making progress. If you continually focus on the things he hasn't managed to attain, he'll feel like a failure, even if your conversations are peppered with meaningless praise.

Show interest in him and his world. Be thrilled for his achievements, even if they don't live up to your expectations. If your child gets a report card full of Cs, but his teacher says he's really tried hard, make a fuss. If your child fails everything, but gets a glowing personal report, focus on the fact that he is a nice, popular child. Praise everything good about your child and what he does. If he feels good about himself, if he believes you like him, flaws and all, he will develop self-esteem that will affect every part of his life.

Only praising a single aspect of your child – his school marks, for example – can put pressure on him to perform at a consistent level. Psychologists at Columbia University, New York, conducted six studies of 412 11-year-olds, comparing children praised for intelligence with those praised for effort and hard work. They looked at children under conditions of failure as well as success. They found that commending children for their intelligence after a good performance could backfire by making them highly performance-oriented and thus extremely vulnerable to the effects of subsequent setbacks. These children learned to believe that intelligence is a fixed trait that cannot be developed or improved, and blamed poor performance on their own lack of intelligence. On the other hand, children who were commended for their effort concentrated on learning goals and strategies for achievement. When these children performed poorly, they blamed their lack of success on poor effort and demonstrated a determination to learn strategies that would enhance subsequent performances. The answer? Use both general and specific praise, so that your child has plenty to feel good about, even when one aspect of his life slips.

Most importantly, however, praise your child for just being himself. Praise his appearance ('you are such a good-looking boy', 'your hair looks nice today', 'you've got such a great smile', 'you look good in those jeans', 'what gorgeous eyes') constantly. Children will define their bodies by how others perceive them. If you make them feel that they are attractive, you will improve their confidence and their self-image. Fat children, skinny children, adolescents with acne, babies with chickenpox – everyone needs to feel that they are lovable and nice to look at. You won't create a big-headed child by praising appearance, you'll simply ensure that your child feels comfortable in his own skin.

If you haven't been as lavish with praise as you might have been, it's never too late. Your child may appear suspicious at the outset, but he will feel proud and flattered underneath. Soon, it will become a way of life, and your child's confidence and self-image will slowly improve in the light of your unconditional love and approval.

Physical affection

Nurturing touch plays a significant role in infant and child development, and research suggests that it continues to be important as a way of communicating love and caring between parents and older children. Most parents continue to share some level of physical closeness with their daughters during the growing-up years, but this can change dramatically for sons. Parents of boys (particularly mothers) find that their physical contact with a son grows more awkward and less frequent around the age of eight or nine. The shift is most dramatic when the son moves into adolescence. Many children naturally withdraw at this stage, particularly in front of their friends, and this reaction has to be expected and respected. However, it doesn't mean that you should give up altogether. Like many other aspects of parenting, physical closeness remains important throughout a child's life. A parent is one of the few people to whom children can turn as they get older, for the emotional comfort of physical warmth in a non-sexual context.

Touch can offer reassurance and love that goes beyond words.

A pat on the shoulder, a warm embrace, a gentle massage, tousling hair or stroking a much-loved little face can all communicate acceptance and affection. Watch for signs that your child needs a little reassurance and make it natural. An attention-seeking child may just need a little quality attention. Sit down together with a book and put your arm around your child. If he's watching television, stroke his feet. If he's struggling with homework, give him a hug. If he cries, don't expect him to be more mature. Get down there and be physical. There is safety in physical affection, and all children will benefit.

Children need to experience physical tenderness if they are to be able to be physical themselves as adults. A child who is not touched will feel ignored, ashamed, unworthy of attention, inferior, lost, alone, unsure and unhappy. Children need to feel good about their bodies and themselves, and physical affection can provide reassurance that they are attractive and lovable. No one touches things that they find distasteful, and if you fail to touch your child, he will get the message – even if only on a subconscious level – that he is something with which you would rather not be in contact. Touch raises self-esteem and it costs nothing to give.

Time and interaction

Communication is one of the most important elements of stress relief, and the majority of children simply do not confide in their parents, either because they fear recrimination, or because they never have a genuine opportunity to do so. Even in families that make a concerted effort to spend time together, children have far too little meaningful time with their parents. Struggles over homework, rushing to activities, grabbing a quick dinner, and scrabbling to prepare for the next day do not allow for an environment that is conducive to interaction and sharing. Children need to be encouraged to talk, and adults need to find or make the time to do this. Asking the same questions of your child at the end of every day, in your half-hour of allotted 'quality time', will not produce genuine and positive communication. Children will either tune out, or reluctantly recite the events of their day.

Converse with your child in much the same way as you would a friend, bringing up interesting situations or elements of your own day, or asking their opinion about a piece of news or even a new colour for the sitting-room wall. Ask them interesting, focused questions that are relevant to their state of mind, their mood and their activities. This doesn't mean treating them like adults, it simply means giving them the respect that you give to other adults. 'What did you have for lunch?' is never going to inspire stimulating conversation, nor is an unhealthy focus on the day's test results. Ask questions that you know will interest him, and take an interest in his interests! Find out the news about his football team, be up to speed on the latest bands, pass on some good gossip, and you'll soon get the ball rolling. Once the channels of communication are opened, you'll establish the type of relationship in which chatting, revealing and confiding are commonplace, as well as a certain level of trust.

The key factor in this type of approach is *time*, and you have to be prepared to make it. If children grow up never forming strong bonds with close family and friends, never sharing problems or working on solutions and coping strategies, they are unlikely to do so in adulthood, and this is very unhealthy.

Essential skills

A significant part of a parent's job is to help children develop skills or tactics to manage challenging situations. It may not always be evident when there is a problem. When you have established good communication (*see above*), you will hopefully find yourself the recipient of news both good and bad, and will be able to gauge where problems might lie.

Children simply do not have the tools, the insight, the experience or the confidence to face every problem on their own. Part of life is learning how to deal with different people and situations, and parents need to be involved along the way, to ensure that the little things don't become insurmountable issues. Give examples of similar experiences that happened to you when you were a child. Ensure that your child feels that his situation and his response are absolutely normal. Never demand 'a brave face', or suggest that he deal with it on his own. Offering a variety of suggestions, from which they can choose, will help them to feel in control. They will be much more likely to ask your advice in future, and feel more confident about their coping skills in general.

Do you have anyone to talk to when you feel stressed?

No, I sit on my own. *Louis, 9*

I don't tell my parents about my problems because they will think it's all my fault. I just work things out by myself or do nothing. Mostly, I guess, I just do nothing and hope it all goes away. *Davina, 13*

Self-esteem and self-respect

Self-esteem is one of the most important qualities that your child can have, but the word has acquired something of a contradictory meaning over the past few years. Children may be young and immature, but they are not stupid. Filling their heads with non-sensical praise and approval that is not genuine will improve neither their self-image nor their self-respect. Children know when they haven't really earned something, and they'll take no pride in an achievement that is not really their own. Furthermore, it has ramifications for the future. A child who has everything altered to appear 'wonderful' and 'perfect' can justifiably expect to be spoon-fed, and for things to go their way, for the rest of their life. When they get out into the big, bad world, they'll be in for a nasty shock.

What's the answer? Realistic appraisal, celebration of genuine effort rather than simply results, constructive, careful criticism, guidance, communication and the identification and acceptance of strengths and weaknesses. There is an element of self-fulfilling prophecy with children. If they are told repeatedly that they are naughty, they are much more likely to act out that behaviour. It's expected and ingrained in their psyche. If they are told repeatedly that they are clever, they'll also believe it. But never be unrealistic or ungenuine. You'll be setting your child up for situations in which he can't cope, and you'll be setting him up for disappointment and failure.

Be honest with your child without being critical. If he fails a maths test because he didn't study, don't say 'well done, aren't you clever?', or show overwhelming disappointment or disapproval. Point out that he can do better next time, and focus on something that was successful that day, even if it was simply remembering to bring his spelling folder home. If children are not taught to indentify weaknesses in their abilities, behaviour and approach, they will never accept them or change them. If they think they are brilliant at everything, they'll get a nasty shock when they realise later in life that they are not. Confidence can get your child far in life, but if he finds out that you've been feeding him a load of rubbish over the years, his confidence will be sorely dented and he'll begin to disbelieve every bit of praise you've ever offered.

Furthermore, children will never develop a respect for their own efforts and achievements. If they never honestly and genuinely succeed, without having their grades altered, their efforts overexaggerated, their matches fixed, and every down on the way glossed over, they'll never experience the elation of real success and meeting personal goals. They will also fail to develop self-respect, which is one of the keys to resilience in childhood and in later life.

PERSONAL FREEDOM AND POWER

Everyone needs some control over their environment. When adults feel powerless – when they are in a situation they can't change, when pressures build up that they cannot alleviate, when they have financial difficulties and the bank refuses to help – they also feel frightened. They may also feel angry and rebellious. They may even feel trapped and depressed. Children feel much the same when they are given no freedom or when they have no power over their life.

Giving personal freedom involves allowing your child to do things that are appropriate for his age and his level of maturity. At some stage, parents have to let go, and allow their child to take that first walk to the shops on their own, take a bus ride or a bicycle ride by themselves, drive a car, light the fire, cook a meal, use a sharp knife. We need to assess when the time is right to offer children some freedom. With freedom comes a sense of responsibility.

WHAT TO DO:

- In every part of their day, offer some time that is your child's own. Allow them to choose what they want to do and let them do it. Give them choices (within the confines of a safe family environment, with household rules) and give them the freedom to enact them.

- Keep an eye on your child's development and gauge his responsibilities and his activities accordingly. Allow him to walk alone to a friend's house when you feel he is ready. Allow him to choose what he wants to eat occasionally. Teach him how to cross the road and let him do it on his own. Teach him to use a knife, and give him space (and a recipe book) to make a family dinner. Give him a watch and send him off to the park with friends, telling him what is expected and when you need him to be home.

- Parenting involves teaching children to behave maturely in every situation. Giving an immature child freedom for which he is not ready will not encourage growth. He'll probably feel frightened, out of control or confused. Assess your child's individual capabilities, and offer freedoms that are appropriate. This doesn't mean sending a child out unarmed into the wide world. It means providing, as your child grows, the tools for dealing with situations and experiences, and then giving space for experimentation.

- Give him a little of his own money and encourage him to choose what he does with it. Money teaches responsibility (*see below*) and offers a little freedom in which to make decisions. Too much money can encourage materialism, but money is a part of life, and a child will need to get used to dealing with it.

- Give responsibility. Get a fish, a hamster or another pet and make it your child's own responsibility. Give your child a plant, or a section of garden to call his own. Leave him in charge of a younger sibling for 10 minutes while you make a telephone call. Responsibility encourages emotional and spiritual growth. It encourages children to use their own resources in order to cope. If you reduce your child's time for freedom to suit your own schedule, he will never learn to rely upon himself, to take pleasure in his own achievements, to feel the glow of completing a task or looking after something successfully. He will never learn to make his own decisions. When he leaves home, he will not have the confidence he needs to find a path to happiness and well-being.

- Older children and adolescents need to be given the freedom to grow and to learn through experience. It can be difficult for many parents to let go, but it's an essential part of growing up. Gauge the correct age for different independent activities by talking to their friends' parents, and working out what is appropriate for your individual child. Set down rules about phone calls home, particularly if your child is late, suitable activities and guidelines. Try to keep the channels of communication open so that your child feels confident confiding in you – you'll feel more comfortable if you have a vague idea of what is going on. Once you've established the ground rules, sit back and give some freedom and responsibility. Your child will inevitably make mistakes, do silly things, and push the rules to the limit, but these are parts of the learning curve and necessary steps to adulthood.

A little power

Like adults, children need to have some control over their environment to feel secure, to learn to make decisions and choices, and to have the self-respect and self-esteem necessary to manage in the modern world. Childhood is a time of fun and experimentation, but it is also a 'training ground' for adulthood. Children need to be given the opportunity to make their own decisions, develop negotiating skills, plan their time and their activities, experience success and failure through experimentation and activities, and feel that they have some control over their environment.

Dominating parents may be able to mould a child into the 'ideal' person, complete with academic, sports and musical qualifications, and other talents and achievements, but that child will be ill prepared to cope with the outside world. Children who are given no power, and stifled by overdominant parenting, are more likely to rebel once they've left the nest. They are also less likely to cope with independence when they finally get it. Over-controlled children have little sense of self and even less sense of the outside world.

A child wrapped in cotton wool is less likely to be injured or emotionally hurt, but one day that child will have to go out into the world, with no experience of correct behaviour or knowledge of the strategies that will keep him safe. Giving a child some freedom, at an appropriate age, teaches decision-making and encourages self-esteem and confidence. Children will undoubtedly make some dubious decisions at times, but they will learn from their mistakes.

POWER AND DISCIPLINE

All children need to know that you (or another adult such as a teacher, baby-sitter or policeman) are in authority. That doesn't mean you have to be *authoritarian*, it simply means that your child must learn to respect people in charge. Establish early on that they have rights and choices, but within certain guidelines. No child will benefit from being allowed to run wild. Emotional health and freedom need the confines of a structured environment. Children of any age feel more secure when they know where they stand, and too much freedom can be alarming. Be consistent, stick to the family rules, and ensure that your child respects your authority to make overall decisions.

Children need to be given licence to debate and to ask questions, and you must be willing to negotiate on the basis of a sound argument. However, rudeness or argumentative behaviour suggest disrespect, and every child needs to learn that this is always inappropriate.

If you do have a problem with lack of respect for authority, empowering your child can help. If he feels that he has some control, and some scope for making choices and decisions, he will be less likely to challenge you on everything. For example, if your overall rule is that your child must dress himself in the morning, and you face a battle every single time, give him some choices. Do you want to get dressed before breakfast or after? Vest or underpants first? The red trousers or the blue trousers? Allowing choices makes him feel that he's in charge to some degree. The rule is the same – he still has to get dressed – but you have given him some personal power.

It works for older children, too. If your child regularly refuses to do his homework, offer choices: 'If we do it now, I can help you, or you can do it on your own after dinner.' 'Do you want to borrow my computer or do you want to write it out?' 'Do you want to do maths first or reading?' 'Do you want to do it in your bedroom or at the kitchen table?' Present it as an accepted fact that the homework *will* be done, but offer some choices as to how, when and where.

Remember that discipline is not about control. No one has the right to control anyone else. It is about guidance and respect, and teaching your child how to behave and act in every situation. Use praise, rules, choices, star charts, rewards, penalties and chats to indicate what is acceptable and what is not. Allow your child to make choices based on a knowledge of what will happen when he behaves appropriately and what will happen when he does not. Focus on the good, and ignore the bad.

Above all, give your child an outlet (*see* page 136), and don't expect angelic behaviour all the time. Everyone needs to let off steam and children need to be allowed to be children. Children do not have the self-control or the sense of propriety of an adult, or an understanding of societal expectations. As they grow up, they learn, through you, and through the reactions of everyone else around them, what is appropriate. Until then, give their natural enthusiasm space to grow, within guidelines that your child understands and accepts.

Discipline

All children need discipline. It defines their world, and makes it a safe place to live. It lets them know their boundaries, and they can express themselves and show some independence within those boundaries. Children without discipline are effectively without a guide, and are forced to make decisions and choices for which they are not equipped.

Many modern parents leave children to their own devices for long periods of time, and expect them to behave in an adult fashion, literally looking after themselves. Many of these children have too much freedom, but none of the guidance they need to use it healthily and successfully. Others are overdisciplined, expected to behave beautifully at all times, and to achieve and succeed, but given no personal freedom; the results are equally disastrous.

One of the most important jobs a parent has is to teach life lessons to their child, including behaviour. A basic level of respect for others is essential. You need to respect your child, and he needs to learn to respect you, and everyone else around him. Teaching respect is the art of discipline.

Parental expectations are crucial to discipline, and you need to assess whether yours are appropriate. Do you expect your child to sit quietly through a play at the theatre, or during an adult dinner party? Do you expect your child to walk by your side in the supermarket? Do you expect your child to behave impeccably in all situations? If so, your expectations are probably too high. Children have abundant natural energy; it can be channelled, but it should never be suppressed. Many parents feel the need to control their children because of the way they will be perceived by others. 'Bad' behaviour is too often considered to be a sign of poor parenting, or lack of parental control.

The best parents are those who allow their children some free rein, some scope to be children, some freedom to be themselves, while still respecting the rights and needs of others. What children need is guidance, and an understanding of the world around them. You can teach children that people go to the theatre to relax and enjoy a performance and that rustling sweet wrappers or jumping up and down on the seat will ruin the pleasure of others. You can teach children that running up and down the aisles of the supermarket will be frustrating for shoppers who are in a hurry and need to get their shopping done quickly. You can teach children that they must keep their voices low in the library, or that they should not interrupt when adults are speaking without saying 'excuse me', or that jumping on the sofa can upset many adults who are proud of their home. Provide your child with an understanding of how other people feel and think, and what will be expected of them in certain situations. No child knows instinctively how to behave, and even with the best guidance, there will always be times when emotion overtakes logic, or exuberance overtakes wisdom, or temper overtakes self-control.

Be realistic in your expectations, make allowances for age and temperament, and ensure you have made clear your expectations before every situation. If they let you down (which they inevitably will, from time to time), you need to consider ways of discipline that will get the message across in the most positive way possible.

Love

When I asked George Marsh, headmaster of Dulwich College Preparatory School, what he believed parents could do to help their children through stressful times, he answered without hesitation, 'Love them'. In his view, 'Love might be an old-fashioned word, but it entails acceptance and gives a child a sense of value. Most of all it entails time, which many people feel they have too little of.' He regularly sees parents struggling with the need to be good parents and to earn a living, but feels that what children need most – unconditional love – is often forgotten in the battle to keep everything going. He feels that, although most parents have their children's happiness at heart, they sometimes need to be reminded of that fact.

Although love isn't qualified by the amount of time a parent spends with a child – obviously, there are some extremely loving parents whose time is at a premium – this may well be the case from a child's perspective. If you do not have the time to express your love in a physical or verbal context, your child may not be aware of the extent of your love for him. All too often, material goods take the place of the interaction that is a true expression of love. Children learn to equate love with the number of presents they receive, rather than equating it with the relationships that form the backbone of their society, growth, development and ability to interact with the outside world.

George Marsh feels that it is unfortunate that it all comes down to time, but says that a willingness to provide children with the time they need and an unqualified acceptance make all the difference to their well-being. He believes that parents often undermine their children's self-esteem by trying to push them into a mould that they will never fit. In the end, he feels that happiness in children comes down to love and acceptance and liking themselves, which has no relation to their success or lack of it. With love comes acceptance, no matter what your child's abilities or achievements.

But why do children need love? The answer may be obvious from an experiential point of view, but there are many reasons why it is crucially important.

A child's sense of being loved has a dramatic impact on his behaviour outside the home. While they still need the love and approval of their peers, children who feel loved and are secure in their family life do not react as strongly to peer pressure. If the love is lacking at home, children look for a peer group that will give them a sense of acceptance and community, and may lead them into anti-social behaviour.

Self-esteem can also be defined as the combination of feelings of capability with feelings of being loved. A child who is happy with his achievements but does not feel loved may eventually experience low self-esteem. Likewise, a child who feels loved but is hesitant about his own abilities can also end up feeling poorly about himself. Healthy self-esteem results when the right balance is attained.

I don't really like myself too much because I am not as good as my friends at a lot of things and it makes me sad.
Nat, 8

Children who are loved like themselves. That is the greatest attribute any child can have, and underscores their ability to adapt to life, and all of the stress that it entails. Love creates a positive self-identity and self-belief that is the cornerstone of resilience. It's the greatest gift that any parent can offer. Of course you love your children, but you need to make it clear. Remind them constantly and show it through acceptance, friendship, approval, praise, encouragement, tolerance and appreciation. Ensure that your child knows that your expectations, your hopes and dreams for their future, their marks, their achievements, all come second to the most important issue of all – the fact that they are loved for who they are, not for what they achieve. If your child knows this, feels it, and understands it, you will have presented him with the most effective tool for dealing with stress and distress that he could ever have.

CHAPTER SIX

Supporting the process of change

When children have all the elements of a healthy lifestyle, they are better able to adapt to stress. Any parent who takes steps to ensure that children have what they really need will be well on the way to bringing up children who have a marked advantage in life, both in childhood and as adults.

The question of personal resilience remains important, however. Most children, at some time or other, will face situations and experiences that take them past their individual threshold. While parents can control stress as much as possible, and do as much as they are able to improve their children's response to stress – in other words, their ability to cope – there will always be times when children need extra support.

Adults and children can improve their health and well-being in a wide variety of ways; many parents will find the methods useful not only on a short-term basis, but as a part of a healthy lifestyle for their children. Natural therapies, such as homeopathy and massage, can be enormously effective in relieving the symptoms of stress in children. And there are a number changes that your child can make to ensure that his life is as stress-free as possible. In the next chapter we'll look at ways to adapt to specific, stressful situations and experiences; in this chapter, however, we'll focus on providing external support that can make all the difference to the way your child feels.

Natural therapies

There has been an unprecedented growth in this industry over the past decade, with people taking more and more responsibility for their own health. Many parents have found natural remedies and therapies effective in looking after their children. Such therapies are ideal for youngsters because they support the healing, growing, developing process, rather than acting as another toxin on an already overloaded system. They also address the root cause of ill-health and poor sense of well-being, putting a child in a better position to cope with both illness and stress when all the 'wrinkles' in his physical and emotional fabric are ironed out.

You don't have to adopt a completely 'natural' lifestyle in order to make use of these therapies. Simply be aware that they are available, and that they may be a crucial factor in dealing with the symptoms of stress, and your child's overall resilience to stress in life. If you decide to take it one step further, and choose natural treatments instead of conventional medicine for common health problems, you will find that they are gentle and encourage a holistic balance.

Aromatherapy

Few therapies are as immediately pleasurable and effective as aromatherapy, and many children (boys included!) respond well to a variety of oils. A number of studies show the efficacy of aromatherapy on young children, and it can make a big difference to the way your child responds to pressure. Older children struggling through exams or finding the transition between childhood and adolescence difficult can also benefit from regular aromatherapeutic massage or baths. Aromatherapy can balance a system under pressure and improve a child's sense of well-being.

The therapy uses essential oils, which are the 'life force' of aromatic flowers, herbs, plants, trees or spices, for therapeutic purposes. The word 'aromatherapy' literally means 'treatment using scents', and the therapy has evolved as a branch of herbal medicine. Unlike the herbs used in herbal medicine, essential oils are not taken internally (except in very rare cases), but are inhaled or applied to the skin. Each oil has its own natural fragrance and a gentle healing action.

No one knows exactly how different scents can have such a dramatic effect on health, but studies show that they do work. It seems that receptors in the nose convert smells into electrical impulses, which are transmitted to the limbic system of the brain. Smells reaching the limbic system can directly affect moods and emotions, and improve mental alertness and concentration. Certain oils also have an affinity with particular areas of the body and their properties have a balancing, sedating, stimulating, or other effect on body systems.

How to use essential oils

There are many ways to use essential oils at home, and some are more appropriate for children than others. A drop of oil in the bath is probably the best way, but remember that smaller children need far less of these oils than adults, and too much can be toxic (*see below*). One of the best choices is massage, not only because it ensures that the oils come into direct contact with the skin, but because massage is also therapeutic in its own right (*see* page 176).

SAFETY NOTES

Aromatherapy is compatible with conventional medicine and most other forms of holistic treatment. However, if your child is taking medication, you should consult your doctor before using aromatherapy. Some oils are not compatible with homeopathic treatment. Aromatherapy is safe to use at home for minor or short-term problems provided certain guidelines are followed:

- Do not take essential oils internally.

- Do not put essential oils in or near your child's eyes.

- Store all oils away from children.

- Do not apply oils undiluted to the skin, unless specifically recommended in this book, or by a qualified practitioner.

Many conditions benefit from aromatherapy. Babies, small children, adolescents and parents can all use the oils safely, provided all the guidelines are followed:

■ Stressful times: exam time? A big match coming up? Or just problems in the playground or at home? A drop or two of lavender oil in the bath every evening will relax and rejuvenate, reduce the physical and emotional symptoms of stress. Lavender oil also works to counter stress hormones, leaving your child feeling fresher and more relaxed. Chamomile works in much the same way.

■ Sleep problems associated with stress: add a blend of chamomile and lavender oil to the bath. The bath should be warm, not hot (which is stimulating). Drop a little oil on a handkerchief and tie it to your child's bedpost.

■ Groggy mornings: if your children have trouble getting going in the morning, place a few drops of rosemary oil in a water-filled pan on the stove. Bring to the boil and let the kitchen fill with invigorating steam. It's a great pick-me up and gives your child a good start to the day.

■ Stress-related digestive problems: essential oil of chamomile or fennel, blended in some warm olive oil, can be rubbed gently into the abdomen.

■ Headaches: dab a drop of lavender oil (neat) around your child's nostrils, or dilute in a little olive oil and massage his neck, shoulders and temples.

■ Problems with the immune system: immunity is compromised when we are under pressure, but a wide range of aromatherapy oils can boost the immune response, and make a big difference to health and well-being. Essential oils can support and strengthen the immune system in two ways: by opposing the threatening micro-organisms (such as viruses, fungi and bacteria), and by stimulating and increasing the activity of the organs and cells involved. A number of essential oils, including lavender, bergamot, eucalyptus and rosemary, combine both of these actions. Geranium supports the adrenal glands, and also stimulates the lymphatic system. Tea tree combines bactericidal, anti-viral and fungicidal properties with a powerfully stimulant action on the immune system.

- High blood pressure: lavender or ylang ylang in the bath or in gentle massage may reduce high blood pressure. Long-term studies in a London teaching hospital have shown that regular massage effectively reduces high blood pressure and that this reaction persists for several days at a time.

- Liver function: a number of oils are 'hepatic', meaning that they have a tonic and beneficial effect on the liver, which is under pressure during stress. The best ones to choose for children are chamomile, peppermint and rosemary. Used regularly, they can improve liver function and, through that, the stress response.

- Mental fatigue: basil, peppermint and rosemary are classified as 'stimulants', and are most suitable for a short-term problem. They should not be taken on a long-term basis. In the middle of exams, or during a particularly stressful period, they can be a godsend. A drop of rosemary on your child's wrist on the morning of an exam will undoubtedly help concentration. Suggest they inhale it whenever they feel unable to carry on.

- Oils that support and strengthen the action of the adrenal glands may help in the long term but they should not be overused. The best of these are geranium and rosemary. Peppermint can also help when stress leads to exhaustion.

- Oils that are sedative, anti-depressant and relaxant include bergamot, chamomile, jasmine, lavender, neroli and rose.

Homeopathy

The gentle therapy of homeopathy is eminently appropriate for children. It offers no danger of toxicity or side-effects, and it can be used alongside many other complementary therapies to provide relief from a wide range of health conditions affecting your child's emotional and physical health.

Homeopathy is a system of medicine that supports the body's own healing mechanism, using specially prepared remedies. It works with the body's vital force (natural energy) to encourage healing and to ensure that all body systems are working at optimum level. Homeopathy is often confused with herbalism, partly, perhaps, because some of the remedies are made from herbs. However, herbalists use material concentrations of plants, while homeopathic remedies use plants, minerals and even some animal products as a base. They are prepared through a process known as 'potentisation' to bring out their subtle healing properties.

Homeopathic remedies

A homeopathic remedy is an extremely pure, natural substance that has been diluted many times. In large quantities these substances would cause the same symptoms that the patient is trying to cure. In small, diluted doses, it is not only safe and free from side-effects, but it will trigger the body to heal itself.

Many scientists have claimed that a study of the remedies themselves has proved that there is little or even no trace of the original substance in the tablet. This is the basis of the scientific assertion that homeopathy effects cure through positive thinking alone. In fact, homeopathy is an extremely subtle medicine, based on the concept of 'vibrational medicine'. Because the remedies are so diluted, they often contain only a vibration of the original substance, and it is this vibration that works on the body's natural energy field. It's like a radio signal rather than an overt substance, but it is that subtle signal that effects a cure.

Homeopathic remedies are classified into three levels of potencies: X, C and M, referring to 10, 100 and 1,000 in terms of the amount of dilution. The more a tincture is diluted, the more potent it becomes. So, while a C is more dilute than an X, the C is more powerful. M-classified remedies are extremely potent, and are normally prescribed by homeopathic practitioners on a constitutional basis.

If you plan to use homeopathic remedies for your children, you'll need to learn to take into account many factors apart from overt symptoms. Choosing the correct remedy involves 'matching' the symptom picture of the remedy as closely as you can to your child's symptoms. Symptom pictures, or descriptions of symptoms, take into account the condition of the whole child, not just one symptom. If two remedies seem to be very close and it is difficult to decide between them, pick the one that best matches your child's most prevalent symptom.

Seeing a professional

Homeopaths treat the same range of complaints as a general practitioner. A skilled homeopath can treat both psychological problems (depression, anxiety, even shyness or phobias) and serious chronic illnesses such as MS. Deep-seated problems, such as allergies (eczema, hay fever and asthma) and repeated infections often respond very well to homeopathic treatment, but you will need to put your child in the hands of an experienced practitioner. Many chronically ill children suffer from high levels of stress, and stress itself can cause illness. Most children will respond to homeopathy, which works by dealing with the underlying cause of the problem and improving your child's overall energy balance in order to achieve a sort of 'status quo' of good emotional and physical health.

Homeopaths differentiate between acute illnesses – usually short illnesses that blow up quickly and blow over quickly as well – and more serious (chronic, or long-term) 'constitutional' problems. In constitutional treatment a single homeopathic remedy is often chosen to address the physical, mental and emotional symptoms. Constitutional treatment may involve monthly sessions over several months, or even years, depending on how long your child has been suffering from health problems.

Always seek professional advice from a registered practitioner in the following cases:

- When your attempts to treat your children don't work. If you have tried two or three remedies, with no effect, it's time to get some help.

- If your child is very run-down and suffering from general, low-grade symptoms (tired, irritable or tearful; not fighting off infections, for example). A constitutional remedy will probably be required.

- If your child seems very out of balance – either emotionally or physically, or both. Again, constitutional treatment is necessary.

- If your child suffers from serious health problems of *any* nature.

Putting homeopathy into practice

There are literally thousands of remedies available, addressing a wide range of symptoms; it can be daunting for a first-time home practitioner. There are, however, some commonly used remedies for a variety of health conditions, and you may want to experiment with some of these first, until you feel more confident prescribing. Children respond very well to homeopathic remedies, probably because they have fewer 'layers' to peel away before the root cause becomes apparent. One of the remedies listed below may fit your child's symptoms.

- Remember ABC when treating a sick child. It stands for Aconite, Belladonna and Chamomilla. Many children's acute health conditions (fevers, coughs, colds, earaches, and so on) that come on suddenly respond to these remedies, taken in ABC order. Leave about 20 minutes between each remedy.

- For a crying, irritable, inconsolable child, try Chamomilla. This remedy is also indicated for teething.

- For a tearful child with green nasal discharge and no apparent thirst, try Pulsatilla. This is a great remedy for the heart-breaking tears of a child who is under pressure.

- For children who are fearful, find it difficult to concentrate, lack self-confidence and cannot explain why they feel anxious or afraid, try Arg nit. Also useful for pre-exam nerves.

- For a child who is tired, exhausted, shy, and dreads performing on the stage or in front of a class, try Gelsemium.

- Children who are very apprehensive about a new situation, insecure, tend to show off to compensate, and regularly crave sweets, may respond to Lycopodium.

- For children who are mentally sluggish, apprehensive, lack initiative, have poor physical stamina, are clumsy, poor at sports and hate being laughed at, try Calcarea.

■ For burning the midnight oil, and excessive demands of any nature, try Nux vomica. It's also useful for children who are prickly, hypercritical, and touchy.

■ For headaches brought on by studying, Silicea might be useful.

■ When school work tends to cause headaches, and your child is slow in talking and fairly solitary by nature, try Natrum mur. It's also useful for a child who bottles up emotions, rejecting sympathy because it is embarrassing, and feels like crying or hiding away a lot of the time.

■ When emotional problems make it difficult for your child to concentrate while studying, try Anacardium.

■ For a child who is very pale, highly strung, fearful, desperately in need of affection and reassurance, try Phosphorus.

■ For insecurity that has come on after an incident that has caused great emotional distress, try Ignatia.

■ Children who are apprehensive, feel tension in their stomach, hate to be left alone and are very sensitive to noise, Kali carb might be the remedy.

■ For a child who is feeling totally worthless, suicidal, disgusted with himself, and tends to be the sort of person who pushes himself far too hard, aiming for perfection, choose Aurum in the first instance.

Flower remedies

This delightful therapy is misleadingly simple, but the results can be dramatic. Children are often more expressive than adults, wearing their heart on their sleeve and their temper on the tip of the tongue. For that reason, negative emotions – the basic tool for assessing appropriate remedies – are often easily recognised and treated.

Flower essences, or flower remedies, as they are more commonly known, are used therapeutically to harmonise the body, mind and spirit. The bottled flower essences are said to contain vibrations of the sun's energy, absorbed by the flowers' petals when immersed in sun-warmed water. The remedies use the vibrational essence of the flowers to balance the negative emotions which lead to and are symptoms of disease. They are a simple natural method of establishing personal equilibrium and harmony.

How they work

Flower remedies do not work in any biochemical way and because no physical part of the plant remains in the remedy, its properties and actions cannot be detected or analysed as with a drug or herbal preparation. Therapists believe the remedies contain the energy or 'memory' of the plants from which they were made and work in a way that is similar to homeopathic remedies – on your child's energetic balance.

Flower remedies are made in water, preserved with alcohol, and employ the ability of flowers to change and enhance mood, and to balance the negative emotions which contribute to disease. Negative emotions depress the mind and immune system, repress activity and contribute to ill-health. Some of the most common negative emotions include fear, uncertainty, loneliness, oversensitivity to influences and ideas, despondency, overconcern for the welfare of others, and despair. There are many others, and you will recognise some of them when your children become ill. Just before physical symptoms set in, you may notice tearfulness, irrational fears (of being alone, for example), depression or anxiety. These are all negative emotional states that can be addressed using flower essences.

Flower essences work to right the negative emotion, improving well-being on an emotional level that transmits to good physical health. They can be used to prevent and treat illness by working on an emotional level.

Using the remedies

Flower remedies are ideal for home use. Dilute them in water, drop them on your child's tongue, or add them to drinks. Some parents are concerned about using a remedy preserved in brandy or another alcohol, but only a drop is required and this will have no effect on your child's health. If you don't want to offer an alcohol-based treatment orally, rub a few drops into a child's pulse points or put a few drops in the bath. The effects may be slower, but the remedies will still work.

Flower remedies can complement other types of therapy such as herbalism, homeopathy or aromatherapy, or may be used alone. Flower essences are simple and effective, and can be used as follows:

- for support in times of crisis;

- to treat the emotional symptoms produced by illness;

- to address a particular reoccurring emotional or behavioural pattern;

- to help prevent illness by identifying negative emotional states that are the precursors to ill-health.

Dr Bach's system

Dr Edward Bach's set of 38 remedies became the inspiration for the world-wide development of hundreds of different remedies. The doctor's remedies are still the cornerstone of flower essence therapy, and remain some of the simplest to use, and the most widely available. They are an excellent starting point for any parent who wants to experiment with the therapy, and they come with literature explaining exactly how they work and in what situations.

A good way to begin using flower essences is to understand the types of negative emotions they address. Dr Bach's system is straightforward, and covers the majority of negative emotions. From here you can progress to other essences (*see below*).

Agrimony	For those who hide their feelings behind humour and put on a brave face
Aspen	For fear of the unknown; for vague, unsettling fears that cannot be explained
Beech	For the perfectionist who tends to be intolerant of other people's methods and experience

Centaury	For those who find it impossible to say no to others' demands and thus exhaust themselves by doing too much
Cerato	For those who lack confidence in themselves and are constantly seeking the advice of others
Cherry Plum	For fear of losing the mind and having irrational thoughts or behaviour
Chestnut Bud	For those who find it hard to learn from life and keep making the same mistakes
Chicory	For the self-obsessed, mothering type who is overprotective and possessive
Clematis	For the absent-minded day-dreamer who needs to be awake and have the mind focused on the here and now
Crab Apple	For those who feel unclean or polluted on any level, physical, emotional or spiritual. For those who need a purification ritual
Elm	For those who suffer temporary feelings of inadequacy brought on by their high expectations of themselves
Gentian	For despondency and those who are easily discouraged and set back in life. For pessimism
Gorse	For those who suffer hopelessness and despair after a long struggle and who are stuck in a negative pattern
Heather	For those who like to be the centre of things and talk constantly about themselves. Poor listeners
Holly	For those who develop the victim mentality and suffer bouts of anger, jealousy and envy
Honeysuckle	For those who suffer from nostalgia or who dwell in the past to escape a painful future
Hornbeam	For those who are stuck in a rut and exhausted so that work which used to be fulfilling is now tiresome
Impatiens	For impatience and irritability. For those who are always in a rush and are too busy to slow down
Larch	For those who feel worthless and who are suffering from lack of confidence or low self-esteem

Mimulus	For the fear of known things. For the strength to face everyday fears and all fears which can be named, for example, fear of flying
Mustard	For depression and those who feel they are under a dark gloomy cloud, for no apparent reason
Oak	For the fighter who never gives in and is exhausting themselves by being too narrow-minded in the same old fight
Olive	For those who are exhausted on all levels, fatigued and drained of further optimism and spirit
Pine	For those who suffer self-reproach and guilt. For those who say sorry even when they are not at fault
Red Chestnut	For those who are overanxious for the welfare of family or friends
Rock Rose	For those who feel helpless and experience terror or panic. There may or may not be a reason, but the feeling is real
Rock Water	For perfectionists who are hard on themselves and demand perfection in all things
Scleranthus	For those who suffer from indecision
Star of Bethlehem	For shocks of all kinds – accident, bad news, sudden startling noise and trauma
Sweet Chestnut	For utter despair and hopelessness, for when there seems to be no way out
Vervain	For overstraining and stress. For the perfectionist, hard on themselves and overstrained by trying to meet their own exacting ideals
Vine	For the overstrong and dominating leader who may tend towards tyranny. For bullying
Walnut	For change. For breaking links so that life may develop in another direction
Water Violet	For people who are aloof, self-reliant and self-contained. To relax the reserved and enable sharing
White Chestnut	For tiresome mental chatter and the overactive mind, full of persistent and unwanted patterns of thought

Wild Oat	For those who need help in deciding on the path and purpose of their life
Wild Rose	For those who drift through life resigned to accept any eventuality. Fatalists
Willow	For those who feel they have been treated unfairly. For pessimism and self-pity

Rescue Remedy (also called 'Five-Flower Essence') is made from equal amounts of the five following essences:

- Cherry Plum – for feelings of desperation;

- Rock Rose – to ease terror, fear or panic;

- Impatiens – to soothe irritability and tension;

- Clematis – to counteract the tendency to drift away from the present;

- Star of Bethlehem – to address the mental and physical symptoms of shock.

Other good essences

There are a number of flower essences now available from around the world, including in South Africa, Australia and Tibet. Remedies are pre-blended to deal with things like exam stress, bowel problems, impatience, and there are some designed specially for parents (try Parent Essence, a South African blend). Some of the following may be useful for children under pressure:

- Emergency Essence, which works in much the same way as Rescue Remedy but with a different blend of essences.

- Aloe Vera for energy and revitalisation.

- Black-Eyed Susan for awareness of hidden emotions (when your child is always sweet, for example, but clearly hiding hidden anger or fears).

- Strelitzia Essence for indecision (particularly important in adolescence, which is a time of great decision-making and change) and to assist in finding the right path.

- Adolescence Essence is specifically designed to assist teenagers in the transformative process. It is a combination of the following seven South African essences, each of which can also be used individually when it seems appropriate: Cape Almond, Dune Calendula, Loquat, Maple, Mountain Cabbage Tree, Plumbago and Wild Pear.

- Ixia Essence strengthens self-confidence and is indicated for shyness, timidity or introversion.

- Oreganum allows your child to be at ease with himself, without the need to pretend to be what his peers expect him to be.

- Wattle for unexpressed emotions.

- Dog Rose for grief which is being denied or not verbalised.

- English Hawthorn for broken-heartedness, intense grief or remorse.

- Cancer Bush for inner turmoil and torment.

- Peach for the effects of past trauma or even for a melancholic state of mind.

- Loquat Essence, when your child complains of being bored, and doesn't want to get out of bed in the morning.

- Freesia is also a wonderful essence for apathy.

- Cucumber for lack of vitality and interest in life, for a sense of being defeated, and pessimism.

- Australian Tea Tree or Jacaranda are useful for procrastination.

- Maple Essence is for those who burn the candle at both ends, possibly depleting their physical resources. It is particularly recommended for periods of physical growth and brings about a sense of balance and harmony.

- Zimbabwe Creeper brings a sense of moderation for children who drive themselves too hard to achieve, for whom no success is enough, or who feel they have to do it all themselves, by themselves.

- Belladonna Essence is for the desire to blame and punish and for uncontrollable temper, Wild Pear is for bitterness, resentment, holding grudges and the inability to forgive and Fuchsia is applicable when the anger is suppressed and emotional expression inhibited.

Putting flower essences into practice

The blend you choose for your child will be unique to his personality and character. For that reason, it is difficult to give general suggestions. There are, however, some tried and tested remedies for some situations and types of children.

- If your child is afraid of anything 'known' – in other words, something tangible, such as the dark, cats, school, his best friend's mother, exams, public speaking, etc. – use Mimulus. This is also a good remedy for stage fright before the school play, or exam nerves.

- In the case of any shock, injury, trauma, bereavement or emotional or physical disturbance, use Rescue Remedy (*see above*). Rescue Remedy rebalances the body after any upset. It's great when you have a hysterical child or baby on your hands, and the first choice for any child who is feeling traumatised or upset by pressure in his life.

- If your child has been chronically ill, seems to have little energy or enthusiasm for anything, and seems to be slow to heal, try Olive, which works to alleviate feelings of utter fatigue.

- If your child has started a new school, changed teachers, gone through a parental divorce, lost a loved one, entered adolescence or experienced significant change, offer Walnut.

- For an impatient child, who cannot seem to accept life's pace, his own shortcomings or those of others, and who seems to be set back by his own inability to wait, try Impatiens. It's also a good remedy for parents at the end of their tether – and temper.

Herbalism

Western herbalists take a different approach from practitioners trained in the East (China, Japan or India, for example), and their version of the therapy has strong roots in Western folk traditions, and in early medicine. Herbs are very good remedies for children, and can complement a broad range of other therapies.

Herbalism embraces the use of plants, particularly herbs, for healing. Like many other complementary therapies, it is based on a holistic approach to health. Treatment by any practitioner is only undertaken after a full assessment of your child's individual symptoms, as well as lifestyle factors and overall health, on a physical, emotional and spiritual level. For many parents, herbalism is an easy therapy to apply and use, and it appears to be closest to conventional medicine. Like drugs, many herbs have a specific effect on symptoms or a part of the body. The difference is, however, that they do much more than work on a physical level.

How it works

Herbal medicine is designed to be gentle, stimulating the body to return to health by strengthening its systems as well as attacking the cause of the illness itself. Probably the most important principle of herbal medicine is the taking of extracts from the whole plant (or the whole of a part of the plant, such as the leaves or the roots); the extracts are not isolated or synthesised (made synthetically) to perform specific functions. This aspect of herbalism is important. Many common drugs are based on herbal medicine. The difference is that scientists have often isolated the active ingredient and used this as the basis of the medicine. In some cases, they synthesise it, which takes it one step further from nature. Many drugs, even those with a natural, herbal base, have side-effects. In herbalism, herbs are used in their natural form, and the problems caused by using single ingredients do not exist. In fact, most herbs have very few side-effects.

Professional advice and treatment is always tailored to individual needs, so there is far less chance of having an adverse reaction to treatment. The aim of herbalism is to help the body to heal itself, and to restore balanced health, not just to relieve the symptoms of the disorder being treated.

Using herbs

Herbal medication is designed to help the body as a whole, to stimulate a response in order to cure disease. One or many herbs may be administered in the following forms, depending on your child's symptoms and the information you have provided to the herbalist. Herbs can also be used successfully at home, but it's important to remember that they are powerful healing agents and can be toxic in high doses (*see* Safety notes, page 172).

The fresher or more recently picked the herb, the stronger its active properties. Dried herbs, which are more readily available, are about a third as strong as the fresh product, and in some cases they *must* be used.

Herbs can be taken internally or applied as a compress, or used in the bath. Tablets or tinctures (herbs suspended in water or alcohol) are probably the easiest for children; choose the alcohol-free tinctures if you can.

Putting herbalism into practice

Herbalism is not a miracle cure and, like any other therapy, works best for specific conditions. Having said that, almost anyone can benefit from the prudent use of herbs as a form of restorative and preventive medicine. As well as having healing properties, herbs are a rich source of vitamins and minerals, and can be an important part of your child's daily diet, eaten fresh, or perhaps drunk as a tisane (herbal tea). For example, a herbal tonic is useful in the winter months, when it is less easy to incorporate fresh fruit and green vegetables into our diet; echinacea or garlic can be taken regularly to improve the general efficiency of the immune system.

There are literally hundreds of herbs and herbal products now widely available, and it makes sense to educate yourself about any herb that you propose to use. Make sure it is suitable for children, and always follow the dosage instructions. There are many herbal treatments that work extremely well in children:

- If your child has difficulty falling asleep or unwinding, try a warm mug of chamomile tea before bedtime. Sweeten with a little organic honey to taste, and make it part of a good bedtime routine for as long as the problem persists. Babies can have a teaspoon of cooled chamomile tea before bedtime. This will not interfere with breastfeeding.

- For indigestion, offer a cup of cooled fennel tea after eating, or serve it iced, with a little honey and lemon.

- To boost your child's immune system, choose herbs with an immuno-stimulant action, such as echinacea, astragalus or garlic, and herbs that help your child's body to detoxify (such as nettles or dandelion root).

- For migraine headaches, particularly those that are associated with stress and occur regularly, give your child a feverfew tablet daily. The effects of this are cumulative, but you will see a difference over a few weeks.

- Milk thistle cleanses and protects the liver, and has antioxidant properties. It's great for adrenal disorders, bowel disorders, a weakened immune system, and liver problems.

- Hops are ideal for anxiety, hyperactivity, insomnia, nervousness, pain, restlessness and all the effects of stress. They can be placed in a small pillow in your child's bed.

- Ginkgo biloba aids proper brain function and good circulation. It can help with poor concentration, and in children who are overstretched. It is useful for depression, headaches and trouble with memory.

- Skullcap is particularly good for nervous disorders associated with stress, including irritability, poor concentration, inability to get to sleep, or stay asleep, and digestive problems. It also relieves headaches.

- Catnip (catmint) is an effective anti-stress herb and encourages drowsiness in overactive children.

- Valerian helps to keep the nervous system from being

overwhelmed, and is a powerful aid to sleep when taken at bedtime. It also helps to ease stress-related headaches.

- Dong quai supports the kidneys, adrenal glands and the central nervous system. These organs are particularly susceptible to the effects of stress.

- Slippery elm is useful for regular digestive complaints, such as diarrhoea, irritable tummy and indigestion. It soothes the entire digestive tract and helps with ulcers and the treatments of colds and flu.

- Peppermint enhances digestion by increasing stomach acidity. It also slightly anaesthetises the mucous membranes and the gastrointestinal tract, so it's useful for diarrhoea, indigestion, nausea and poor appetite.

SAFETY NOTES

Unless you are only purchasing herbal teas or products specially designed for children (for some good sources, *see* page 269), it is wise to consult a registered medical herbalist before offering your child herbal treatment. The majority of herbs are safe for most people, but there are also many contra-indications – especially in children, and particularly if they suffer from a long-term, chronic or serious health condition (for example, epilepsy). Herbs are natural, but they are very powerful. There is some evidence that they can affect the uptake and efficiency of some conventional drugs, so make sure you tell your herbalist about any medication your child is taking, and tell your doctor about any herbal products.

Acupuncture

Many parents will be surprised to see acupuncture suggested for children, but it can have a dramatic effect on overall health, and can be used to treat many chronic and acute health conditions. Most children are not naturally frightened by needles, and acupuncture is not painful – indeed, in the hands of a good therapist, it can be a pleasurable experience. Always choose a therapist who has experience in treating children.

Acupuncture works by balancing the body's energy to encourage it to heal itself. It can be used to treat a wide range of conditions, including disorders where conventional medicine has not been able to provide a cure or even to find a cause. It's also brilliant for acute conditions brought on by stress, and can help to encourage your child's overall resistence to the effects of stress.

Traditional Chinese medicine theorises that there are more than 2,000 acupuncture points on the human body, connecting with 12 main and eight secondary pathways, or meridians. Practitioners believe that these meridians conduct energy, or 'chi', between the surface of the body and internal organs. When this vital force, or energy, becomes blocked or stagnant, disease and disharmony result. Acupuncture works by stimulating or relaxing points along the meridians to unblock chi and encourage its flow.

Chi regulates spiritual, emotional, mental, and physical balance, and is influenced by the opposing forces of yin and yang. According to traditional Chinese medicine, when yin and yang are balanced they work together with the natural flow of chi to help the body achieve and maintain health. Acupuncture is believed to balance yin and yang, keep the normal flow of energy unblocked, and restore health to the body and mind. Traditional Chinese medicine practices (including acupuncture, herbs, diet, massage, and meditative physical exercises) all aim to improve the flow of chi.

The treatment

The first consultation will last for up to 90 minutes, and your child's therapist will take great trouble to make an accurate diagnosis, since the success of the treatment depends upon it. He will ask you questions about your child's health, lifestyle, medical history, symptoms, sleep patterns, sensations of hot and cold, any dizziness, eating habits, bowel movements, emotional problems, relationships and many other factors.

The therapist will note your child's general appearance, particularly facial colour. He will look at your child's eyes and tongue, then listen to his breathing patterns, speech and the tone of his voice. Next, he will use his sense of smell to decide where your child is imbalanced. Finally, he will take pulse readings on each wrist – there are three basic Chinese pulses on each.

Your child will have to lie on a table or couch and undress so that the acupuncturist can reach the relevant points on his body. In some cases only the socks need to be removed! The fine needles will be inserted into the skin, and manipulated to calm or stimulate a specific point. The therapist will use up to eight needles, which will be left in for about 30 minutes, or removed very quickly. The acupuncturist may also suggest some Chinese herbal treatment, or dietary or lifestyle changes to go alongside treatment.

Treatment may continue for as long as it is necessary for your child's condition. Chronic (long-term) conditions such as asthma and eczema take a little longer to treat than acute conditions such as flu (which has been lifted by acupuncture almost immediately in some cases). You should, however, see some improvement after three or four treatments. Many people return to their acupuncturist every two to three months after their initial illness has been cured, for a 'rebalancing' session. Acupuncture can also work preventatively, to improve general health.

Acupuncture points also can be stimulated by pressure, ultrasound, and certain wavelengths of light. Occasionally, herbs are burnt at acupuncture points in a technique called 'moxibustion'.

People experience acupuncture needling differently. Your child should feel only a tingling sensation as the needles are inserted; some feel absolutely nothing at all. Once the needles are in place, there is no pain. Acupuncture needles are very thin and solid and are made from stainless steel. The point is smooth (not hollow with cutting edges like a hypodermic needle) and insertion through the skin is not as painful as injections or blood sampling. The risk of bruising and skin irritation is much reduced. All acupuncturists carefully sterilise their needles using the same techniques as for surgical instruments, or use disposable needles, so there is no risk of infection.

As energy is redirected in the body, internal chemicals and hormones are stimulated and healing begins to take place.

Occasionally, the original symptoms worsen for a few days, or other general changes in appetite, sleep, bowel or urination patterns, or emotional state, may be triggered. These should not cause concern, as they are simply indications that the acupuncture is starting to work. With the sessions, it is quite common for your child to have a sensation of deep relaxation or even mild disorientation immediately after the treatment. These pass within a short time, and are easily overcome with a bit of rest.

Cranial Osteopathy

The complementary therapy of osteopathy is widely accepted by conventional medicine, and is used to treat a wide range of health conditions in people of all ages. While general osteopathy is commonly and successfully used to treat children, it is cranial osteopathy that has most recently attracted the most attention. This type of osteopathy can have a dramatic impact on your child's health. Studies show that 80 per cent of children with learning difficulties, including autism and dyslexia, suffered a traumatic birth. Taking that a step further, osteopaths point to research showing that some 80 per cent of all children suffer trauma at birth, which can affect immunity, overall health, development and even language skills. By reversing the damage caused at birth, osteopaths – particularly cranial osteopaths – can cure chronic health conditions, improve well-being and sleeping habits, and make a big difference to a child's health on every level.

The philosophy of osteopathic medicine is based on the theory that the human body constitutes an ecologically and biologically unified whole. All body systems are united through the neuroendocrine and circulatory systems. Therefore, when looking at disease and other health problems, osteopaths address the whole body, not just symptoms.

How does it work?
Cranial osteopathy is a specialist technique used to manipulate the bones of the skull with a touch so light that many people claim they can barely feel it.

The human skull is made up of some 26 bones that can move

slightly. Inside the skull the brain is surrounded by cerebrospinal fluid. The fluid is secreted in the brain and from there flows out of the skull and down the spine, enveloping the spinal cord and the base of the spinal nerves. Practitioners believe that cerebrospinal fluid is pumped through the spinal canal by means of a rhythmic pulsation, which has its own rhythm, unrelated to the heartbeat or the breathing mechanism.

When the bones of the skull move normally, the cranial rhythm remains balanced, but any disturbance to the cranial bones can disturb the normal motion of the bones and, consequently, alter the cranial rhythm. This affects the functioning of other parts of the body.

A trained osteopath can feel the rhythm of the cranial pulse anywhere in the body, but principally at the skull and the sacrum. By holding and exerting very gentle pressure on the skull the practitioner can feel the rhythm of the cranial pulse and detect irregularities. The technical approach used involves extremely gentle, but specifically applied adjustments to the movement of body tissues. Cranial osteopathy is both gentle and non-invasive, making it a very safe method of diagnosis and treatment for children, and even for new-born babies.

Massage

The therapeutic effects of massage are well documented, and although sceptics insist that any health benefits derived from treatment are the result of an improved sense of well-being, rather than any biological response by the body, there is no doubt that massage works on many levels to improve overall health. Even ticklish children enjoy a soothing massage, and this is one therapy that you can undertake at home in a variety of situations. A professional massage may be a luxury for a young child, but older children who are under stress of any type, or suffer from chronic health conditions, will undoubtedly benefit.

How does massage work?

Massage is one of the oldest and simplest forms of therapy and is a system of stroking, pressing and kneading different areas of the body to relieve pain, and relax, stimulate and tone the body. Massage does much more than make your child feel good, it also works on the soft tissues (the muscles, tendons and ligaments) to improve muscle tone. Although it largely affects those muscles just under the skin, it is believed that it also reaches the deeper layers of muscles and possibly even the organs themselves. Massage also stimulates blood circulation and assists the lymphatic system (which runs parallel to the circulatory system), improving elimination of toxic waste throughout the body.

KEEPING IN TOUCH

The importance of touch for babies is now clear, and physical contact, including bed-sharing, is no longer frowned upon in quite the same way as it was in the past. As children grow older, physical contact often declines. Children become busy, there are siblings to consider, and then pride and self-consciousness come into play, and children prefer not to be seen touching, kissing or hugging (in some cases even speaking to) to their parents in front of their peers. Despite all this, growing children need touch. Being held is a sign of love and reassurance, and children sometimes need a way to express their emotions physically as well. Incorporating massage into your daily life can be a link for both children and adults. They can 'touch' you, with a quick stress-relieving shoulder massage, and you can touch them in the same way. There is no question of unnecessary or embarrassing affection. Many adolescents receive little or no touch from their parents, or, indeed, from anyone, until they begin exploring in the context of a sexual relationship. Remember that all children need to touch, and to be touched. Don't be alarmed by any sexual connotations. Massaging an adolescent is a way to keep in physical contact without the intrusion of any pseudo-sexual elements. Even if it's just a shoulder rub or a foot massage, this kind of touch can keep open the channels of communication between you and your children as they get older.

Massage has a number of proven physical effects:

- Massage is known to increase the circulation of blood and flow of lymph. The direct mechanical effect of rhythmically applied manual pressure and movement used in massage can dramatically increase the rate of blood flow. Also, the stimulation of nerve receptors causes the blood vessels (by relaxation) to dilate, which also encourages blood flow.

- For the whole body to be healthy, the individual cells must be healthy. These cells are dependent on an abundant supply of blood and lymph because these fluids supply nutrients and oxygen and carry away wastes and toxins.

- The oxygen capacity of the blood can increase 10–15 per cent after massage.

- Massage balances the nervous system by soothing or stimulating it, depending on what your child needs at the time.

- By indirectly or directly stimulating nerves that supply internal organs, blood vessels of the organs dilate, allowing a greater supply of blood.

When to see a professional

It's certainly possible to practise massage at home on your children, and there are books and courses available teaching the basics of the therapy. A number of basic strokes help to produce the therapeutic benefits, and it is important to learn these if you aim to produce significant health changes. An amateur massage at home will, however, work on several levels, including enhancing well-being, which will affect your child's physical and emotional health. There are times when a professional should be called in, including cases of chronic illness (colic, insomnia, colds, ear infections, asthma, non-weeping eczema, juvenile arthritis, diabetes and others).

Reflexology

This is a gentle and effective therapy for children, and most of them enjoy the experience of having their feet, and sometimes their hands, massaged. The effects can be dramatic, but longer-term health problems can take some time to treat effectively.

Reflexology involves stimulating, massaging and applying pressure to points on the hands and feet, which correspond to various systems and organs throughout the body, to stimulate the body's own healing system. These points are called 'reflex points', and each point corresponds to a different body part or function. Reflexologists believe that applying pressure to reflex points can improve the health of the body and mind.

Reflexology can be used to ease tension, reduce inflammation, relieve congestion, improve circulation and eliminate toxins from the body. Like many other complementary therapists, reflexologists do not claim to cure anything. Their aim is to work on the physical body to stimulate healing at the physical, mental and emotional levels.

Pressure applied to nerve endings can influence all the body systems, including the circulation and lymphatic systems. Improvements in these systems result in improved body functioning because nutrients and oxygen are transported more efficiently round the body and toxins are eliminated with greater ease. Energy pathways are opened up so that the body is able to work more effectively, and harmony or 'homeostasis' is restored.

BODY ZONES

Reflexologists believe that the body is divided into 10 vertical zones or channels, five on the left and five on the right. Each zone runs from the head right down to the reflex areas on the hands and feet and from the front through to the back of the body. All the body parts within any one zone are linked by the nerve pathways and are mirrored in the corresponding reflex zone on the hands and feet. By applying pressure to a reflex point or area, the therapist can stimulate or rebalance the energy in the related zone.

Each zone is a channel for energy (or chi), and stimulating or working any zone in the foot by applying pressure with the thumbs and fingers affects the entire zone throughout the body. For example, working a zone on the foot along which the kidneys lie will release vital energy that may be blocked somewhere else in that zone, such as in the eyes. Working the kidney reflex area on the foot will therefore revitalise and balance the entire zone and improve functioning of the organ.

Trying it at home

A full treatment will involve working all of the areas on the right foot and then all of the areas on the left foot – starting with the toes and working each section of the sole of the foot and then the sides and top of the foot. Chronic conditions should be treated by a registered practitioner, but it is possible to treat acute conditions (such as colds, headaches, colic, backache and coughs) at home. If you don't have any success, get some professional help.

The main parts of the body are reflected in the following areas of the feet:

- the head and neck: within the toe areas;

- the spine: down the inner border of both feet;

- the chest: between the levels of the shoulder girdle and the diaphragm on both feet;

- the abdomen: below the level of the diaphragm to just above the pad of the heel on both feet;

- the pelvis: over the pad of the heel;

- the limbs: on the outer side of the feet;

- the reproductive glands: on the sides of the feet near and over the ankles;

- the lymphatic system and breast: on the top of the feet.

The diagram below shows which parts of the feet correspond with different areas of the body:

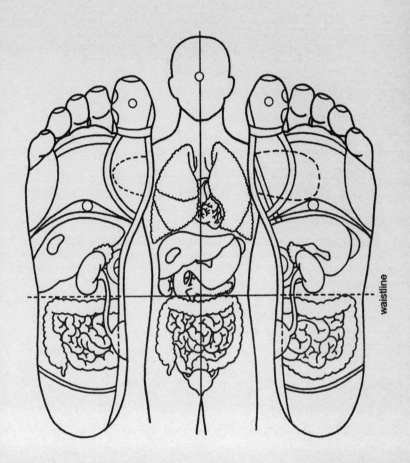

waistline

Here are some suggested treatments for common ailments which you could try at home:

- If your child has a headache, try massaging the big toe on both feet, working upwards with firm strokes.

- For indigestion, use your thumb to press into the stomach, intestine, diaphragm and solar plexus areas on both feet.

- For colds, work the head area. Then work with your thumb on the affected areas such as the nose, throat and chest. If your child has a temperature, work on the pituitary gland reflex.

- For constipation, start by stroking both feet and, beginning with the right foot, work thoroughly all over the small intestine area on both feet. Then rub your thumb along the colon which runs across both feet. Finally, press firmly on the solar plexus area. Repeat on the left foot.

- For insomnia, work all over the foot, giving special attention to the head area. Press on the solar plexus and then press your thumb down the spine. Finish by gently stroking the top of your child's feet from the toes down towards the ankle.

Meditation

Meditation works best for older children, for obvious reasons! The techniques, however, are useful for children of all ages, to help them to relax, focus on relaxation, and take time for themselves to do something positive.

The word 'meditation' comes from the Latin *moderi*, meaning 'to heal'. Western medicine has been slow to catch on to the benefits of meditation, but research has shown that it can slow the heart rate, reduce negative emotions and produce a sense of calm. Meditation makes us aware of the peace within us, a place that the outside world cannot touch or influence. All children will be stronger and healthier if they learn how to find their own 'place of peace' within.

A SIMPLE MEDITATION EXERCISE

Ideally, meditation should be learned from an experienced instructor, but you can encourage your child to practise the techniques at home, either alone or with the whole family. Meditation should be done at the same time each day and in the same place if possible. Your child's form of meditation will be unique to him. The idea is simply to clear and purify the mind and allow your child's own natural energy or life force to flow within. It may help to visualise this. There is no wrong way to meditate.

Breathing should be gentle and with a regular rhythm from the abdomen. Begin with five minutes or so of deep breathing and then breathe more gently. Sit cross-legged on the floor with your hands outstretched and your palms facing upwards. You can meditate with your eyes opened or closed, whatever feels best.

Encourage your child to try this simple exercise to begin with. Why not try it with him?

1. Sit cross-legged on the floor, comfortably with your back straight.
2. Close your eyes and breathe in and out five times.
3. Look at a place inside yourself where it is quiet and peaceful.
4. Continue to breathe evenly while you focus your mind on the drifting of your thoughts. Do not hold on to any thoughts. Let them go and watch them pass.
5. Breathe slowly and calmly and allow your mind and body to relax completely.
6. Focus all of your attention inwards.
7. After a while, try to breathe more deeply.
8. Open your eyes and take a few minutes to rest.

Hypnosis

Hypnotherapy has been very successful in treating many emotional and physical problems in children. From the age of about six (or as soon as they can understand what is being said), children can benefit from treatment. Younger children can be hypnotised or taught self-hypnosis (positive affirmations) for relaxation. (In 1981, self-hypnosis was introduced into the national curriculum in Sweden.)

Hypnosis is a tool for reaching and dealing with problems of the mind and body using a state of mental relaxation in which the patient is open to suggestion. In the hypnotised state, emotional problems can be addressed and resolved, and body functions can be improved to restore normal activity. There is evidence that hormonal problems, respiration, heart rate, circulation and digestive activity can be influenced by hypnosis, and many people find they can cut off completely from sensations of pain.

Hypnotherapy is especially useful in the treatment of behavioural and habitual difficulties, such as eating disorders, phobias, and so on. Other conditions treated include arthritis (including juvenile), asthma, digestive troubles, eczema, insomnia, migraine, stress and many childhood problems, like colic, bedwetting and hyperactivity. It is also very good for chronic pain, such as sciatica and headaches.

Yoga

Yoga encourages flexibility, relaxation skills and breathing. Used therapeutically, the practice can help with the muscle and joint mobility, flexibility, breathing disorders, musculo-skeletal pain, nervous system and endocrine disorders, digestive problems, fatigue, insomnia and stress-related conditions.

The word 'yoga' means 'unity or oneness', and is derived from the Sanskrit word *yug*, which means 'to join'. In spiritual terms it refers to the union of the individual consciousness with the universal consciousness. On a practical level, yoga is a means of balancing and harmonising the body, mind and emotions, allowing a withdrawal from the chaos of the world into a quiet space within. It utilises the innate life force within the body and teaches how to tap into it and direct it skilfully. Yoga uses movement, breath, posture, relaxation and meditation in order to establish a healthy, vibrant and balanced approach to living.

Traditional forms of yoga may be difficult for some children, requiring enormous self-discipline and concentration; however, a variety of courses now teach yoga in children's terms. Many of the poses have animal names, which children are encouraged to remember. Oki-do yoga, introduced to the West in the 1970s, has both dynamic and relaxing aspects. It was developed in Japan by Masahiro Oki, combining Indian yoga, Eastern healing methods and martial arts in a programme that is brilliant for kids.

BASIC YOGA

Enrol your child in a yoga class with other children, to ensure that he is properly taught. (Children also need to learn to make time for relaxing activities; enrolling them in a series of classes will start a good habit for later.)

Yoga exercises are comprised of *asanas*, or poses, in six main groups: standing, inverted, twist, back bend, forward bend and side bend. Each posture had a specific therapeutic effect. Relaxation and breathing exercises are designed to increase alertness and to enhance the benefit of the poses.

The best time to practise yoga is first thing in the morning, or late in the afternoon. Each sequence should take between 10 and 15 minutes. Never hold your breath while practising yoga. Encourage your child to concentrate on his breath, clear his mind, and stop if it becomes painful or difficult to carry on.

Salute to the Sun (*surya namaskar*)
One of the best yoga exercises to try at home, a beautiful series of movements that loosen and energise the entire body. Older children can practise it first thing in the morning.

1. Stand tall, feet together, palms touching in front of the chest. Inhale and stretch your arms up and back. Tighten your buttocks.

2. Exhale, bend forward and place your hands on the floor. Take your head towards your knees, keeping your legs straight. Inhale and extend your right foot as far back as possible, with your toes touching the floor. Your left knee should be bent at a 90-degree angle.

3. Exhale and draw your left foot back to meet your right. Your head, back and legs form a straight line. Hold your breath.

4. Turn your hands in slightly, bend your arms and knees so that your toes, knees, chest, hands and forehead are touching the floor.

5. Inhale, straighten your arms, as you bend backwards. Your lower body should be resting on the floor.

6. Exhale and raise your hips into the air, keeping your hands and feet on the floor.

7. Inhale. Bring your right foot forward knee to chest and raise your face to look up.

8. Exhale. Draw your left foot to join your right. Draw your head to your chest. Keep your legs straight.

9. Inhale. Raise your arms above your head and bend backwards.

10. Exhale and draw your arms together in front of your chest.

Perform the whole sequence twice, relaxing after each completed sequence.

Positive visualisation

This technique can be easily learned and used to great effect. Visualisation is the conscious use of the imagination to create images that your child can use to heal or change aspects of his life. It can help to deepen the relaxation process and overcome many of the mental and emotional problems that can lead to ill-health. It is often goal-directed, which means your child sets himself a mental goal such as, 'I feel calm and in control', or, 'I don't mind what people think of me', and his mind learns to accept it. Relaxation therapists encourage you to use the skill to picture yourself overcoming a problem or an illness and to replace negative and destructive emotions with positive, life-enhancing alternatives.

Visualisation uses the power of the mind to enhance the benefits of physical relaxation. The brain is divided into two hemispheres: the left is concerned with logic and reason and the right relates to creativity, imagination and emotions. Most of the time we use the left side to work, study and cope with daily life. The right side is used much less, but any images created in it are believed to be directly linked to physical responses in the body. Remembering an embarrassing situation, for example, can bring on all the symptoms of the stress experienced at the time. Given that children have such intense and strong memories of anything they consider to be traumatic, it's extremely useful to learn the balancing art of positive visualisation. Soothing or positive images can provoke a corresponding sense of calm or well-being in the body.

Visualisation encourages right-brain activity and uses the images it provides to override destructive effects wrought by the left side. It is based on the belief that imagination is stronger than intellect. If we give our mind a positive image it will accept it, providing the image is strong and believable.

How to do it

Visualisation often involves the use of a special imaginary place. When your child is relaxed and lying with his eyes closed, suggest that he finds a special place in his mind, such as a lovely warm beach, a secret garden or a castle. Ask him to tell you all about it in detail – the temperature, the smells, what he sees, and hears. If your child gets stuck, offer some ideas and guidance. The important thing is to paint a picture that his imagination will hold and expand upon.

Once he has this 'special place' established in his mind, he can 'go there' when he feels tense, stressed or upset. When the place is established, his mind will be relaxed and open to suggestion. This is when positive visualisation works best, although it can be used in a rather less structured way, such as in the bath every night, or at bedtime.

Encourage your child to make positive statements about himself. For example, 'I am popular', 'I am a good footballer', 'I am pretty', 'I like my body', 'I am good at taking exams', 'I am calm under pressure'. These affirmations must always be positive, relevant and set in the present tense in order to make an imprint on your child's mind. It is important to practise the visualisation every day to ensure that the message gets through.

Other appropriate therapies

Other therapies that are appropriate for children include healing, Ayurveda (Indian medicine), traditional Chinese medicine, nutritional therapies, chiropractic, Alexander Technique, colour therapy, shiatsu and naturopathy. New therapies appear all the time, and it's worth experimenting and exploring. Make sure that any therapist you visit has experience with children, and can show evidence of training and an affiliation with a recognised body. The therapies detailed here are all appropriate for children in the right hands, and many can also be undertaken safely at home on a basic level. Use the best of both worlds – complementary and conventional – to get the most appropriate treatment for your child. In times of pressure, and as a preventive measure, the combination can work wonders.

CHAPTER SEVEN

Skills and schedules

A longside a healthy programme of natural healthcare and preventive medicine, your child will also benefit from learning
some basic skills that will help to reduce the stress in his life, and
make it easier to cope when things do go wrong. Every child has
his own unique combination of strengths and weaknesses. Some
children are tidy and well organised from the word go, while
others approach life in a more haphazard fashion. Neither is right
or wrong, but all children will benefit from learning skills, such
as time management, that will be carried through to adult life.

Time management for children

One of the greatest skills that any adult can learn is time management, which helps to ensure not only that activities are pri-
oritised, but also that time is used most effectively, allowing space
for essential leisure, relaxation and fun. Because children's schedules are now as busy as most adults', they will undoubtedly benefit from learning about time management, both now and in the
future.

If your children are fairly young, you'll need to be heavily
involved in the process, perhaps planning out their time and
schedule for them, with their approval and input. Planning a
schedule also offers a good opportunity to discuss activities and

priorities. Use it to find out areas where your child is most stressed or overworked, or undertaking activities that he either no longer enjoys or finds too much pressure. Listen carefully; it's easy to continue a hectic schedule out of habit and because of a desire to give children skills and abilities that will help them in the future. However, there is a fine line between stimulation and stress, and dropping activities along the way is an essential part of maintaining a balance. As children grow up, their needs and interests change. Parents are not always right about what is best for their children. If their schedule is the subject of frequent conversations, you'll be able to keep tabs on areas that could become problematic.

Older children and adolescents should be encouraged regularly to manage their time by developing schedules and listing their preferences and priorities. The same system can be applied to children of all ages, but you need to be involved at some stage, if only to spot changes in your child's interests or to see areas of potential stress.

Setting priorities

Sit down with your child and have a pen and paper ready. Begin by writing down priorities. The obvious ones are exercise, sleep, eating together, talking time, school, homework, free time, time with friends and family activities. Next, add the activities that your child enjoys enormously, and finds relaxing. List all the current activities and ask him to rate them according to their importance to him, and how much enjoyment he gets from them. Use the list as a talking point. If you feel some of the lower-rated activities are worthwhile, explain why and be prepared for concessions on both sides. The aim here is to reduce overscheduling, and make it possible to set up a routine that allows all of the important aspects of life to be fitted in easily.

Consider the fact that some activities may be undertaken at times that are difficult for you to manage, and that some of your child's activities may actually be detracting from family time and/or adding to your own stress load. Talk about this with your children. You may be able to come to a compromise, with a shared lift system with other parents, or perhaps rescheduling the activity to a more appropriate time. If it's going to cause problems with your child's schedule, it might be best to drop it, and agree to pick it up again when the coast is clearer.

Planning a schedule

The purpose of the schedule is to set a routine, which will help to encourage your child to get on with the job at hand, particularly if he knows that some 'fun' activities are planned as well. Make sure there is a good balance between play, fun and work, and that you leave some periods completely free.

In order for this type of time management to be successful, you'll need to produce a schedule for the family and for each individual child. Post them up on the wall or the fridge, so that every family member knows what to expect, and when. Be prepared to be a bit flexible – unexpected events, illness, or just fatigue may mean that some activities need to be shifted from time to time, but if you are working to rough guidelines, it will be much easier to plan.

Make sure your child is involved in the process. Ask him to have a go at scheduling his activities before you begin, then work with him to fine-tune it.

An 11-year-old's schedule could, for example, look something like this:

7.15	Wake, bath and clean teeth
7.30	Breakfast
8.00	Head off for school
8.30–3.30	School
3.45	Snack and free time (preferably with some exercise involved)
4.15	Homework
4.45	Free time
5.30	Instrument practice
5.45	Swimming lesson
6.30	Family dinner
7.30	Reading

7.45	Family time
8.15	Organise books and sports bags for the following day
8.30	Free time (with unwinding activities)
9.00	Bed

Some children's days might be much busier, in which case, the schedule needs to include short breaks more often. Choose a day or days when they have friends round, and try to keep at least one day a week free from homework, for complete relaxation and choosing activities.

Family management

Parents need to ensure that they build time into their own schedules for relaxation, family meals, interaction and support. Working parents cannot always be there for an early homework session, or make it home for dinner every night – find compromises that work for your family. Choose the 8.30 to 9.00 slot for family time if you have to, and take the time to relax together. Shift the homework slot later, if you want, or if your child needs you to be involved.

Take the time to plan things in advance, in much the same way as you would schedule appointments. Children will know when they can expect to share some time with you, and they'll be able to plan their own time around family events, activities and interaction. Try to stick to your schedule as much as possible, so that every family member knows where they stand.

A family schedule could look like this:

Time	Mother	Father	Son	Daughter
7.00	Waken	Waken		
7.15	Prepare breakfast		Waken	Waken
7.30	Family breakfast	Family breakfast	Family breakfast	Family breakfast
8.00	Prepare for school run	Leave for work		

Time	Mother	Father	Son	Daughter
9.00	Exercise	Work	School	Toddler gymnastics
10.30–3.00	Housework, activities with youngest child, shopping, lunch, time off when baby sleeps			Nap, playtime with mum or other carer, lunch with friends, session with toddlers, droppped at birthday party
3.30	School run			
3.45	Supervise kids		Snack and free time	
4.15	Supervise homework		Homework	
4.45	Prepare dinner		Free time	Dropped off by another parent
5.15	Drive to swimming lesson and read the paper		Swimming lesson	Along for the ride
5.45	Collect from activities			Snack or light dinner
6.00	Bath baby	Exercise	Reading and free time	Bath and free time
6.30	Family dinner	Family dinner	Family dinner	Family dinner
7.15	Time with partner	Time with partner and youngest child	Instrument practice	Reading with parent and bedtime
8.00	Free time	Free time	Free time	

Time	Mother	Father	Son	Daughter
8.30	Family time	Family time	Family time	
9.00	Free time	Chat with oldest child and relax	Free time, reading with parent and prepare for bed	
9.15	Time with partner	Time with partner	Bedtime	
11.00	Reading and bed	Reading and bed		

Although this schedule might not look anything like your own, it shows that it can be possible to allow for time for family, time alone with each child, exercise, meals together, free time and sleep. The important thing is to prioritise your commitments, and make sure that all family members get the things they feel they need.

When your child will be doing homework, studying or practising, it helps for them to start each session with a clearly defined goal – finish his list of French vocabulary, master a song on the clarinet, or get that front crawl stroke smoother. If he takes a minute or two at the beginning of a study session to plan his time – 10 minutes for French, 20 for geography and two minutes to clear the desk – he'll know where he stands and have a game plan that can reduce any potential stress.

If you tend to procrastinate or overbook yourself, or forget to plan in advance with the help of a schedule or calendar, stop and consider why. Why are you resistant to careful planning? Is your schedule full of boring activities? If you continually procrastinate about a particular thing to do, complete, or even start, consider why. If there is something in your schedule that you really don't want to do, drop it immediately.

Do you feel that managing your time involves constraints, and means that you can't be spontaneous or flexible? In fact, done properly, time management can free you up to be much more flexible, enjoying activities such as reading, exercise, listening to music or chatting to friends, which you may not be able to fit into your daily life at present.

Time management also helps you to keep sight of your goals, and to make changes in order to reach them. If your goal is to spend more time with your family, you can plan for it. If your goal is more free time for yourself, slot it in. If you feel you need more time for creativity, or want to take up an evening class, or a social group, shift the blocks. Rather than being constraining, good time management allows you and your children to meet personal goals and realise dreams.

Try to find a good balance between 'being' and 'doing'. With better time management, both you and your children can be more productive, experience improved relationships, and enjoy more good times with the minimum of stress and anxiety. Doing more is not the ultimate goal of effective time management. Cramming your schedule full of 'to do' items will only increase the stress load. Choose a manageable load of activities and goals for each day, and leave it there. Things inevitably run late, and it's better to have some free slots to catch the overflow.

The art of pacing

Pacing has two components: learning to monitor stress and energy levels, and then pacing yourself accordingly. It is about awareness and vigilance; knowing when to extend yourself and when to ease up. It is also about acting on the information your body gives you. It's a concept that all children need to learn. They will be able to recognise signs of stress in themselves, and will be in control, and capable of making changes. That's a skill that can, ultimately, make all the difference to stress levels, and lead to an ability to deal with stress and overscheduling both now and in the future.

Increased stress produces increased performance, initially. After a certain point, more stress results in decreased performance. Trying harder at this point is unproductive or even *counter-*productive. The only sensible move is to take a break. In order to function well, we need a certain amount of stress or healthy tension (eustress, or good stress). However, stress becomes harmful (distress) when there is too much, when it lasts too long or when it occurs too often.

One of the first symptoms of distress is fatigue, which is often ignored. Cardiologist Dr Peter Nixon advocates a healthy respect for fatigue and doing something about it before it becomes exhaustion. When your child gets tired, encourage him to relax and stop. Help him to see when he's got too many balls in the air. Cutting down, getting some sleep and simply relaxing will make all the difference, and help to prevent the symptoms of stress causing havoc with mind and body.

The other key to pacing is taking periodic time-outs. Too many children go far too long without breaks. In *The 20-Minute Break*, author Dr Ernest L. Rossi wrote that, just as we all have cycles of deep sleep and dream sleep throughout the night (at roughly 90- to 120-minute intervals), we also have cycles through the day (peaks of energy and concentration interspersed with troughs of low energy and inefficiency). The main point is that we need to watch out for these troughs and take 20-minute 'healing breaks' when they occur, as opposed to working through them and building up stress.

It is not always convenient for children to take a time-out when they feel that they need a break, but they can try! For example, in a stressful day, using their mid-morning break to do something relaxing rather than trying to get their homework done can make all the difference. In a busy schedule, it's healthy to take little regular naps, do some meditation (*see* page 182), daydream, have some time with friends, take a walk, or have a snack. The aim is to change to low-concentration activities, which can include listening to music or doing some painting or drawing. Although time is at a premium in the life of most children, learning to use time effectively and positively can help reduce stress and increase productivity.

Learning

Childhood is a period of intense learning, and children are increasingly pressured to learn more quickly, more efficiently and to produce results. An understanding of how people learn and remember is useful for all parents. Given the emphasis on exams, helping your child acquire the skill of learning will enhance performance, make him feel more in control and less stressed, encourage confidence and raise self-esteem.

Memory

Most scientists break memory into three parts. First is the working or 'scratch pad' memory. People use this to recall phone numbers or other information they need for a short period of time – usually about a minute. After that, it is usually forgotten.

The mid-range or intermediate memory (also called short-term memory) keeps all the information consciously and unconsciously absorbed within the past few days or hours. Eventually it is either forgotten because it is not important, or transferred to long-term memory (LTM), where permanent recollections, such as important phone numbers and memories of childhood, are stored.

Learning is a relatively permanent change in behaviour as a result of experience. Clearly, without memory we could not benefit from such experience. The uses we have for memory and the amount of information we can store almost defy belief; an average brain weighing around three pounds can store more information than the world's most advanced computer!

Practical strategies

One of the best ways to reduce the stress of studying, homework and other 'essential' activities is to plan in advance, offer support, and teach the basics of successful, productive working time. These are skills that your child can use now and in the future.

- Create a good study environment. It is most dispiriting if the workplace fills you with gloom. Try to keep a particular space, room or part of a room for work. Make this place attractive, with an inviting tabletop and minimum clutter.

- Encourage your child to leave the workplace tidy, instead of trying to tidy up and find things at the beginning of the next session. An untidy workplace acts as a barrier to getting going. It's a good idea to spend the last few minutes of any session organising for the next.

■ Find your child's best time of day. He may have little choice when to study, but some people work better or more easily at particular times of the day. If your child has preferences, try to accommodate them.

■ Encourage your child to plan beforehand what he wants to achieve. A little advance planning – writing a list of things to do, and the order in which they should be done – can save a lot of time. While most children will resist homework and studying, they will be more inclined to get down to it if they have a game plan. If they cross off each item as they complete it, they'll feel a sense of achievement, and there will be an end in sight. But ensure that they aren't overambitious! Set specific targets that can be managed in the time available.

■ Space study sessions: several short sessions usually result in better retention than a single, longer session (*see box below*). Many children are reluctant to do their homework because they believe that once they get down to it they will be at it for hours. This is so daunting that they end up doing nothing at all. It is much better to have more modest goals and actually do the work.

■ Encourage your child to reduce material to a manageable amount: looking at a chapter, and writing out the four or five key points that summarise what it is saying, works well for term tests and exams. Big projects can be daunting at the beginning and dispiriting in the middle, and need to be tackled systematically. Help your child to set small, manageable tasks that will eventually lead to his dealing with the large task.

■ Encourage 'periodic retrieval'. Instead of passively reading and re-reading material, ask him to test himself periodically to see if he has actually remembered anything. Breaking the work into small chunks, and quizzing your child at the end of each, will help to see whether it's actually going in.

- Don't stop when he reaches 100 per cent accuracy. One researcher found that he could improve his retention of material by repeating it once or twice more after he had effectively learned it. Once your child is at that point, a quick review might be all he needs to remember it all.

- Encourage your child to finish whatever he starts.

- Use breaks and rewards. Humans can only function for so long at maximum efficiency before concentration begins to wane. Encourage your child to take a break every so often, and do something rewarding or have a snack in between sessions, and he should return to work refreshed. Rewards make children more inclined to do the work again. Allow an hour at the end doing whatever your child finds relaxing. At the end of an exam period, plan a big outing or treat!

- Try to encourage your child to develop a time management schedule (incorporating spaced study sessions), in which certain times are devoted to study and certain others to leisure (*see* page 189).

THE 35-MINUTE STUDY PERIOD

The 35-minute daily study period is an efficient way of learning. Thirty-five minutes is a period during which most people can concentrate well. If your child studies, or does homework without a break for as long as an hour, the last 20 to 30 minutes are likely to be less efficient, as concentration diminishes. It's also much easier to encourage your child to get down to work knowing that it is for a 35-minute stretch. If your child has a huge workload, break it into 35-minute segments, with breaks and fun in between.

Encouraging learning in children

It is now well established that without attention to self-esteem children are not likely to make long-term scholastic progress. Research shows that, in general, people's levels of achievement are influenced by how they see themselves and, more specifically, that self-esteem and academic performance are strongly associated.

Parents are in the best position to influence the way that their children feel about themselves, primarily through their relationship with them. When this is valuing and caring in nature, the children's self-esteem will be elevated. Success and failure in themselves have no effect on a child's motivation to learn, but the reactions of parents, teachers and other significant adults to success and failure can have a devastating effect. It is important for parents to be aware that while unrealistic demands lead to low self-esteem, no demands at all lead to the same end. In both cases, children are doomed to low academic achievement or over-achievement. The ideal is to apply optimum pressure – just enough to cause children to feel challenged and positive but not so much that they become distressed.

The following guidelines will help parents encourage learning in children:

- Parents should never persist in encouraging learning when the child demonstrates a lack of interest or reluctance.

- Children's efforts should never be criticised or the child made aware that parents are disappointed with the progress being made.

- Parents should make sure that there are times when the child has their full attention.

- Children should share in their parents' everyday activities and be included in their daily life as much as possible.

- Children should be talked *to*, not talked *at*. Parents should create opportunities when they and their children can respond to one another.

- Parents should try to see things from the child's perspective, acting as 'guides' rather than 'teachers'.

- Parents should be serious about directing their child towards experiences that provide opportunities for learning and discovering.

CHAPTER EIGHT

Becoming resilient

All the therapies, techniques and strategies described in the preceding chapters can help to make things more manageable for your child on a day-to-day basis. Teach the basics of relaxation, productive work and the importance of free time. A busy child with a busy lifestyle and a busy family life has the ability to manage it, as long as he has this kind of support. But what happens when a child reaches and passes his stress tolerance level? Inevitably, there will be times in your child's life when things become too much, or events will occur that he simply cannot control. Fortunately, there are ways to get through such stressful situations and periods, and deal with the symptoms of stress when they occur.

Recognising and acknowledging problems

To enjoy a stress-free environment, we need to have the ability to find hope, in thinking through solutions, and be able to anticipate stress and learn ways to avoid it. Children need to learn to lean on people during difficult times, as social support is one of the most important aspects of dealing with stress.

Some children may be naturally more inhibited when it comes to expressing themselves. Boys in particular may find it harder to communicate; in fact, studies show that girls are more likely to report positive and supportive peer relationships than boys. Furthermore, boys define themselves as being more competitive and achievement-oriented than girls; given the overly competitive and achievement-oriented nature of the average child's life today, this is a massive disadvantage.

All parents need to watch for changes in behaviour – regression, withdrawal or sudden aggression – which may mean that something is wrong. Be vigilant about quarrels with friends, little give-aways in conversation, and periods when they seem to be under more pressure than usual, without any obvious or vocalised reason.

It is most important for a parent to acknowledge a child's feelings and to provide the child with an emotional vocabulary. No children feel confident and well all the time, and they need to know that it's normal and acceptable to feel angry, frightened, lonely, jealous, sad and alone. Help your child to put into words how he is feeling: for example, express it yourself first ('You must be feeling very sad not to have been invited to that birthday party', 'You must be very angry that your teacher treated you like that', or 'I can understand why you feel jealous that your brother has made the team and you haven't'). You may get it wrong, but you will be providing words for them to express their feelings without fear of rancour or embarrassment.

Express your own emotions regularly, so that children learn that this is acceptable. Keep the channels of communication open. If a child becomes used to opening up, he'll be much less likely to allow stress to build up to an unhealthy level. Get into the habit of having regular conversations, and develop a good rapport. Share his interests so that you can use these subjects as ice-breakers. If you seem genuinely interested in your child, he will feel loved, important and respected and he will be more likely to open up.

Be positive without belittling your child's perception of events. If your daughter is enormously anxious, upset and stressed after falling out with a friend, it may be tempting to trivialise it. But, if she *perceives* it to be stressful, then it is. Parents need to ensure that children see the positive in every situation, and that they feel good about themselves. If they feel positive and self-assured, they'll be more likely to take things in their stride.

The most stressful thing in my life is my friends. It makes me feel left out when they turn on me. *Beth, 8*

Similarly, suggest that your child focuses on the particular problem or issue and thinks it through. Ask him what most worries him, and what the worst possible outcome could be if his fears are realised. By preparing him for the worst-case scenario, he'll know what to expect. Discuss some coping strategies that he might use if the worst comes to the worst. Events probably won't turn out as badly as he fears, but if he's prepared, he'll feel more confident about facing the challenge.

Learn to identify future potential problems. While this may seem like an alarmist strategy, it genuinely helps children to anticipate and plan for stress. Find out what could cause stress, and plan ways to avoid it or deal with it. If you know that exams are coming up, and your child always responds badly to this type of pressure, talk it through well in advance. Develop some coping skills, study methods, stress reduction, rest and rewards. Your child will be much better prepared to adapt.

Expressing feelings

Some schools have developed time for co-operation and interaction that is not competitive. Dulwich College Preparatory School in London has adopted a 'Nurturing Programme', turning over just over an hour a week to airing issues and problems, and promoting personal power and self-esteem within the children. The children are given space to express themselves, in a supportive environment, and often in the context of group games and talking. Dulwich headmaster George Marsh feels that the wealth of information recently published about children's needs has brought to light all sorts of problems that can now be addressed. Because children are now not only encouraged but expected to speak out, we are forced to listen, and can, therefore, make the appropriate changes.

George Marsh warns that the programme is relatively new, and that they are yet to see full results, but he is convinced that there has been a general movement forward with the boys. The boys now seem better able to understand their peers, and to interact, which balances the sense of competition.

The most stressful thing in my life right now is GCSE coursework and making and breaking friendships that I thought would last for ever. **Rachel, 14**

Teaching children to think through a problem is an important part of dealing with crises and adapting to stress. If they don't find it easy to discuss it, suggest that they write about it, or develop a strategy that you can work on together. Ensure that they express it in one way or another, and don't just hide it away. A problem can only be dealt with when it is faced.

Books, art, puppetry, plays, play and writing can all help children think through and name their feelings. If children can act out their problems, or express themselves through dramatic interplay, they'll reduce the stress burden. Seek out books that show children adapting to similar situations, and read them together to encourage conversation. For older children, simply offer them as a treat and let them know that you are there.

Encourage your child to find solutions to problems. If you suspect that there has been some bullying at school (*see* page 208), but haven't had it confirmed, propose some hypothetical situations and ask what he'd do. Invent a friend's child who is undergoing some stress in exams, for example. Ask your child what he thinks that child could do to feel better, and adapt. If children have practised thinking through the problems of others, they'll be much better placed to work out solutions to their own issues.

Let children express some personal power (*see* pages 144–9). If they are used to making decisions, having choices and voicing their opinions, they'll feel more confident about doing so in the framework of a problem situation. This experience cannot be underrated. A child who is used to making informed choices and decisions, within the context of normal expectations, will show a marked advantage over children whose parents do everything for them.

I feel I have to live up to my cousins, who are a bit older than me, to make my parents proud. *Caroline, 14*

Parents have a responsibility to set a good example. Express your emotions rather than 'sparing' your child. Children certainly do not need to know all the ins and outs of your adult problems, but you can let them understand if you are feeling unhappy, frightened or exhausted by something in your life. Show them that you have an action plan, or plan with your family to take off some of the pressure. Teach children how to adapt to stress by using healthy tactics yourself. Try not to lash out in anger, keep calm, don't rely too heavily on alcohol, coffee or tobacco to get you through tough periods, and make sure you relax, exercise and eat well.

> Seventy-six of the 80 children I surveyed said that they felt more stressed when their parents were stressed.

You can't always prevent or remove negative stress from your children's lives, but you can help them manage it: show faith in your children and their ability to cope. Remind them of times when they found a solution to a problem. Suggest they use the same strategies, or help them to come up with different ones. Encourage independence and interdependence. There is a time for each, and a well-rounded child will develop skills from both that will stand him in good stead in the outside world. Show solidarity, as a team or as a family. If your child knows that he has the unconditional support of his family or parents behind him, he will feel more confident, take more risks and exercise his own judgement. Above all, celebrate good coping skills. When a child handles things well, praise his efforts and achievement.

The most stressful thing in my life was having a massive argument with my best friends and parents at the same time. I couldn't sleep, I stayed in my room, didn't talk and cried a lot. *Kellie, 14*

Treating stress

Dr Robert Dato makes it very clear that stress is not simply something with which we should cope, but that it is actually a physical and emotional condition that requires treatment and education. There are many ways to help children to cope, but when they suffer from stress, this approach may need to be supplemented with actual treatment. Some parents may feel concerned enough to suggest counselling for their children, which may be of some use, particularly if the whole family is involved. Others might be tempted to control the situation by using drugs – this is a last-resort solution, to be used only when symptoms are spiralling dangerously out of control. Relying on drugs is not a viable or healthy long-term solution. Some of the more natural options will support your child's mind and body in crisis, contributing to the equilibrium that is necessary for health, happiness and well-being.

HELPING REDRESS THE BALANCE

No child is perfect, and all have their own individual idiosyncrasies. In certain situations, you'll will need to adapt your game plan to take into consideration their personality and overwhelming character traits. Here are some ways to help a child that may be considered 'more difficult'.

- Shyness: a child who is shy or clingy should be introduced to new situations gradually. Talk about what's coming beforehand and then allow him to proceed at his own pace. Don't be tempted to push him into the limelight or force him to perform. There's nothing wrong with being shy, and many children develop confidence and people skills at different ages.

- Overenergy: consider how stimulating every situation may be in advance, and make sure you allow time for letting off steam and cooling down.

- Strong will: try to avoid inflexible confrontations. State your position gently but firmly, and do not allow his stubbornness to prevail over what you know is right, but be open to negotiation. Look for an occasional situation where his position can be shaped to being acceptable, and praise good efforts and persistence. Remember that later in life a strong, determined character will be applauded.

- Rebellion: some children find it difficult to fall in with expectations (even those that are fair and reasonable). He may have trouble going to sleep, eating his dinner, or even toilet-training. Don't despair. Put good routines in place for the whole family and ensure that your child takes part in all of them. Ensure that he goes to bed at a reasonable time, even if he doesn't sleep, and ensure that he sits at the table, even if he doesn't eat. Take him to the lavatory, but don't force him to go. Eventually he will become used to the pattern of daily life and settle in.

- Moodiness: some children naturally have emotional highs and lows. These may be balanced using natural remedies (see Chapter 6), alongside some practical strategies: try to let him act out his moods for a while, and then distract him by involving him in other activities that you know he enjoys. Try not to let negative moods overshadow the rest of the family's fun. When he comes round, show extreme pleasure and he'll get the message that being happy is much more fun.

- Overexuberance: with a highenergy, overexuberant child who is extreme in every way – yelling, barging into conversations, interrupting and generally ensuring that you know he's there – you will need to adjust your tolerance level. When the child is older you will be able to channel this energy more effectively. In the meantime, try to control volume, and overreactions, and stop activities until he settles down. Explain that some people find noise and energy alarming. Encourage him to control himself in some situations, but leave plenty of space for letting off steam.

■ Resistance to change: some children find change completely disruptive and may even develop something approaching a phobia. Some children adjust slowly to new situations, while others simply cannot face them. Provide regular routines in the home, to provide a basic level of security. Be as consistent as possible. When a new situation is on the cards, talk about it well in advance, pointing out exactly what to expect and what your child can do in different situations. Focus on the positive aspects of change whenever you can.

Common situations and solutions

Children may not experience any of the following problems; others may sail through them without a murmur. But some will come up against such major issues, and you will need to know how you can help your child to adapt. Small problems can create negative energy. Even if such situations represent a small proportion of the stress in your child's life, learning to deal with the little things clears the path and allows a focus on greater and bigger issues.

Bullying

Many children experience some level of bullying at some stage (*see* page 50), even if it is not full-blown harassment; a recent study by Young Voices and Oxford University was based on 7,000 pupils between the ages of 13 and 19. One in 10 reported severe bullying, including physical violence. Many felt they could not tell anyone what was happening to them as their treatment by other children had sent them into a spiral of depression and misery.

The study found that home life plays a vital part in determining whether a child will be a bully or a victim. 'For both the victims and the bullies, parenting was markedly less positive, colder and more controlling. Bullies were far more likely to see aggression at home,' said Adrienne Katz of Young Voices.

Children were far less likely to be bullied if they lived with both parents. Severely bullied boys reported not having a supportive parent and were highly likely to have an absent or unsupportive father. Of the bullied girls, 79 per cent felt anxious about one parent, and were more likely to say they planned to bring up their own children very differently from the way they were being raised. Racism seems to be a factor. A quarter of children from ethnic minorities reported being severely bullied, as opposed to 13 per cent of white pupils.

Adrienne Katz: 'There are factors which protect children: being bolder and having high self-esteem and positive, warm parenting is overwhelmingly linked to those who are not being bullied.'

Bullying in childhood is known to cause acute misery. It has also been linked to problems in adulthood such as alcohol abuse, violence against children, marital breakdowns and psychiatric disorders. A 12-year-old bully is three times as likely as other pupils to have a criminal conviction by the age of 24. Suicide among adolescents has risen in the past decade, and now attempts among under-14s seem to be going up too. According to Professor Keith Hawton of the Centre for Suicide Research in Oxford, girls largely account for the increase in non-fatal overdoses and self-inflicted injuries. They outnumber boys by at least six to one, while actual suicide, rather than attempted suicide, is actually on the increase in boys.

Previous NSPCC research showed that more than half of children aged eight to 15 sometimes or often worried about being bullied at school and that younger children worried most. According to the NSPCC, 43 per cent of young people had, at some point in their childhood, experienced bullying, discrimination or being made to feel different by other children. Nearly all (94 per cent) of these experiences took place at school.

When asked why they believed this had happened, the reasons given were usually personal characteristics over which the young people had no control. 'Size' was given as the reason by a more than a quarter of the respondents. 'Class' (how they spoke or dressed) and 'intelligence' were each cited as the reason by around a fifth of respondents.

Name-calling, insults and verbal abuse were most common – almost nine in 10 of those bullied said that other children had treated them in this way. This amounted to 37 per cent of all respondents. One in seven respondents had been subjected to physical bullying such as hitting or punching, and one in 10 had been threatened with violence. Bullying and discrimination included damaging or stealing belongings, humiliating, ignoring/not speaking to them, and telling lies about them or deliberately getting them into trouble.

What can you do?

- You may well suspect bullying without having it confirmed. Obvious clues are curiously 'lost' belongings, inexplicable bruises, withdrawn behaviour and mystery ailments that prevent your child from having to go to school. If you are concerned, try to encourage your child to talk about it. Ask about different parts of their day, and about the people they like and don't like. Ask if lunchtime or break is stressful and why. Don't bully them into talking, which will just make matters worse. Just let them know that you are there if they want to share the problem.

- Talk to your child's school and find out what anti-bullying policies they have in place. Chances are they don't know what is going on, and they can take steps to stop it.

- Help your child to develop coping strategies. Suggest some sharp retorts that your child could use, or ways of avoiding the perpetrators. Practise what he could say, for example, 'Stop calling me names now, I don't like it and I'm not going to accept it any more.' This implies a threat that further action could be taken, and even the most robust bully fears recrimination from authorities.

- Don't encourage physical violence, which will turn your child into a form of bully himself. Your child needs to learn to stand up for himself with confidence. The secret is to look strong and confident, keeping his head up, and looking the bully/ies in the eye.

- Children who are bullied tend to have lower self-esteem than their peers, perhaps unconsciously placing themselves in a 'victim' mode. This might be a short-term self-esteem problem, caused by stress or a family problem, for example, or it may be something that needs addressing in the long term. Work on your child's self-esteem (see page 143). A child who feels good about himself will be better able to face up to bullies.

- Make sure your child doesn't feel guilty, which can compound the problem. Many children blame themselves, and believe that their own actions or weakness have led to the problem. Help them to feel that they are not at fault, and that they are good, strong, effective people.

- Explain to your child why some people become bullies. A bully is normally a victim of someone else in their life. If your child is aware that there is a cause for the behaviour that has nothing to do with him personally, he may feel more in control of the situation.

- Don't become too upset. It won't help your child, and he may become alarmed, oversensitive, or concerned that he has made you unhappy. Be calm and supportive, and show him that you are on his side, and that you are prepared to show a little of that all-important family solidarity.

- Many children will feel very vulnerable and need an awful lot of comfort, as well as practical advice. Don't be too business-like or problem-focused. Give them hugs, reassurance, love and empathy. Sympathise and recall any similar experiences that you had as a child.

- Encourage your child to develop a network of friends outside of school, who share his interests and enjoy his company; this will help him to feel stronger and better able to cope with bullies the rest of the time. Encourage a good circle of friends at school, too, if possible. Children in a group are much less likely to be bullied than those on their own.

In a crisis:

- Make sure your child gets lots of sleep, good nutritious food and TLC. It will help him to cope physically and emotionally with the demands.

- Give him a bottle of Rescue Remedy or Emergency Essence (*see* page 166) to carry. It helps to relieve feelings of panic, trauma and upset, and if he knows he has something that will instantly help, he'll feel more in control.

- Try one of the following South African flower essences: Black-Eyed Susan for nervousness, Fringed Violet for shock, Dog Rose for anxiety.

- *See* the advice on insecurity, page 256.

Exam stress

Of course, exams are a major source of stress in children and adolescents, and that situation is unlikely to change. All stress-relieving strategies are relevant to helping children to cope with exams, and becoming and staying calm. Practical coping strategies and productive studying are the keys to getting through it all. The most important thing is for parents to offer support rather than nagging or criticism. A little sympathy and understanding go a long way.

If your child knows that his exam results are neither going to ruin nor 'make' his future, it will help to reduce the pressure. Failing an exam is not the end of the world, no matter what your child's age. If it means he doesn't get into a school that he'd hoped to attend, so be it. Focus well in advance on the other options, and don't encourage your child to pin his dreams on one goal. The most resilient people in life are able to deal with change. Your child will benefit from taking a more flexible approach to life, accepting defeat or failure and finding the positive in a new situation.

ChildLine, the UK charity that offers confidential advice for young people, has published its own suggestions for both parents and pupils for taking as much stress as possible out of exams. They claim that young people facing exams should recognise the importance of performing well, but should remember 'that there is a life beyond revision and exams'. Parents are advised to show an interest in children's preparations for exams, but in a way that does not add to the pressure. ChildLine urges parents to offer support rather than criticism if they have concerns.

Tests have shown that people operate best in exam conditions with a medium level of stress. Some perform badly in exams when they are under too little stress just as when they have too much stress. Encourage your child to find a happy medium, and leap in when the going gets tough.

In a crisis:

- Rescue Remedy or Emergency Essence can be dropped on the tongue and rubbed into pulse points regularly.

- If your child is genuinely frightened of exams, give a few drops of Mimulus several times a day for a few days before they begin. This is for fear of known things, and is remarkably effective. The homeopathic remedy of Arg nit is equally good for exam fear. Vervain is useful if your child sets exacting standards for himself, and pushes himself too hard to attain them.

- Treat your child to a relaxing and/or stimulating massage, either at home or with a professional. Massage raises self-esteem, concentration and even immunity. Lavender and chamomile oils will work well if your child is intensely stressed.

- Try a few drops of lavender or chamomile oil in a vaporiser in their study room, too. Alternatively, choose oils for mental fatigue, which may be making the problem worse (*see* page 156).

- For exhaustion, try giving Olive flower essence, which will restore energy levels.

Sibling rivalry

The sibling relationship is quite different from the parent-child bond. One may be stronger or more dominant, but brothers and sisters rarely exert the kind of power and authority over one another that parents hold over their children. There are no codes of behaviour insisting that siblings must respect and honour one another as they do their parents. As a result, siblings are generally freer, more open and more honest with one another than they are with their parents, and less fearful of punishment or rejection. As children, they say what is on their mind, without worrying about the long-term effects of their emotions on one another. Even as adults, many siblings speak more bluntly to each other than they dare do to friends or colleagues.

Making comparisons

It is perfectly normal, natural and appropriate for parents to have different feelings towards each of their children, and to treat those children differently. Their challenge is to appreciate what is unique about each child, and to show that appreciation in a balanced way so that all their children feel equally loved and valued. The knack is to distinguish between *different* treatment and *preferential* treatment.

The highest-achieving child, the most affectionate one, the first-born or the youngest, the one most like or unlike a parent or relative, can all move unwittingly from a position of equality with other children to receiving or seeming to receive special attention. Parents may not be aware of slipping from treating children differently to giving preferential treatment to one, but siblings are highly sensitive to such slips. Young children monitor their parents' treatment of their siblings, just as they monitor their own treatment, and that relationship of parent to siblings becomes as important as the relationship of parent to self.

Despite their best efforts, most parents find it almost impossible to avoid making comparisons between their children. Long before siblings begin to take stock of each other, parents decide that their first baby was easy, the second more difficult; the oldest was placid, the youngest active. It's when those comparisons turn into 'labels' that it can become problematic. Those labels can define the internal image children have of themselves and, later, their role in the family and elsewhere.

Whatever child-rearing methods parents use, they create a different environment for each child. The differences can act to shape the different personality and outlook that each child develops.

What young children label as 'favouritism' may be far from that, but it is perception rather than reality that colours a sibling relationship. If a child perceives that he is being treated less fairly, or not getting enough attention, even if parents are scrupulously fair, he will feel disempowered and will be more likely to initiate rivalry.

Sibling rivalry is exhausting for everyone, and often siblings provide the only outlet for a stressed child to exert control, to lash out, to scrap, fight, bicker, taunt, tease and harass. When a child exhibits awful behaviour with his siblings, it can be a sign that things are just too much.

Coping with sibling rivalry

Sensitive parenting can restore the balance, in many cases preventing serious rivalry from taking hold. If you are concerned that sibling rivalry may be affected by birth order, consider the following:

- Make each of your children feel special. Older or younger, every child needs to feel that they are as important as anyone else in the family. If one child thinks that a sibling is held in higher esteem by parents, jealousy will arise. Do your best to listen to each of your children and respond to them positively.

- Show enthusiasm for the achievements of all your children. You may find that you are less excited about a younger child's milestones (the first step, the first word) than you were with your first child. It is not that you love the youngest less, but it is less of a novelty. If you do feel this way, try not to let it show. Your youngest children need you to be interested.

- Give each of your children responsibility. Resist the trap of giving the oldest child all the household chores. Younger siblings can help, for example, by tidying toys. And oldest children do not need to take younger siblings with them whenever they go out to play.

- Respect all your children. Every child has the same psychological need to be loved and accepted by his parents, regardless of his position in the family. He has feelings and ideas that he wants to express, and has a right to receive respect, and to be taken seriously.

- If a new baby is the cause of problems, remember that most new babies require little more than warmth, love, feeding, and nappy-changing on a regular basis. A lot of this can be undertaken by a partner, grandparent or carer, while you focus time on your older child. The point is to ensure that your elder child/children feel that their position has not been usurped, and that they are still as important and worthy of your time. Spend time together with the new baby, and ask your older children to take responsibility for some of her care. You'll be showing trust and inspiring them to feel included and important, which will help them to feel more secure. Remember to remind them, however, that the baby is there to stay, and that everyone must welcome her into the family, and be prepared to make some changes!

In a crisis:

- For jealous children, try Holly Flower essence, which helps to balance these negative feelings. Vine is for children who have a tendency to bully, and are dominating and tyrannical at home. In all situations, Rescue Remedy or Emergency Essence (*see* page 166) will be helpful, to lower the pitch and ease the trauma – whatever it may be! Impatiens will also help with the ubiquitous irritability of children among their siblings.

- The homeopathic remedy Lycopodium is ideal for children who are jealous of others, and feel a powerful sense of injustice.

- Pulsatilla will help for constant outbreaks of tearfulness and fretting that may accompany sibling rivalry.

Moving house

Our transient society, job instability, and other factors mean that the average child will move home at least once before the age of ten. In the USA, one in five Americans aged one and over moved last year. It's a disruptive experience for the whole family, but children can find it even more traumatic, particularly since they are virtually powerless to do anything about it.

If you are the type of person who thrives on change, you may need to curb your instincts if you have small children. Children thrive upon familiarity and routine, and their social development can be hampered (usually only in the short term, but stressful none the less) if you constantly seek change. Consider your children carefully before putting a move into action. If your child has suffered a recent trauma, such as a death of a loved one or a divorce, you may want to hold off moving until things settle a little. Many people make a quick move following marital break-up, often because finances dictate this. However, it can intensify the problems and stress for young children. Wait as long as you can, if possible.

The most important thing is to exhibit positive behaviour. If it's not a move you particularly want to make, try not to let your negative feelings influence your child's approach. Your child may sense that you are not 100 per cent happy with having to do it, and keep quiet in order to avoid further upset. All children find change difficult, and you need to draw out, face and find ways to discuss and cope with any fears and concerns.

Talk about things well in advance so that your child is well and truly prepared. It might seem overly pedantic, but if they know what to expect in every situation, they'll feel prepared and find it easier to cope. It's perfectly acceptable to commiserate with a child, but you should try to point out the positive elements of a move, and actively find things that will cause your child to look forward to the change. For example, talk about the nearest park, the nice new school, the other children you saw playing, the social clubs, the big new bedroom and the ease of communication with friends left behind.

Involve children in the decision-making process as much as possible. If redecorating is on the cards, ask them to choose their own room colour, or a new piece of furniture. If you are choosing between two houses, ask for and listen to their opinions. Don't look upon a move as a perfect opportunity for a mass clear-out. Your child will appreciate having lots of his old familiar belongings around, even those that he cherished as a child and no longer looks at. These are links to his past, and are important, if only in the short term, for a successful move.

For school-age children, try to move in the summer, or at a stage at which they would be facing change anyway. No child wants to feel different or be the 'new kid on the block', so make the change when there is the least possible disruption. Try to arrange get-togethers before your child starts at the new school, so that he knows at least one or two familiar faces. Have realistic expectations for your child. Teachers generally expect an adjustment period of about six weeks; some children may take less time, some may need more. Your child will need your continuing support.

With teenagers, you may find dramatic scenes and rebellions become the norm for some time. It's often difficult to establish a trusted group of peers, and the prospect of starting all over again can be very daunting for an adolescent. Take note of his feelings, and suggest that a girlfriend or boyfriend, or a few of his old mates, can come to stay from time to time. Don't discount the importance of adolescent relationships. Show empathy and respect for his concerns, and do as much as you can to ease the transition.

In a crisis:

- Use Walnut Flower essence, for change, and offer regularly to all family members.

- The homeopathic remedies Aconite and Ignatia will help your child to cope with the trauma.

Homework

Far too much importance has been invested in this after-school 'activity', which is probably the biggest cause of familial battles on a day-to-day basis. The best way to cope with a reluctance to do homework is to encourage a routine and a family schedule that allots a certain amount of time where homework and only homework will be done. If everyone is sitting down working together (even if younger family members are colouring or reading), you are much less likely to face a showdown. Similarly, once a routine is established, and your child knows that fun will follow, he'll be more likely to fall in, even if the early days of establishing routine are fraught with rebellion.

Sometimes, the demands placed upon your child may be too high. If he's expected to do too much work in the evenings or in the holidays, talk to his teacher about the fact that he is over-loaded. Chances are that he is not alone. Ask that homework be set for a specific period, rather than on a task-completion basis. A friend of mine was incensed that her child had homework over the holidays, when she felt he should be resting and spending time with his family. She brought it up at a parent-teacher forum and the result was that holiday homework was abolished. Sometimes it just takes one brave individual to make the difference.

Don't become too involved in the homework, or try to do it for your child. Encourage and reward initiative and hard work, but don't overemphasise it. You don't want your child spending hours labouring over something to please you. Homework is merely an extension of what he's done all day long. Underplay it and suggest he does his best for an agreed period of time. You'll get no brownie points for doing your child's homework, and you could even hamper his development (*see* page 41). Teachers know that if work improves dramatically when it's done outside the confines of the classroom, it's not likely to be down to the individual child. Give your child a chance.

George Marsh of Dulwich College Preparatory School is one headmaster who feels that parents should offer a supportive but ultimately non-interventionist approach to homework. He says that too much involvement can be undermining, produce resistance to doing homework together in the future and, ultimately, cause problems. Teaching techniques change and a nifty maths tip you had as a youngster might completely confuse your child.

Teach your child not to procrastinate, but to knock it on the head and get it out of the way. Offer rewards for a job well done; this approach doesn't need to last long, but it can be an effective means of getting your child started. Let your child choose (within reason) when he does his homework, in the process of planning his time. (For more on time-management techniques, *see* page 189.) Talk to him about the advantages of getting it out of the way earlier, freeing him up for a long stretch of relaxing evening or weekend time. If he just won't do it, leave it. Sometimes children are just too tired. Suggest that you'll back him up this time, with a note to the teacher, but that it can't happen again. Suggesting a chat with the headmaster or teacher on the whole homework issue might spur him into action.

In a crisis:

- Lycopodium is for the staunchest procrastinator, who feels a deep sense of injustice that he should be working rather than playing.

- Flower essences are ideal: try Gorse for children who feel hopeless and stuck in a rut. Clematis is perfect for a daydreamer who just can't get down to work. Try Cerato if your child doesn't believe in his own ability to get things done. Child Essence is a good all-rounder, which helps to deal with the normal, negative emotions of childhood – homework included!

- Rosemary oil in a vaporiser will help a child who feels tired and unable to settle down to work, while lavender will relax an overactive child into a more tolerant and tolerable state.

Peers and peer pressure

Children always rate their peers highly, and their status among their peer groups will always be an issue. A recent study showed that most children spend time with their friends either every day or most days (61 per cent), and over two-thirds felt they had extensive friendship networks (68 per cent). This type of peer relationship is healthy, and normal.

Peer pressure only really becomes a problem when your child is forced into situations in which he feels uncomfortable. The pressure from peers can be stimulating rather than stifling, but the key is self-esteem. Your child has to respect and believe in himself. He needs the courage to stand up for himself, and to challenge his peers when he feels threatened or uncomfortable.

All children need a reservoir of self-esteem and self-confidence. Reinforce this quality in your children, and teach them to be independent. Give them some power in the household, so that they are used to exerting some control over their environment. If they feel pressured, ask them why someone else's beliefs should be more important than their own, and ask them to challenge or question friends who put them under pressure. Teach a 'who cares?' approach to pressure. In the end, why should it bother your friends whether you smoke or not? Who cares if you aren't exactly like your friends? Celebrate your child's uniqueness rather than struggling to help him to conform. You'll encourage independence of mind and spirit that will help him through all types of pressure in life.

Be available for communication, and to talk things through. If your child can express his concerns, and rely on your support at home, he'll feel stronger and more able to cope outside the home environment. If you teach your child to believe in himself and his achievements, he will be much more likely to resist external influences, and feel comfortable doing so.

Point out the importance of true friendship. If he's fallen in with a bunch of people who scorn him, or put him under pressure to conform, it may be time to find new friends. Help your child to foster friendships and relationships that are stimulating and non-threatening. If he has a circle of friends who support rather than undermine his confidence, he's much less likely to be pressured into doing things that he doesn't want to do. Encourage plenty of activities that involve a wide variety of different children. If he has some recourse or respite from one peer group, he'll be able to offload and escape when necessary.

The peer group can be a source of affection, sympathy and understanding from people who are experiencing the very same emotions, situations and outlook. Peers act as guinea pigs, as adolescents and children experiment with different personalities and behaviours in the normal course of development. The peer group helps them to define themselves, and it's a step away from being dependent upon parents. It's a normal feature of development.

However, peer relationships can be stressful, largely because adolescents and children invest so much in them. For the first time, they are experiencing conditional affection and acceptance. They are often meeting and developing friendships with people who have different morals, values, and goals. There may be a sense of competition behind it all, as well as new types of relationships, with the opposite sex for example, or a romance. These factors can often make children feel uncertain about themselves, and force them to confront and perhaps even challenge their own ideals. Not surprisingly, this puts pressure on familial relationships; as adolescents begin to explore, experiment, question and define themselves, they often contradict parental expectations and even their values.

The whole issue of peers is a difficult one for children to manage, and can be a source of great stress. Falling out with friends was one of the main stresses that the girls who answered my survey experienced. In fact, for 79 per cent of these girls, it was the most stressful thing in their lives.

It's important for all parents to accept the importance of peers in a child's life, and not to see them as a threat to family harmony. All children grow up eventually, and this is one of the steps on the way to independence. Be understanding and empathetic about problems that develop with peers. It's often difficult to relate to what children are experiencing, particularly if we don't like the company they are keeping, but keeping the channels of communication open gives them a feeling of security. Children also need to know that they can go in and out of peer groups, but always have the love and acceptance of their family. This helps to balance times when they fall out with friends, or have arguments or break-ups.

A child who has a strong sense of self, and high self-esteem and self-respect, is more likely to establish positive peer relationships.

In a crisis:

- Flower essences are most effective and several can be blended for best effect. Consider Cerato for a child who is constantly seeking reassurance from others, and has no faith in himself; Elm for a child who feels like a failure or inadequate because he sets himself such high expectations. Holly is for children who feel envious, jealous and cross, tending to develop a victim mentality. Larch is for low self-esteem and lack of confidence. Most important of all is Walnut, for adolescence and childhood are periods of enormous change. Everyone needs a little support.

- Homeopathic remedies that may help include Aconite, for bottled-up emotions and anxiety, Pulsatilla for tearfulness, Calcarea for excessive pride, Aurum for despair, fear or grief, or an inability to bear opposition or contradiction.

Competition

Competition is part of life, and every child needs to know how to deal with competitive colleagues and friends. Competition is a stressor, but it can be healthy in the short term, raising energy levels and stimulating the senses. It can provide the drive and stimulation to finish a task, and to produce a best performance. However, competition in every area of life is stressful and exhausting.

Headmaster George Marsh defends the fairly intense competition that exists between the boys at his school in London. He claims that it plays a crucial role, particularly in sport, in development and preparing a child for life. In his view, it reflects real life, but within the confines of a safe and structured environment. The boys can choose to compete, to do their best, to sit on the sidelines or even opt out. The balancing factor is choice, and control over their environment. Healthy competition is often experienced in sport, for example, where children work together, learn to be effective as a team, and experience winning and losing.

Within the environment of Dulwich College Preparatory School, George Marsh ensures that there are many opportunities for children to experience the less competitive aspects of school. They are given free time to forge relationships, and can spend time in various clubs, with like-minded individuals in a non-competitive setting. Much of the free time revolves around hobbies and interests, and the boys are encouraged to choose activities themselves; alternatively, they can make the choice simply to relax. Marsh feels that this empowerment is crucial to a child's development. The children seem to feel much less stressed because their day is a 'known quantity'. He believes that, at home, many children are forced to develop the same time-management skills as adults. They have little time for relaxation, interaction, and even sleep, all of which can lead to a poor sense of well-being.

Pressure from parents increases competition. Parents pushing their children to excel can make them doubt their own worth, and feel a need to prove themselves within their peer group and at school. Similarly, parents often encourage competition by showing disregard for effort, and intensely praising results and achievement. This can undermine a child's self-esteem and confidence, and drive them to compete for the wrong reasons. Ultimately, every child needs to learn to satisfy his own personal goals, and to do it for himself, and no one else. Later in life, children who face intense competition can experience debilitating stress, disillusionment and burn-out, often realising that they have been pushed and been pushing for something that simply doesn't exist – perfection.

Children often feel overwhelmed by competition, and it is extremely important for them to take part in plenty of non-demanding activities, which act as an outlet rather than a source of stress. If a child spends his weekends on the football pitch, or in the gym, he'll need to use his leisure time to relax, enjoy and let off steam. If parents place too much pressure on fun time, they will increase the competitive element and, through that, the stress load.

Being alone can help, too, for children cannot be pressured when they are in their own space.

If your child feels under pressure because of competition, you need to show that you understand and sympathise. Resist putting any more pressure on a child who faces competition in many aspects of his life. Assess your own motivation for wanting your child to do well (*see* page 98). Encourage a healthy level of competition, but praise effort and individual progress rather than winning or being the best. If a child feels unthreatened by competition at home, and feels that his efforts are being recognised, he won't feel the need to overachieve in other areas of his life. By all means share your expectations, but make them relevant and realistic, and don't apply pressure to see that they are realised. All children benefit from having goals, targets and an understanding of why it is important to be the best that they can be, but that doesn't mean being the best of all; it simply means making the most of individual talents to carve a niche for themselves in life.

In a crisis:

- Too much competition can cause all of the symptoms of stress, so try some general remedies (*see* page 250) if your child is suffering.

- Offer Olive flower essence when a child is physically at rock bottom, and Vervain when he's reached the end of his tether trying to be the best. Impatiens soothes irritability and tension, and Oreganum will allow him to be at ease with himself, without the need to pretend to be what his peers expect.

- Aconite will help with trauma, particularly if a child is suppressing his emotions to get on with things. Natrum mur will help if sympathy seems to make your child feel worse. For excessive pride, try Platinum and Calcarea. If your child pushes himself too hard but ultimately doubts himself, perhaps becoming depressed and underconfident, try Aurum. Another good one is Bryonia for anger, peevishness and irritability.

- Essential oils can be a quick-fix solution for someone facing intense competition. Try lavender and chamomile to relax and soothe the nerves, and neroli and rose to balance and ease any depression.

- Offer a massage, as often as you can.

Trauma

As well as physical experiences and injuries, the term 'trauma' includes emotional injury, which is essentially a normal response to an extreme event. It involves the creation of emotional memories, which arise through a long-lasting effect on structures deep within the brain. The more direct the exposure to the traumatic event, the higher the risk for emotional harm. Emotional trauma can have a dramatic effect on health.

At different ages, children react differently to trauma, and some children appear to be more affected than others, for reasons that are not clearly understood. Even something like hearing the news of murders at schools (which have taken place in the UK, Canada and the USA very recently) can shock some children and make them fearful. You need to do get to the bottom of your child's fear, and help him to work through it.

Reactions to trauma may appear immediately after the traumatic event, or days or even weeks later. Loss of trust in adults and fear of the event occurring again are responses seen in many children and adolescents who have been exposed to traumatic events. Other reactions vary according to age:

- For children of five and younger, typical reactions include a fear of being separated from a parent, crying, whimpering, screaming, immobility and/or aimless motion, trembling, frightened facial expressions and excessive clinging. Parents may also notice children returning to behaviours exhibited at earlier ages ('regressive behaviours'), such as thumb-sucking, bedwetting, and fear of darkness. The behaviours can lead to problems at school.

- Children aged from six to 11 may show extreme withdrawal, disruptive behaviour, and/or inability to pay attention. Regressive behaviours, nightmares, sleep problems, irrational fears, irritability, refusal to attend school, outbursts of anger and fighting are also common in traumatised children of this age. The child may also complain of stomach aches or other bodily symptoms that have no medical basis. School work often suffers. Depression, anxiety, feelings of guilt and emotional numbing are often present as well.

- Adolescents aged from 12 to 17 are likely to exhibit responses similar to those of adults, including flashbacks, nightmares, emotional numbing, avoidance of any reminders of the traumatic event, depression, substance abuse, problems with peers, and anti-social behaviour. Also common are withdrawal and isolation, physical complaints, school avoidance, academic decline, sleep disturbances, and confusion.

If this sounds extreme, and unlikely to affect your child, remember that almost anything can traumatise a child, even if it appears innocuous to an adult. Think back to your own childhood. There may be a particular event that stands out clearly in your mind – being lost at a funfair, being forgotten at school, being left alone in your cot, being physically or emotionally abused, or witnessing abuse of others. This kind of traumatic event can affect children dramatically. More obviously, a car accident, a death in the family, a parental divorce, the death of a pet, or even a physical injury can also cause emotional trauma. All children differ in the way they deal with the effects.

What to do:

- Encourage your child to express his feelings, and help younger children to use words that help them do so. Don't force discussion of a traumatic event if your child does not want to open up. Make sure your child knows that you are there when he wants to talk. It might help to express your own feelings, and to identify with feelings that he might be experiencing. He might feel better about opening up if he sees you doing so.

- Let children and adolescents know that it is normal to feel upset after something bad happens.

- Return to your normal household routine, which can be reassuring for children. They'll know that whatever goes on outside, they are safe at home.

- Be patient with extra needs. If your child needs a light on at bedtime for a short time, try to accept it. He may need someone with him when he falls asleep, or he may want someone in the room with him at all times. Try to meet his demands until he is able to heal.

- Never make a child feel guilty or childish for expressing feelings, or for crying. These are healthy emotional expressions.

- Some children blame themselves for events that occur around them. Reassure them that they are not to blame, even if you cannot see any reason why they should consider themselves the cause.

- Some children need more time to heal than others, and it is important to be patient throughout the course. It can take many months for some children to get over something as simple as the loss of a pet or a friend, but in order to do so they need your sympathy and constant reassurance.

In a crisis:

- Flower essences can be particularly useful (*see* page 161), and you can create a blend of several types to best match your child's outlook. For example, Aspen and Mimulus can be blended for fears, Rock Rose is appropriate for shock or trauma of any sort, and Rescue Remedy is ideal for all types of shock or trauma.

- Homeopathic treatment will be constitutional, but it can make a big difference to emotional health. Consider some of the following remedies in the meantime: Aconite should be given as soon as possible after any trauma, with Arnica, if there is physical injury; Ignatia should be offered if trauma follows a bereavement or when there is intense grief; Opium is suitable is your child is frightened by the death of the loved one, and numb with grief; Pulsatilla is useful if there is sleeplessness, helpless weeping and catarrh; Natrum mur will help a child who rejects sympathy and prefers to hide his feelings.

Changing schools

Any type of change can be stressful for children, but moving schools – either to a school in a new area, or as part of the progression through the educational system – can be particularly daunting. School represents one of the great 'known' quantities in a child's life, and he will undoubtedly have experienced a period of adjustment before he felt at home and comfortable with his peers. Beginning again, in a different social climate, or with children who are older (as in the progression to a senior school, for example), can leave a child feeling bereft, frightened, unsure and insecure.

The switch from middle to senior or upper schools tends to coincide with several major changes for young adolescents. Most are in the throes of puberty; they're becoming more self-aware and self-conscious, and their thinking is growing more critical and more complex. At the same time, adolescents are often 'in a slump' when it comes to academic motivation and performance. Researchers at the University of Michigan have studied the transition from junior to senior school and have found that, on average, children's grades drop dramatically during the first year of middle school compared to their grades in junior school; after moving to middle school, children become less interested in school and less self-assured about their abilities.

The American Psychological Association suggests, 'At a time when children's cognitive abilities are increasing, middle school offers them fewer opportunities for decision-making and lower levels of cognitive involvement, but a more complex social environment. At the same time, numerous teachers have replaced the single classroom teacher and students often face larger classes and a new group of peers. These factors all interact to make the transition difficult for many youngsters. Studies find the decreased motivation and self-assuredness contribute to poor academic performance; poor grades trigger more self-doubt and a downward spiral can begin.'

Children who believe that effort can affect results, and that intelligence can change over time, seem to make the best adjustment. Studies have found that even children with low self-confidence respond better if they believe that their early results are not 'fixed'. In fact, highly confident children who believe that their intelligence is fixed have the most trouble making the transition. They apparently believe that they should be able to do well because they are clever and that extra effort in order to learn a new skill is not necessary. When 'effortless' learning does not take place, these students lose confidence, motivation and interest.

Because children can be demotivated by change to a school where they are an unknown quantity, having to prove themselves all over again, it's important that they understand that it is acceptable to experience a dip in results. Children who are encouraged to focus on future results and potential rather than carrying on from previous success will have a much better chance of fitting in and excelling in a new environment.

Children will also need encouragement to forge new relationships, and parents can help by setting up activities with new friends, maintaining links with old friends, if possible, and initiating new interests in their children. They will need constant reassurance that they are interesting and fun to be with, giving them the confidence to establish new friendships and join in with group activities and events.

All children will feel shy and probably frightened by a new situation; keeping things at home as sane, similar and comforting as possible will make the transition that much easier. A child who is shy or clingy should be introduced to new situations gradually. Talk about what's coming beforehand and then allow him to proceed at his own pace.

In a crisis:

■ Rescue Remedy or Emergency Essence (*see* page 166) are brilliant for feelings of panic and fear. Other flower remedies include Mimulus for fear of the known, Aspen for fear of the unknown, and Walnut for change. For a child who constantly seeks the reassurance of others because he does not trust his own judgement or intuition, try Cerato, which gives an ability to believe in himself. Elm can help a child who feels overwhelmed or inadequate.

■ Homeopathic remedies can also help. Try Aconite for fear, restlessness and anxiety. Lycopodium helps children who are frightened or worried about new situations, who feel insecure and may show off to compensate. Gelsemium is good for children who are tired and shaky, and who seem to dread things like speaking in front of a class of other children.

■ Essential oils can be very useful in the treatment of symptoms caused by change, particularly those that help to release tension and induce a feeling of calm. Some of the best oils to try are chamomile, geranium, jasmine (for older children), lavender and ylang ylang, which are sedative. They can be used in the bath, in massage with a light carrier oil (such as sweet almond), or in a vaporiser.

■ Calming herbs such as catmint, hops and valerian will help to soothe anxiety.

Learning difficulties

Dr Robert Dato proposes that stress in the mind of a child is the same as static on the radio. They can hear that someone is talking, but cannot really hear what is being said. Stress greatly impedes learning, so the problems of a child who already has learning difficulties will be significantly compounded by high stress levels. There are many different types of learning difficulty, including dyspraxia and dyslexia. Parents need to recognise that children with learning difficulties already feel stressed by their situation, particularly in relation to their peers, and in the context of our achievement-oriented society. As a result, they are probably more susceptible to stress, and hindered by it even more.

There is a relationship between anxiety and problem-solving skills (and more) in all children, and especially those with learning difficulties. Children who are anxious or worry a lot about lots of things are in a chronic state of stress. Stress can also be caused by external factors such as noise or family arguing. (A recent study at Cornell University showed that the constant roar from jet aircraft could affect a child's blood pressure and the production of stress hormones, which in turn affect learning. Other studies show that children living near large airports tend to be poor listeners and do not read as well as children in quieter locations.) Both types of stress – internal and external – can be harmful and can interrupt learning.

Children with learning difficulties are especially vulnerable to stress that affects learning. Many of these children are chronically worried, first and foremost about the usual things – peers, friendship, achievement and expectations – but also about whether they will 'meet the grade', be accepted by other children, be able to attend a college or university of their choice, or bomb out of academic life completely. They will probably be self-conscious about reading in public, and worry about being slower, asking more questions, taking longer to get the gist of a theory or subject, and doing less well at tests.

Most learning difficulties are not 'diseases' to be cured, and children do not grow out of them. Early recognition and appropriate intervention can, however, make a big difference to the extent to which a condition affects your child. Children with learning difficulties accommodate to a greater or lesser degree depending on their own personality and the type of support they receive from home and school. Many individuals will experience difficulties throughout their life; the majority develop strategies to enable them to cope most of the time, but in stress situations all the original problems can recur. It's important, therefore, to teach your child ways to relax and to avoid stressful situations.

What to do:

- A child with learning difficulties is not stupid. A child who struggles with tasks that seem to come easily to other children may be negatively labelled and even teased. In some cases, a diagnosis is not made until children are well into their school careers, by which time they may believe that they are academically sub-standard. For this reason, it is crucial that you build your child's self-esteem (*see* page 143), and offer plenty of praise for even the smallest task completed – or attempted.

- Make home a safe place, with as little expectation or potential for failure as possible. School can be hard work, and it's important for him to know that he can rest and relax, and be accepted at home. It is a mistake to think that you can cure the condition by sheer perseverance and extra work at home. Be patient and loving, and celebrate every small victory along the way. Keep your anxieties about his long-term prospects to yourself. Your child will have the best chance of doing well if he is calm, loved and happy.

- Give your child a night off every now and then. School days can be exhausting, and he will be genuinely in need of a break sometimes. Extra handwriting or reading practice at the end of the day may put him off completely.

- Encourage hobbies such as collecting stamps or fossils, or anything else. Teach him as much as you can in a casual way, so that he will have a wealth of fascinating information and facts at his fingertips. Explore non-traditional study methods, using travel, hobbies or television and theatre to make information fun. Read interesting articles from the newspaper. Create story tapes, reading interesting books or plays. Buy tapes with times tables and other mathematical concepts set to music; numbers may be difficult on a page, but he will be able to remember a song. Make things visual – ask him to draw a story you are reading, or to re-enact a part of history that he is studying.

- Read to a dyslexic child as often as possible, to encourage a love of books and learning that might otherwise be threatened. Even teenagers faced with exams or plenty of homework will welcome a break from the printed page. It can be exhausting trying to remember facts without a visual memory, so study sessions together should be short, with lots of breaks.

In a crisis:

- Homeopathic treatment of learning difficulties has been successful in many cases, but it will need to be tailored to your child's specific needs. While you are waiting to see a therapist, try Lycopodium, taken three times daily for up to three weeks.

- Nutritional medicine has eased some cases of learning difficulties. One 1998 study showed that dyslexic children have lower amounts of zinc than children without the condition, indicating that zinc supplementation may help to reverse some symptoms.

- A good, nutritious diet encourages the best brain health.

- Flower essences (*see* page 161) can do a lot to redress poor self-image, which may be making the problem worse.

Parental separation and divorce

For today's children, the family structure is likely to be far less constant and predictable, which means that their basic emotional foundation is less secure. It's estimated that by the end of the next decade, more than half of all marriages will end in divorce. Given that the family is such a crucial part of building self-esteem in children, it's not surprising that parental problems are a source of great stress.

Children – even very young children – are acutely sensitive to parental tension and unhappiness, and are probably well aware that there is a problem before separation or divorce are even mentioned. Many parents do not want to burden their children, and choose not to discuss the problem. However, family silence can increase the stress load, with children feeling concerned, guilty and even responsible.

Even the most amicable divorce is a difficult experience for children. They may feel the need to be more self-reliant as their basic security system undergoes a profound change. Many divorces are far from amicable, and too many children are exposed to negative comments about the other parent, or put in the position of having to choose sides. Although parents inevitably want to spare their children, it can be difficult to be consistently loving, open and fair when you are suffering a huge trauma and stress of your own.

Parents need to show honesty, sensitivity and self-control, and to allow time for healing. Be aware that your child is under pressure, even if he isn't vocalising it, for fear of adding more pressure to an already toxic situation.

What to do:

- Encourage your children to talk as openly as they can about their feelings. Don't be afraid to let them know that you are feeling sad, tense and frightened too, but don't overload them; simply show them that it's acceptable to feel the way you all do. Carry on the communication; different things come out at different times and they will need you to help in times of uncertainty, even if it is months later.

- Children may feel guilty and imagine that they 'caused' the problem, particularly if they have heard their parents argue about them. Children may also feel angry or frightened, or they may be worried that they will be abandoned by or 'divorced from' their parents.

- Don't say negative things about your ex-partner, no matter how upset or angry you may be. In the end, they'll feel like they've lost both of you, when they need to feel they can still rely on both parents, even if one is not always present.

- Children should not be put in the position or relaying information, or carrying messages between angry partners. Don't quiz your child about your ex-partner's love life, or expect a running commentary of time spent away. Let your child know that you are interested in what he has to say, and that you are there to support him if he is concerned, worried or confused. But communicate directly with your ex-partner, no matter how hard it may be.

- Expect resistance and difficulties in helping children adjust to a new partner and, possibly, to a new partner's children. New relationships, blended families and remarriages are among the most difficult aspects of the divorce process. Step-parenting and remarriage require a tremendous amount of patience, time, humour and talking. It takes a long time; love and affection will never be 'instant'.

- Depending on their ages, conversations with children will vary. In general, young children probably need less detail than older children. Be as concrete and specific as possible about events they have witnessed. If you have spent a lot of time arguing recently, acknowledge it. Leaving it to the children's imagination can make things much worse.

- Prevent unnecessary guilt by making sure children know that any irritability or preoccupation on your part is because of something going on in your life, and not because of them.

- Encourage relationships with other trusted adults and friends. Many children do not feel as confident or comfortable confiding in their parents during times of marital trouble, partly because they do not want to exacerbate the problem, and also because parents are distracted and usually unhappy and/or irritable. Arrange for loving grandparents, godparents, aunts or close friends to spend time with your children, and to encourage good communication. All kids need to talk, and if they can't do it with you, they will need to do it elsewhere.

In a crisis:

- Rescue Remedy and Emergency Essence (*see* page 166) are good standbys. Offer them on a daily basis, or as required, to help keep your child calm, and to reduce anxiety and tension.

- Other useful flower remedies include Mimulus for fear, Aspen for fear of the unknown, Walnut for change and Paw Paw, which will help your child if he feels overwhelmed, unable to resolve problems and burdened by decision-making. Mountain Devil will help with hatred, anger and holding grudges. Illawarra Flame Tree is useful if your child feels an over-whelming sense of rejection, and lacks confidence.

- Suitable homeopathic remedies in the first instance are Aconite and Ignatia.

- Calming herbs, such as chamomile, hops and catmint, are useful to ease anxiety.

Bereavement

Stress and grief are natural reactions to the loss of a person, animal or other loved one, and it's difficult to contemplate the emotions that a bereaved child experiences. Many children bottle up their feelings, or simply fail to acknowledge or accept the death. Other children may show anger, depression and a sense of numbness. There is no right way to respond to bereavement, and the remaining parent or carer must acknowledge that whatever a child is feeling is right and correct for them.

According to a study published in the *Journal of the American Academy of Child and Adolescent Psychiatry* in September 2000, the death of a parent in childhood can increase a child's risk of post-traumatic stress disorder. They found that girls and younger children generally tend to report more PTSD symptoms than boys and older children. They found that the surviving parent's emotional adjustment was directly related to how well a child responded and healed, illustrating the importance of an stable emotional environment.

One thing is certain – no one benefits from suppressing emotion. Although it may take some time for your child to be able to talk about it, it's important that you empathise, show patience, seek to open the channels of communication, and express your own feelings. If you've lost a partner, you will be unlikely to find the prospect of coping with a child easy, particularly if they are exhibiting aggressive, angry or fearful behaviour. However, sharing the experience can help everyone involved, and shift the focus to the future, where hope still remains.

Children may also experience serious and debilitating stress when a beloved pet dies, or even when a favourite and much-loved nursery toy is lost. Don't underestimate their grief, or tell a child that he is overreacting. If your child is extremely upset, respect his feelings and help him to cope.

What to do:

- Don't push anything under the carpet. Talk about the deceased with your child, and encourage him to join in. Provide opportunities to participate in memorialising activities, such as telling stories about the deceased, remembering birthdays, flipping through photograph albums, and reading a diary.

- If your child is old enough, suggest that he attends the funeral and becomes involved in the plans. It often helps children to know that they can play their part in marking the end of a life, and a certain finality will allow the grieving process to begin.

- Make sure your child has a memento. A piece of jewellery, an article of clothing, a well-thumbed favourite book that was shared between parent and child can bring back fond memories many years later and help a child to feel a link. In the case of the death of a pet, find a picture of your child's pet, or a collar or another thing that will help them to feel in touch.

- Be alert to feelings. Grief is a many-staged and many-layered process, and everyone responds differently. You'll need to help your child find the words to express his feelings, and to be vigilant about looking for signs that he is not coping well.

- Don't be afraid to use humour to lighten the pain of loss. While it can seem irreverent, and in bad taste in the early days, it can help a great deal to share laughter and fond, amusing memories. Remind your child about what lousy milkshakes Daddy made, or Mummy's grumpy face in the morning. If it's a pet, talk about its sillier adventures.

In a crisis:

- Rescue Remedy and Emergency Essence (*see* page 166) are musts for any trauma of this nature.

- The homeopathic remedy Ignatia is most suitable, and can be taken at a low potency for several weeks. Arnica will help if your child wants to be left alone, and insists that he feels all right. Aconite helps if your child is fearful, or on the verge of collapse. If your child is very frightened by the death of a loved one try Opium. For helpless weeping, try Pulsatilla. For a child who becomes angry and critical of others, try Nux vomica.

- Try any of the relaxing aromatherapy oils (*see* page 154), to help soothe the emotional and physical tension. Chamomile, lavender and jasmine are good first choices.

School phobia and fear

It may sound dramatic, but school phobia is quite common in children and adolescents. There can be a variety of reasons for the condition. Young children may build up a negative experience in their mind to be something traumatic. They may associate school with trauma, even if it is on a subconscious basis, and no amount of rational discussion will sway them. Consider whether there has been a traumatic event in your child's life, such as moving house, losing a loved one, or fighting with siblings.

Usually a school phobia masks some other problem, and the negative emotions surrounding whatever is causing the upset can translate themselves into headaches, abdominal pains, nausea and vomiting, and even fainting. Symptoms are normally worse on weekday mornings, better at weekends and during holidays. If there is any tension in the family, your child may feel that he needs to stay at home to prevent the occurrence of something terrible (a fight, a divorce, violence, or whatever he may have conjured up). For children who lack confidence, find school work difficult, or have problems with their peers, home is the safest place to be, and they are right to head towards safety.

Never underestimate your child's concerns or fears. There may be a serious problem at school affecting his emotional health, or it may be something simple that has affected your child more dramatically than perhaps it should have done. Whether or not you consider a problem to be valid is irrelevant. If it is enough to cause your child to become upset, and to manifest physical symptoms, something has to be done about it.

What to do:

- Most importantly, get to the bottom of it. Spend as much time as you can with your child talking things through. He may be too traumatised or upset to talk about it, or vaguely embarrassed or ashamed of his concerns. He may not even be able to pinpoint what the problem is – there may just be a general feeling of unhappiness and fear, or self-consciousness. Choose different times of the day for chats, and use personal examples to lead into discussions. For example, recount a childhood experience that upset you greatly. Children respond well to comparisons because it helps them believe that they are not weird or unusual.

- Talk to your child's teacher and, if necessary, other classmates, to find out what is wrong, and then work out a solution. Bullying may be at the root (*see* page 208).

In a crisis:

- Of the flower remedies (*see* page 161), Mimulus is for the everyday fears of known things (school, other children, sports, teachers). Aspen is for those vague and dark fears that are unknown. Rock Rose should be added when the fear is turning into terror and perhaps panic. Cherry Plum is for the fear that everything will fall apart (particularly useful if your child thinks he *needs* to be at home rather than at school) and Red Chestnut is for the fear for the safety of others. The most important Bach Flower Remedy for fear, anxiety and phobias is Rescue Remedy.

- Essential oils can be very useful in the treatment of school phobias, particularly those that help to release tension and induce a feeling of calm. Some of the best oils to try are chamomile, geranium, jasmine (for older children), lavender and ylang ylang, which are sedative. They can be used in the bath, in massage with a light carrier oil (such as sweet almond), or in a vaporiser.

- A school phobia (or indeed any type of phobia) should be treated constitutionally by a good homeopath. Some of the best remedies are as follows: Arnica, when fears are brought on by an obvious trauma or accident; Arg nit, when your child finds it difficult to concentrate, lacks self-confidence and cannot explain why school is so terrifying (and may also be suffering from diarrhoea); Lycopodium helps children who are frightened or worried about new situations, feeling insecure and perhaps showing off to compensate; Gelsemium is good for children who are tired and shaky, and who seem to dread things like speaking in front of a class of other children; Natrum mur is indicated when your child is afraid to use the school toilets, and fears having an accident.

- If a child's diet is high in refined and processed foods, or if there is too much sugar, he may become more highly strung and sensitive to new situations.

- Ensure that your child is getting enough restful sleep (*see* page 118), which can affect his emotions.

- Valerian tea, sipped at night before bed, can help to reduce tension.

Birth of a new baby

See 'Sibling rivalry' (page 214); all of the information is relevant.

Eating disorders

Stress can exacerbate and even cause eating disorders, and eating disorders rob the body of key nutrients, and play havoc with physical health to the extent that the stress response is often initiated, and sufferers are much more susceptible. There are two main types: anorexia and bulimia.

Anorexia nervosa

Around 5 per cent of young girls in the UK are estimated to have anorexia nervosa. Boys are much less likely to be affected, although that situation is changing. The condition results in death in 20 per cent of cases within 20 years of onset of the illness. Only around 60 per cent of anorexics recover.

Psychiatrists have singled out several characteristics as being typical of anorexics, including a dominant, overprotective and critical mother and a passive or withdrawn father; a tendency to perfectionism; a strong desire for social approval; and a need for order and control. However, many of these characteristics have been the subject of dispute, particularly those relating to parenting. Whatever the case, a poor self-image is almost always at the root of an eating disorder, and it is this that needs to be addressed before there can be any hope of a cure. The media and its emphasis on super-thin models is also blamed by some for influencing the way people, particularly girls, see themselves.

In the USA, over 60 per cent of fourth-grade girls (aged about nine) in an Iowa study reported a desire to be thinner. By age 18, nine out of 10 teenage girls in a California survey were dieting to lose weight. This perception of fatness is common even among girls with little body fat. In one study, 58 per cent of girls aged nine to 18 thought of themselves as fat, whereas only 15 per cent *were* fat, based on height and weight measures. Fear of fatness, restrained eating, and binge eating were found to be common among girls by the age of 10.

Anorexia nervosa is a form of intentional self-starvation. What may begin as a normal diet is carried to extremes, with many reducing their intake to an absolute minimum. It is also characterised by obsessive behaviour. The majority of anorexics deny they have a problem (*see* the advice on warning signs, below). The average age for onset of the illness is thought to be 16, although the age range of anorexia is between 10 and 40. Around 90 per cent of cases are female. Most have no history of being overweight.

Symptoms of anorexia include extreme weight loss for no discernible medical reason; ritualistic food habits, such as excessive chewing; denying hunger and exercising excessively; choosing low-calorie food; and hiding feelings. A person with anorexia may be excessively thin but still see themselves as overweight.

Some of the main warning signs include the following:

- Does your child seem obsessed by fat or by the calorie content of food? Has he put himself on a 'diet' for any reason, from which he cannot be swayed?

- Does your child exercise obsessively, carefully calculating the number of calories burned during physical activity?

- Is your child frequently 'not hungry' or 'too busy' at mealtimes?

- Does your child disappear into the lavatory after meals?

- Have you noticed any mood changes, including angry out-bursts, isolation from friends, withdrawn behaviour, chemical abuse or depression? Studies indicate that starvation tends to increase feelings of depression, anxiety, irritability and anger, and mood changes can be a sign that all is not well. Many teens are subject to mood swings, however, so if this is the only symptom, look elsewhere for a cause.

- Has your daughter failed to start her period at a normal time, or have her periods stopped?

- Alongside weight loss, does your child suffer dry skin, hair loss, rashes and itching?

Bulimia nervosa

Bulimia is thought to be two to three times more common than anorexia, but is generally not as dangerous physically. However, excessive use of laxatives and self-induced vomiting can cause rupture of the oesophagus, mineral deficiency and dehydration, which can have serious effects on health.

Bulimia was only officially recognised in the 1970s and is characterised by a cycle of bingeing and starving. Many bulimics seem fine, but experts say that, under the surface, they often suffer from poor self-esteem and self-image. Bulimics may have irregular periods or stop having periods at all because of excessive use of laxatives and vomiting. Using laxatives can also cause kidney

and bowel problems and stomach disorders. It can be more difficult to recognise this condition, because your child may stay
around the same weight, or lose weight more slowly. However, a
puffy face, swollen fingers, muscle weakness and stomach pains
can indicate problems when associated with an obsession with
weight and obvious signs of bingeing and purging.

Some experts believe bulimia is the result of an imbalance of
chemicals to the brain, but others think the illness is more likely
to be linked to a lack of self-worth. It is thought that up to half
of anorexics also suffer from bulimia and some 40 per cent of
bulimics are reported to have a history of anorexia.

Preventing eating disorders

- Avoid talking about weight or diets, even if your child does
  have a weight problem. Anorexic children are much more likely
  to come from families that are overconcerned about weight
  and the calorie content of food. Parents send strong messages
  to their children when they constantly complain about their
  bodies, discuss diets and obsess over the fat, calorie and sugar
  content of food.

- Make family meals a daily occurrence. Many parents are surprised to find a child is anorexic because they have not eaten
  with them, or seen them eating, for many weeks or even
  months. A new UK study shows that many children no longer
  eat with their parents on a regular basis. Children should not
  be made responsible for their own food choices. Apart from
  the fact that they can make unacceptable choices that can
  damage their health, parents need to model positive eating
  habits, which will go a long way towards instilling healthy
  attitudes to food.

- Always provide a variety of fresh foods from all food groups
  at meals. Don't force a child to eat, and give small helpings,
  even when children are small. They can always ask for more.

- Parents have a powerful influence on their children's self-esteem
  and body image. In one study, self-esteem scores of children
  aged from nine to 11 were lowered when they thought their

parents were dissatisfied with their bodies. Encourage your child to feel good about himself, no matter what his weight. Even overweight children need high self-esteem (*see* page 143). Make sure your child feels loved and accepted for what he is, not what he looks like. Children with high self-esteem naturally gravitate towards habits that are good for them – taking exercise, good hygiene habits, dressing well, and taking pride in their appearance (flaws and all!).

Dealing with an eating disorder

- All anorexics should be given a good multivitamin and mineral complex. All nutrients are needed in extremely high doses, because food passes through the gastrointestinal tract rapidly and nutrients are poorly assimilated.

- If your child does suffer from an eating disorder, you will need to address emotional issues to uncover problems affecting self-image and self-esteem (*see* page 143). Support and love your child. Showing disgust when he is overly thin or fat will reinforce a poor self-image. Let your child know that you love him and care about him. You can certainly show concern about his health, but make sure he is aware that your love and concern are not judgemental.

- Encourage hobbies and activities that will help your child to feel good about himself – choose something at which he is bound to succeed. Draw attention to successes, and overlook failures of any kind.

- Get some help for yourself. Join a support group with other parents in the same situation. Try not to blame yourself. The finger of suspicion is often pointed at parents. Even secure children can suffer from self-esteem and emotional problems after some kind of upset, or there may be problems at school about which you know nothing. Get to the root of the problem, and find ways of addressing it.

When it's all too much

Children cannot be programmed to adapt, and they can't be bullied into coping. Some children suffer from stress that sends them beyond the normal, unpleasant symptoms and feelings. There are many natural and practical solutions to stress, but there may be times when a child's health, development and well-being are severely threatened; at this point, they may need drug therapy and/or counselling or psychiatric help. There is no need to be ashamed if your child requires this type of assistance. In the long term, a short period turned over to this type of intervention can make a difference to your child's future ability to adapt to the world around him, and to find health and happiness as an adult.

It's also important for parents to understand that a child's inability to cope with the rigours of modern life is no reflection on parenting skills or a child's future capability and success. It is abundantly clear that the stress of modern life is taking its toll on even the most robust of us, and children are no exception.

Counselling

Counselling is a treatment for the mind – a form of psychotherapy. It is not aimed specifically at children who are ill, but at healthy people who wish to deal with a crisis, or to improve their lives or relationships. It can be useful for children who feel that they have no one to whom they can turn, and need encouragement to express and deal with conflicting emotions, problems and issues in their lives.

The link between the mind and body has been long established on scientific grounds, and a physical illness can give rise to psychological symptoms, while an emotional problem can affect overall health. The clearest example of this is stress, which affects both mind and body. Counselling can help children to understand the link between various problems, and help them to learn to manage them.

A counsellor should aim to help your child to gain an insight into his motives and needs, giving him the confidence to deal more effectively with problems himself.

Behavioural therapy

Some doctors or therapists recommend behavioural therapy. This therapy, introduced at the turn of the 20th century, is based on learning theories. It aims to predict and control behaviour using scientific means. It concentrates on observing and analysing behaviour and cognitive functioning, diagnosing unproductive habits and ways of dealing with life, and instituting changes in order to alter and improve the outcome.

A therapist will discuss methods and expectations with your child, who then agrees to participate at a negotiated level. Measures to monitor effectiveness are then established. The techniques used include the following:

- Counter-conditioning, which involves replacing an undesirable response to a stimulus with a new one.

- Role-playing, in which the therapist demonstrates more effective behaviours in a session, which your child can then try in real life.

- Aversion conditioning, which involves pairing a stimulus that is attractive to your child, but would lead to undesirable results, with an unpleasant event or thought, in order to break the pattern.

- Desensitisation, which involves relaxing your child and then exposing him gradually and gently to anxiety-provoking situations.

- Cognitive Behavioural therapy is a type of psychotherapy that highlights the fact that it is our beliefs, interpretations and perceptions of life events that determine our feelings, moods, responses and actions.

Other therapies

Children below the age of five would likely respond to play therapy, which involves developing self-control, self-responsibility and self-esteem. A child is offered a safe and consistent environment in which feelings can be explored with the help of a therapist. Children are allowed to talk, remain silent, play alone or involve a therapist.

Family therapy is very effective for older children, and involves working with the whole family unit to help children to adapt in stressful situations. This is one therapy that I would highly recommend as it addresses problems with both the support of the family and a therapist or doctor, and in the context of a child's day-to-day life. All elements of lifestyle and scheduling can be examined, as well as interactions, anxieties, inappropriate responses and behaviours.

Drug therapies

Drugs will be prescribed according to your child's overwhelming symptoms, but in general, you can expect treatment in the form of anti-depressants (such as the selective serotonin-reuptake inhibitors (SSRIs) in the form of fluoxetine (Prozac), sertraline (Zoloft), paroxetine (Paxil), citalopram (Celexa), and fluvoxamine (Luvox)). For a mix of generalised anxiety and depression, doxepin (Adapin, Sinequan) may be beneficial. Some children are prescribed Ritalin, which works as a mild depressant.

Conclusion

The key to parenting in the modern age is awareness. If you know what's going on, you can make changes that will affect the health and well-being of your entire family. Give your child the best possible chance of a healthy, happy childhood, and a rosy future, by making sure that his stress load is stimulating and invigorating, rather than painful and discouraging. There are many ways of doing this, all practical, relevant and easy to follow. Your child's future is in your hands, and the choices you make will decide ultimately whether he becomes one more casualty of the 21st-century rat-race, or someone who makes the most of his life. Exhibit your love by having the courage to make changes, no matter what your child's peers or their parents are doing, no matter what your time or society dictates. Follow your instincts and your child wil flourish and grow into adulthood with a set of tools that will see him through any situation he might face. Above all, he'll experience the kind of deep-seated happiness and fulfilment that he deserves.

Appendix I:
Common symptoms and natural treatments

Around 80 per cent of visits to doctors' surgeries are caused or exacerbated by stress, but the majority of patients are sent away with a prescription for drugs to ease their symptoms. However, antacids, painkillers and anti-depressants all fail to get at the root cause of the health condition. If your child is suffering from the symptoms of stress, you should address the causes of the stress, not the symptoms. Changing your child's lifestyle, adopting a healthy approach to eating, sleeping, exercise and leisure, and learning the skills of relaxation will all substantially reduce the stress your child faces.

Treating the symptoms of stress will do nothing to improve your child's health or general well-being. However, relief of symptoms can help your child to feel well enough to carry on, and able to address the issues that are really behind the problem. This section, therefore, outlines some basic tips for treating various symptoms. The treatments – all tried and tested, natural ways of encouraging health – should only be used in the short term, and as a complement to making fundamental changes towards well-being.

If your child suffers repeatedly from any of the following symptoms on a long-term basis, see your doctor to rule out illness.

Anger and irritability
• A variety of different homeopathic remedies will be effective, but you'll probably need the help of a homeopath to get it exactly right. You could try Aconite, Chamomilla, Ignatia or Bryonia in the first instance.
• Of the flower remedies, Mountain Devil flower essence is your best bet. Rescue Remedy,

Emergency Essence, Child Essence and Impatiens should also help. Holly will help in cases of jealous anger or rage.

• Choose some of the sedative aromatherapy oils to soothe and calm the nervous system. Good choices are lavender, chamomile and a tiny drop of marjoram for extreme situations.

• Soothing herbs include chamomile, hops and catmint, which can be drunk as a tea or taken as a tincture.

Anxiety

• Constitutional homeopathic treatment will be appropriate for chronic conditions, and there are a number of remedies which will be useful for acute attacks; these include: Aconite for a panic attack that comes on suddenly; Arsenicum for a child who feels insecure, restless, tired and tends to fight anxiety by being obses- sively tidy or organised; Natrum mur may be useful for a child who dwells on morbid topics and hates fuss; Ignatia if anxiety fol- lows the loss of a loved one or a specific, distressing event.

• Herbal remedies can calm the nervous system and relax your child. Skullcap and valerian are useful, blended together for best effect. Offer as a tea when symp- toms arise.

• Flower essences can be brilliant for anxiety: consider Elm for anxiety accompanying a feeling of being unable to cope, or Red Chestnut for anxiety over the

welfare of others. Anxiety for no apparent reason might be treated with Aspen. Rescue Remedy or Emergency Essence are useful during attacks.

• A relaxing blend of essential oils of lavender, geranium and bergamot in sweet almond oil or peach kernel oil may be used in the bath at times of great stress and anxiety.

• Ensure your child gets plenty of B vitamins, which work on the nervous system.

Colds and flu

• If your child suffers repeatedly from colds and flu, it might be a good idea to seek constitutional homeopathic treatment. In the short term, however, the fol- lowing homeopathic remedies should help: Aconite in the first stages of a cold, particularly if it seems to have come on suddenly, after your child has been outside, for example; Belladonna, for colds with a high temperature, and great thirst; Natrum mur, for watery colds, particularly if accompanied by cold sores; Kali mur for catarrhal colds; Ferrum phos for hot colds; Arsenicum, for watery colds, particularly if your child is prone to frequent colds; Euphrasia, for colds affecting the eyes; Pulsatilla is useful if your child is clingy and irritable, and when there is thick yellow discharge; Bryonia helps an irritable child who is thirsty and wants to be left alone; Mercurius for a child with an earache, and swollen lymph nodes in the neck.

• Rescue Remedy will soothe any distress – rub the cream into the chest area to calm.

• Olive flower essence will help with fatigue.

• Golden Seal and Elecampane are useful for chronic colds to clear mucus from the lungs and nasal passages.

• Elderflower, drunk as an infusion, will reduce catarrh and help to decongest. Peppermint is another decongestant and will also work to reduce a fever.

• Chamomile will soothe an irritable child and help him to sleep. Chamomile also has an antiseptic action, which will help to rid the body of infection, and it works to reduce fever and feverish symptoms.

• Herbs to strengthen the immune system, including Echinacea, can be taken throughout a cold, and afterwards to stimulate healing and prevent subsequent infection.

• To ease congestion, sit your child in front of a steaming bowl of water with a few drops of essential oil of cinnamon in it. Place a towel over the head to make a tent, and let him breathe in the steam for four or five minutes.

• Try a few drops of lavender or tea tree oil in a warm bath to encourage healing and help to open up the airways.

• Blackcurrant tea is excellent for catarrh and infections.

• Offer plenty of fresh garlic and onions, to reduce catarrh and cleanse the blood. Garlic is also antibiotic and boosts the immune system.

Poor concentration

• Try a few drops of rosemary essential oil in a vaporiser in your child's room. This is uplifting and stimulating.

• Watch blood-sugar levels, making sure that your child eats regularly and sensibly. Also make sure your child gets enough sleep, which can affect concentration in the short term.

Depression

• Homeopathic treatment should be constitutional, and based on a wide variety of factors. Aurum is good for feelings of worthlessness or self-disgust. Your child may be intensely driven and competitive, but suddenly give up. Pulsatilla is for bursting into tears at the smallest slight. Use Arsenicum if your child feels chilly, tired, restless and obsessively tidy. Ignatia is used if the depression has a specific external cause, such as bereavement, breaking up with a girlfriend, or exams.

• Flower essences can be amazingly effective. Try the following: Agrimony for deeply held emotional tensions which are hidden from others; Gorse for feelings of great hopelessness; Gentian for a mild depression and despondency; Mustard for blacker and deeper feelings when the joy is missing; Sweet Chestnut for anguish and if your child feels stretched beyond endurance.

• A number of anti-depressant oils can be used in the bath, in a vaporiser, on a light bulb and in massage. Try geranium, melissa, lavender, rose, ylang ylang, and chamomile.

• The best anti-depressant and nervine (having specific action on the nerves) herbs include balm, borage, limeflower, oats, rosemary and vervain. These can be taken as herbal teas, added to the bath, or taken as tablets or in tincture form (herbs suspended in alcohol). St John's wort can be enormously useful – see a registered herbalist for appropriate applications. Ginkgo biloba has also been used in the treatment of depression. Offer it on a daily basis for as long as necessary.

Digestive problems

• Homeopathic remedies can be taken hourly, as required. Consider Arsenicum, for burning pains in the abdomen and great thirst; Pulsatilla, for symptoms that are worse at night, and tearfulness; Phosphorus, for a burning sensation when stools are passed, with vomiting and cravings for cold water which is then vomited; Colocynth, for diarrhoea accompanied by griping pains, with yellowish, thin and copious stools; Arg nit, for diarrhoea caused by anxiety, characterised by belching and cravings for sweet and salty food.

• Arrowroot or slippery elm tea can be sipped during the worst symptoms to soothe the digestive tract, and afterwards to help restore bowel health.

• Offer acidophilus to restore the healthy flora in the intestines, to help in the fight against infection.

• Very ripe bananas will ease nausea, act as a gentle constipant, and help to restore the healthy bacterial growth in the intestines.

• Massage chamomile and geranium oils into the abdomen to bring relief from pain and discomfort. The essential oils of peppermint or lavender can be used in a vaporiser and inhaled to alleviate nausea and vomiting.

• Make a cup of very weak blackcurrant or chamomile tea and offer to your child in small sips after it has cooled. This will help to soothe the digestive tract, and boost the immune system.

• Rescue Remedy or Emergency Essence will be useful for prolonged or distressing vomiting; it will help to reduce panic and calm the mind and body. Holly or beech may help if the vomiting is linked to emotional problems.

• Chamomile and vervain can be taken internally to soothe a child whose illness is exacerbated or caused by emotional upset, or who is distressed by the vomiting.

Eczema flare-ups

• For dry skin that feels hot, use Calendula or Rescue Remedy cream. To relieve itching, Urtica urens lotion or ointment will help.

• The most nourishing gentle moisturiser is olive oil, which can be rubbed into the skin following a bath. Never put moisturising oils in the bath until after your child has soaked for some time. Otherwise the oil forms a barrier between the water and the skin, which prevents rehydration. Drop olive oil into the bath after about five to 10 minutes of soaking, or apply it afterwards. Add a drop of lavender oil to soothe.

• Add a cup of chamomile tea, or a few drops of Rescue Remedy, to your child's bathwater to soothe inflammation and itching.

• Offer a good multivitamin and mineral tablet to prevent any minor deficiencies that may be exacerbating the problem.

• Evening primrose oil has been used successfully in the treatment of eczema.

• Eczema requires 'constitutional' homeopathic treatment, but the following remedies may be useful in the meantime: Sulphur, when the skin is burning, red, hot and itching; Graphites, when the skin appears infected; Petroleum, when there are deep cracks with a watery discharge; Urtica urens for a nettle-rash type of itchiness; Rhus tox, with blisters that are worse at night, and improve with warmth.

• Aloe vera gel, from the leaf of the plant, will encourage healing.

• Flower essences can be very useful, and will help babies and children, particularly because eczema is so strongly linked with emotions. Impatiens is useful for itching, and can be taken internally or mixed into a neutral cream. Rescue Remedy, taken internally, or used externally in a cream or wash, helps most skin problems.

• A gentle massage with a blend of chamomile, lavender and/or melissa essential oils in a little carrier oil can be used to treat eczema.

Growing pains

• Homeopathic constitutional treatment may alleviate the problem in many children, particularly if it is common. For rare occurrences, try one of the following remedies: Calcarea, for dragging pains in the ankles and knees that are worse for walking; Phosphoric Acid, when your child feels weak and the pains come on after prolonged stress, and are sometimes worse after exertion; Guaiacum for pains that are worse in cold, wet weather, and made worse by heat, but normally better when pressure is applied to the area.

• During an attack, warm a little olive oil and add one drop of lavender oil. Massage into the legs, working from top to bottom and then bottom to top, to improve circulation, release tension and encourage flow of any lactic acid build-up.

• Offer Rescue Remedy during an attack.

• Ensure that your child has plenty of calcium, vitamin D and magnesium in his diet, which may be lacking in times of stress.

• The tissue salts Calc fluor and Calc phos, taken three times a day, are often helpful.

• If your child seems agitated or overexcited at bedtime, offer a little valerian tea to calm and relax.

Headaches

• Frequent headaches could be a signal that your child is low on some important vitamins and minerals. Low levels of niacin and vitamin B6 can cause headaches, for example, and all the B vitamins are needed to help combat stress and avoid tension headaches.

• A relaxing cup of mild herbal tea is often good for a tension headache. Good choices are peppermint, spearmint, chamomile, rosehips, meadowsweet or lemon balm.

• Valerian root tea can also be helpful, but it may make your child sleepy, so use it at night, or when he has time to take a nap.

• Researchers are studying the benefits of the herb feverfew for treating chronic headaches and migraines. The leaves of this plant contain a substance that relaxes the blood vessels in the brain. Studies suggest that children who eat a few fresh feverfew leaves or take an extract of the leaves every day have fewer and less severe migraines. The herb has no unpleasant side-effects.

• Homeopathic remedies can be very effective, particularly for chronic headaches. In the short term, try some of the following remedies: Ignatia for headaches caused by emotional stress; Nux vomica for headaches caused by overindulgence or stress (after a birthday party, for example); Nux vomica or Pulsatilla are useful in many cases of migraine; Aconite for a sudden headache, that feels worse for cold, and characterised by a tight band around the head; Apis, for stinging, stabbing or burning headaches, when the body feels tender and sore; Belladonna, for throbbing, drumming headaches with a flushed face; Bryonia, for sharp, stabbing pain when the eyes are moved; Hypericum, for a bursting, aching headache with a sensitive scalp; Ruta, for a pressing headache caused by fatigue, and made worse by reading.

• The relaxing qualities of lavender oil make it a good treatment for a tension headache. This essential oil is very gentle, so you can massage a drop into your child's temples and at the base of the neck (dilute it in a carrier oil first), or add to the bath.

• Chamomile tea is soothing and will ease the symptoms.

Hives

• The best homeopathic remedies to try are Apis, for burning or swelling, particularly of the lips and eyelids; Urtica, for a rash that feels like a nettle sting, worse for touching or scratching, and Rhus tox, for burning, itching and blisters. These remedies should be taken every three hours.

• The Bach Flower Remedy Impatiens is very useful for itching. Take internally or mix into a neutral cream and apply to the affected area.

• Urtica urens cream, available from health-food shops and some good pharmacists, will soothe and promote healing.

• Aloe vera can be used topically to soothe the rash.

• A warm bath with essential oil of chamomile or melissa will soothe the skin and help to prevent stress-related attacks.

• Add a few tablespoons of baking soda to the bath to relieve itching.

• Offer an infusion of valerian at bedtime.

• A warm bath with essential oil of chamomile or melissa will soothe the skin and help to prevent stress-related attacks.

Insecurity

There are natural treatments for insecurity, but they will be most effective when the whole picture is taken into consideration.

• Homeopathic treatment should be constitutional, although you may find some of the following remedies help: Aconite for insecurity brought on by a traumatic experience; Ignatia, for insecurity stemming from a particular incident or cause, such as a bereavement; Pulsatilla, if your child feels tearful, and longs for company.

• Marjoram essential oil is cheering and can boost self-image. It can also put your child to sleep, so use it at night in a vaporiser for best effect.

• Flower essences can work wonders for insecurity. One of the best options is Mimulus, for insecurity caused by fears of any sort. Larch is great for children who have little confidence and may feel inferior. Elm can help if your child feels overwhelmed or inadequate. Use Walnut in times of change.

Jealousy

The best one for this is the Bach Flower Remedy Holly. Try also the homeopathic remedy Lycopodium.

Mood swings

Keep an eye on blood-sugar levels in the first instance, and make sure that your child is getting enough sleep. These can dramatically affect mood swings in the short term. Otherwise, *see* the advice on the various mood, such as anxiety, anger and tearfulness.

Sleep problems

• Vervain is a gentle sedative, and can help children fall asleep – particularly if they are fighting it.

• Limeflower will be useful for children who are nervous and sensitive.

• Motherwort can be useful for calming a frightened child or baby.

• A strong infusion of chamomile,

hops, lavender or limeflower can be added to a warm bath to soothe and calm a child.

• Tincture of catmint, added to a little honey, can be given to a distressed child as required.

• Homeopathic treatment should be constitutional, based on your child's exact requirements and symptoms. However, the following remedies may be appropriate for short-term problems, or while waiting for a consultation (remedies can be taken an hour before going to bed, for up to 14 days; repeat the dose if your child wakes in the night, and cannot get back to sleep): Calcarea and Ant tart for night terrors; Colocynth or Bryonia for constant crying; Arsenicum, when your child wakes between midnight and 2am, restless, worried and apprehensive; Rhus tox, when your child cannot sleep, is irritable, restless and wants to walk around, and may complain that something 'hurts'; Aurum, when your child has vivid dreams about dying, hunger, or problems at school, and may wake depressed; Aconite, when sleep problems are worse after shock, leading to restlessness, nightmares and perhaps even a fear of dying; Phosphorus if there is thirst, and alternating anger and affection; Pulsatilla, for a weepy, clingy child; Chamomilla, if sleep is being disturbed by teething, or if your child cannot settle without being hugged, rocked or patted to sleep; Nux vomica, for irritability, after a busy day, or too much food or fun; Coffea when your child's mind is overactive and he can't switch off.

• Older children may suck a zinc lozenge before bedtime to help them sleep.

• Flower essences can be enormously useful. Create a blend of some of the most appropriate (*see* pages 163–6), or see a flower therapist for advice. Generally, the following are useful: White Chestnut for children with overactive minds; Rescue Remedy will calm a distressed child or baby; Rock Rose for night terrors; Aspen for fear of the dark; Walnut for change; a few drops of Mimulus to soothe a distressed or fearful baby or child.

• A few drops of chamomile, geranium, rose or lavender can be added to bathwater to calm and soothe.

• Lavender oil on a hanky tied near the cot or bed will help a baby or child to sleep. Lavender or chamomile can be used in a vaporiser in the room with the same effect. A gentle massage before bedtime, with a little lavender or chamomile blended with a light carrier oil, may ease any tension or distress.

Sudden shyness

• Constitutional treatment with homeopathy is extremely helpful if your child is chronically shy, and it is affecting his interactions with others. There are also remedies that can help in different situations, according to your child's individual characteristics: for a child who is quiet and tends to cry a lot, Pulsatilla is most appropriate, particularly if he tends to blush; Lycopodium is good for children who are shy in new situations, and who tend to hide behind false bravado (although you know how shy he is feeling, and he's made it clear in the lead-up to the situation); Phosphorus for a child who constantly seeks affection and reassurance, and is pale and highly strung; Silicea is useful if your child is bashful, with a tendency to burst into tears, although he can sometimes be obstinate. It's most appropriate if your child feels the cold.

• Flower essences come into their own here. For some good examples, *see* page 167, or try Mimulus, which is suitable for children who are shy, nervous and blush easily. Your child probably feels uneasy with people he doesn't know, feels self-conscious and doesn't like parties. Larch is for children who suffer from poor confidence, which holds them back. They probably feel inferior and self-doubtful. Elm will help if your child feels overwhelmed and inadequate due to pressure from family, work, friends and other commitments. Cerato is good for children who constantly seek the reassurance of others because they do not trust their own judgement.

Tearfulness

• There are a number of effective homeopathic remedies. Try one of the following in the short term: Pulsatilla, when your child is woefully tearful and you feel sorry for him; Chamomilla for angry crying; Lycopodium for tears brought on by a sense of injustice, or not wanting to try new things.

• Try Chicory flower essence if your child needs constant reassurance. Mimulus is for tears of fear of known things, while Gentian might be appropriate for children who are easily set back. Olive is for a child whose tears are caused by overwhelming fatigue. Mustard will help children who feel that they are under a dark cloud and don't know the reason why. English Rose will help if your child feels broken-hearted.

• Try any of the relaxing essential oils, such as lavender and chamomile, which will soothe and restore. A drop of rosemary in a vaporiser will help to lift feelings of gloom and despair.

Teeth-grinding (bruxism)

• Constitutional homeopathic treatment will be appropriate, particularly since this condition seems to have an emotional basis. In the meantime, try Arsenicum for grinding of teeth during sleep, especially between midnight and two or three in the morning.

• Herbal remedies can calm the nervous system and relax your child. Valerian is a gentle herb, which encourages the health of the nervous system and helps to keep him calm. Encourage your child to sip this several times daily during periods of stress. Lime Blossom may also work to ease anxiety and tension that may be exacerbating the condition.

• Flower essences are particularly useful, but treatment should be aimed at each individual child. Consider Elm for anxiety accompanying a feeling of being unable to cope, or Red Chestnut for anxiety over the welfare of others. Anxiety for no apparent reason might be treated with Aspen.

• A relaxing blend of essential oils of lavender, geranium and bergamot in sweet almond oil or peach kernel oil may be used in the bath to calm and prevent attacks.

Tummy aches

• Add a drop of chamomile oil to a little apricot kernel oil, and massage into the abdominal area to ease the symptoms.

• The homeopathic remedy Bryonia is useful if your child is very irritable and screams at the slightest movement, and Chamomilla is good if your child seems better for comforting, but otherwise is almost impossible to please.

• If indigestion is the problem, a warm cup of peppermint or chamomile tea may help.

• Flower essences can be appropriate for nerves (Mimulus), or try Impatiens if your child does everything in a hurry and seems impatient. Again, Mimulus is good for pain caused by fears. Walnut will help if your child is undergoing change of any sort (adolescence, exams, a new school, a new girlfriend, a new carer).

• Nervous tummy aches can be eased with chamomile tea, or valerian at bedtime.

Appendix II:
The Dato Stress Inventory

The Dato Stress Inventory is a stress assessment and evaluation instrument designed for adult use. The DSI is comprised of the Personal Symptoms Profile, the Personal Needs Profile and the Personal Skills Profile. The accuracy of your scores will depend on your comprehension of the profile items, and your honesty in responding.

Follow the inventory procedures and guidelines to score and interpret the DSI.

Results	Scales	Symptoms	Needs	Skills
DSI	Raw Scores			
	Percentage Scores			
%				

Interpretations

Stress Level	DSI (Raw Scores)	DSI (Percentage Scores)
Mild Stress	50–98	20–39%
Moderate Stress	99–148	40–59%
Severe Stress	149–198	60–70%
Extreme Stress	199–250	80–100%

Strategic Stress Management Guidelines

Recommended Programme Components	Average DIS Stress Level			
	Mild	Moderate	Severe	Extreme
	50–98	99–148	149–198	199–250
	20–39%	40–59%	60–79%	80–100%
Education	●	●	●	●
Consultation		●	●	●
Medication			●	●
Hospitalisation				●

Strategic Stress Assessment Guidelines

Recommended Assessment Frequency	Average DIS Stress Level			
	Mild	Moderate	Severe	Extreme
	50–98	99–148	149–198	199–250
	20–39%	40–59%	60–79%	80–100%
Quarterly	●			
Monthly		●		
Weekly			●	
Daily				●

Personal Symptoms Profile Definitions

1. Headaches   Pain or tightness in the head

2. Muscle Tension   Pain or tightness in the muscles

3. Fatigue   Tiredness or exhaustion without exercise

4. Overeating   Eating too much or too frequently

5. Loss of Appetite   Having little or no interest in food

6. Constipation   Infrequent or difficult bowel movements

7. Diarrhoea   Frequent or loose bowel movements

8. Rapid Heartbeat   Fast pulse without physical activity

9. Hypertension   Elevated blood pressure while at rest

10. Insomnia   Difficulty in falling or staying asleep

11. Inattentiveness   Reduced awareness and responsiveness

12. Forgetfulness   Diminished short-term memory

13. Poor Concentration   Inability to remain focused

14. Irritability   Hypersensitivity and overreaction

15. Restlessness   Urgency to move or do something

16. Hyperactivity   Constant or fast-paced activity

17. Frustration   Feelings of impatience or powerlessness

18. Anger   Feelings of resentment or rage

19. Anxiety   Feelings of nervousness or fear

20. Depression   Feelings of helplessness or hopelessness

Personal Symptoms Profile

Directions. Circle the *frequency of your specific physical and psychological symptoms* at this point in time. Please use the definitions provided. Be sure to circle only one number per item and to complete all items. Do not score this Profile until the entire Inventory has been completed.

General Symptoms	Specific Symptoms	Symptom Frequency				
		Very Low	Low	Moderate	High	Very High
Physical Symptoms	Headaches	1	2	3	4	5
	Muscle Tension	1	2	3	4	5
	Fatigue	1	2	3	4	5
	Overeating	1	2	3	4	5
	Loss of Appetite	1	2	3	4	5
	Constipation	1	2	3	4	5
	Diarrhoea	1	2	3	4	5
	Rapid Heartbeat	1	2	3	4	5
	Hypertension	1	2	3	4	5
	Insomnia	1	2	3	4	5
Psychological Symptoms	Inattentiveness	1	2	3	4	5
	Forgetfulness	1	2	3	4	5
	Poor Concentration	1	2	3	4	5
	Irritability	1	2	3	4	5
	Restlessness	1	2	3	4	5
	Hyperactivity	1	2	3	4	5
	Frustration	1	2	3	4	5
	Anger	1	2	3	4	5
	Anxiety	1	2	3	4	5
	Depression	1	2	3	4	5
	Circled Items					

Scores   RS____   PS____   %

Procedures. Connect each response to the following response with a straight line. Enter the number of circled items at the bottom of each column. Multiply each column total by its column weight (1, 2, 3, 4 or 5). Enter results on next line. Add results to determine Raw Score (RS). On this Profile, RS and Percentage Score (PS) are identical.

Personal Needs Profile Definitions

1. **Nourishment**   Sufficient and well-balanced diet

2. **Activity**   Regular physical exercise

3. **Rest**   Adequate relaxation and sleep

4. **Protection**   Insulation from injury or harm

5. **Stability**   Personal constancy and consistency

6. **Control**   Influence over conditions in your life

7. **Acceptance**   Belief in yourself

8. **Approval**   Favourable opinion of yourself

9. **Understanding**   Self-knowledge and self-insight

10. **Identity**   Awareness of your unique individuality

11. **Purpose**   Clear and specific goals

12. **Commitment**   Strong attachment to your goals

13. **Responsibility**   Willingness to be accountable for your actions

14. **Co-operation**   Successful interactions with others

15. **Achievement**   Accomplishment of your goals

16. **Respect**   High regard for your integrity

17. **Admiration**   High regard for your achievements

18. **Appreciation**   Understanding of your value or worth

Personal Needs Profile

Directions. Circle the *degree to which you have satisfied your own spe-cific needs* at this point in time. Please use the definitions provided. Be sure to circle only one number per item and to complete all items. Do not score this Profile until the entire Inventory has been completed.

General Needs	Specific Needs	Need Satisfaction				
		Very Low	Low	Moderate	High	Very High
	Nourishment	5	4	3	2	1
Survival	Activity	5	4	3	2	1
	Rest	5	4	3	2	1
	Protection	5	4	3	2	1
Security	Stability	5	4	3	2	1
	Control	5	4	3	2	1
	Acceptance	5	4	3	2	1
Support	Approval	5	4	3	2	1
	Understanding	5	4	3	2	1
	Identity	5	4	3	2	1
Selfhood	Purpose	5	4	3	2	1
	Commitment	5	4	3	2	1
	Responsibility	5	4	3	2	1
Success	Co-operation	5	4	3	2	1
	Achievement	5	4	3	2	1
	Respect	5	4	3	2	1
Satisfaction	Admiration	5	4	3	2	1
	Appreciation	5	4	3	2	1
	Circled items					
Scores	RS ___ PS ___ %					

Procedures. Connect each response to the following response with a straight line. Enter the number of circled items at the bottom of each column. Multiply each column total by its column weight (1, 2, 3, 4 or 5). Enter results on next line. Add results to determine Raw Score (RS). To obtain Percentage Score (PS), divide RS by 90, then multiply by 100. Round off Percentage Score.

Personal Skills Profile Definitions

1. **Objective**   Perceives clearly and without bias

2. **Perspective**   Possesses insight and foresight

3. **Imaginative**   Can generate new ideas

4. **Thorough**   Thinks carefully and completely

5. **Judicious**   Exercises sound judgement

6. **Decisive**   Makes choices with conviction

7. **Dynamic**   Is proactive and forceful

8. **Persuasive**   Can influence others

9. **Flexible**   Accepts and adapts to feedback

10. **Confident**   Is certain of one's abilities

11. **Enthusiastic**   Finds joy in achievement

12. **Optimistic**   Expects continued success

Personal Skills Profile

Directions Circle the *level to which you have developed your own specific skills* at this point in time. Please use the definitions provided. Be sure to circle only one number per item and to complete all items. Do not score this Profile until the entire Inventory has been completed.

General Skills	Specific Skills	Very Low	Low	Moderate	High	Very High
				Skill Development		
	Objective	5	4	3	2	1
Perceptual	Perceptive	5	4	3	2	1
	Imaginative	5	4	3	2	1
	Thorough	5	4	3	2	1
Cognitive	Judicious	5	4	3	2	1
	Decisive	5	4	3	2	1
	Dynamic	5	4	3	2	1
Behavioural	Persuasive	5	4	3	2	1
	Flexible	5	4	3	2	1
	Confident	5	4	3	2	1
Emotional	Enthusiastic	5	4	3	2	1
	Optimistic	5	4	3	2	1
	Circled Items					
Scores	RS____ PS____ %					

Procedures. Connect each response to the following response with a straight line. Enter the number of circled items at the bottom of each column. Multiply each column total by its column weight (1, 2, 3, 4 or 5). Enter results on next line. Add results to determine Raw Score (RS). To obtain Percentage Score (PS), divide RS by 60, then multiply by 100. Round off Percentage Score.

Resources

The author is happy to answer questions on any issues relating to this book. Please contact her care of her publisher, or email her on childheal@aol.com (please note: not childhealth!)

UK and Ireland

Action Against Allergy, 43 The Downs, London SW20

Alcoholics Anonymous, PO Box 1, Stonebow House, York YO1 7NJ
Tel: 0845 769 7555 Website: www.alcoholics-anonymous.org.uk

The Bach Centre, Mount Vernon, Sotwell, Wallingford, Oxfordshire OX10 9PZ

Barnardos, Tanners Lane, Barkingside, Ilford, Essex IG6 1QG Tel: 020 8550 8822

British Hypnotherapy Association, 67 Upper Berkeley Street, London W1H 7DH

British Medical Journal website: www.bmj.com

British Nutrition Foundation, High Holborn House, 52–54 High Holborn, London WC1V 6RQ Tel: 020 7404 6504 Fax: 020 7404 6747 Email: postbox@nutrition.org.uk

British Sleep Society website: www.british-sleep-society.org.uk

British Society for Allergy, Environment and Nutritional Medicine, PO Box, Totton, Southampton S040 2ZA Tel: 01703 812124

British Society for Nutritional Medicine, Stone House, 9 Weymouth Street, London W1N 3FF Tel: 020 7436 8532

Child Psychotherapy Trust, Star House, 104-108 Grafton Road, London NW5 4BD Tel: 020 7284 1355

Childnet International, Studio 14, Brockley Cross Business Centre, 96 Endwell Road, London SE4 2PD Tel: 020 7639 6967 Fax: 020 7639 7027 Website:www.childnet-int.org

ChildLine, 2nd Floor, Royal Mail Building, Studd Street, London N1 0QW Tel: 020 7239 1000 Helpline: 0800 1111 Fax: 020 7239 1001 Website: www.childline.or.uk

ChildLine Northern Ireland, PO Box 1111, Belfast BT1 2DD, Northern Ireland Helpline: 0800 1111 Tel: 02890 327773 Fax: 02890 818131

ChildLine Scotland, 18 Albion Street, Glasgow Tel: 0141 552 1123 Helpline: 0800 1111 Fax: 0141 552 3089

Children First – Royal Scottish Society for the Prevention of Cruelty to Children, Melville House, 41 Polwarth Terrace, Edinburgh EH11 1NU Tel: 0131 337 8539 Fax: 0131 346 8284 Email: children1st@zetnet.co.uk

The Children's Society, Edward Rudolf House, Margery Street, London WC1X 0JL Tel: 020 7837 4299 Fax: 020 7837 0211 Email: information@the-childrens-society.org.uk Website: www.the-childrens-society.org.uk

Children's Trust, Tadworth Court, Tadworth, Surrey KT20 5RU Tel: 01737 357 171

The Council for Nutrition Education and Therapy (CNEAT), 1 The Close, Halton, Aylesbury, Buckinghamshire HP22 5NJ

Eating Disorders Association, Sackville Place, 44 Magdalen Street, Norwich, Norfolk NR3 1JE Tel: 01603 621 414

Galen Homeopathics, Lewell, Dorchester, Dorset DT2 8AN Tel: 01305 263996/265759 Fax: 01305 250792 For homeopathic remedies

Get Connected, PO Box 21082, London N1 0QW Tel: 020 8260 7373 Helpline: 0800 096 0096 Email: admin@getconnected.org.uk Website: www.getconnected.org.uk

Health Plus Ltd, Dolphin House, 30 Lushington Road, Eastbourne, East Sussex BN21 4LL Tel: 01323 737374 Sell extensive range of supplements

Higher Nature also supply a good range of vitamin, mineral and herbal products, and supply a magazine entitled Get Up and Go. Send for a free colour catalogue to Higher Nature, Burwash Common, East Sussex TN19 7LX Tel: 01435 882880

Hyperactive Children's Support Group, 71 Whyke Lane, Chichester, West Sussex PO19 2LD Tel: 01903 725182

Institute of Optimum Nutrition, Blades Court, Deodar Road, London SW15 2NU Tel: 020 8877 9993 or contact its founder, Patrick Holford on www.patrickholford.com. They also run the Food for the Future Project, to promote the importance of optimum nutrition to children, adolescents, adults, parents and teachers.

Institute of Stress Management, 57 Hall Lane, London NW4 4TJ Tel: 020 7203 7355

Institute for Complementary Medicine, PO Box 194, London SE14
1QZ Tel: 020 7237 5165

International Stress Management Association (ISMA), PO Box 348,
Waltham Cross EN8 8ZL Tel: 07000 780430 Fax: 01992 426673
Email: stress@isma.org.uk Website: www.isma.org.uk

Kidscape, 152 Buckingham Palace Road, London SW1W 9TR
Tel: 020 7730 3300

National Asthma Campaign, Providence House, Providence Place,
London N1 0NT Helpline: 0345 010203 Tel: 020 7226 2269

National Children's Bureau, 8 Wakley Street, London EC1V 7QE
Tel: 020 7843 6000 Fax: 020 7278 9512 Email:
membership@ncb.org.uk Website: www.ncb.org.uk

National Council of Psychotherapists and Hypnotherapists, 46
Oxhey Road, Oxhey, Watford, Herts WD1 4QQ

National Eczema Society, 163 Eversholt Street, London NW1 1BU
Tel: 020 7978 6278

NCH Action for Children, 85 Highbury Park, London N5 1UD
Tel: 020 7704 7058 Fax: 020 7704 7006
Website: www.nchafc.org.uk

NSPCC, 42 Curtain Road, London EC2A 3NH Tel: 020 7825 2500
Fax: 020 7825 2525 Helpline: 0808 800 5000 Textphone: 0800
056 0566 Websites: www.nspcc.org.uk and www.bullying.co.uk

NSPCC, Jennymount Court, North Derby Street, Belfast BT15 3HN,
Northern Ireland Tel: 02890 351135 Fax: 02890 351100

Nutrition for Kids website: www.nutritionforkids.com

Organic Food Federation, The Tithe House, Peaseland Green, Elsing,
East Dereham NR20 3DY Tel: 01362 637314 Fax: 01362 637398

Parent Network, 44-46 Caversham Road, London NW5 2DS Tel: 020
7485 8535

Play Leisure Advice Network (PLANET), Save the Children,
Cambridge House, Cambridge Grove, London W6 0LE Tel: 020
8741 4054

Positively Children, Unit F7, Shakespeare Commercial Centre, 245a
Coldharbour Lane, London SW9 8RR Tel: 020 7738 7333

Royal College of Psychiatrists, 17 Belgrave Square, London SW1X
8PG Tel: 020 7235 2351 Email: infoservices@rcpsych.ac.uk
Website: www.rcpsych.ac.uk

The Samaritans Tel: 08457 909090 Email: jo@samaritans.org
Website: www.samaritans.org.uk Offer a confidential listening and
e-mail service 24 hours a day.

Save the Children Fund, 17 Grove Lane, London SE5 8RD Email:
enquiries:cfuk.org.uk Website: www.savethechildren.org.uk

Save the Children Northern Ireland, Popper House, 15 Richmond
Park, Belfast BT10 0HB, Northern Ireland Tel: 02890 431123 Fax:
02890 431314

Shape Up website: www.shapeup.org

Single Parent Action Network, Millpond, Lower Ashley Road, Easton,
Bristol BS5 0XJ Tel: 0117 9514231

Sleep Matters, Medical Advisory Service, PO Box 3087, London W4
4ZP Helpline: 020 8994 9874

Sleepnet website: www.sleepnet.com

The Traumatic Stress Clinic, 73–75 Charlotte Street, London W1P
1LB Tel: 020 7380 9462

UK Council for Psychotherapy, 167-169 Great Portland Street,
London W1N 5PB Tel: 020 7436 3002 Website: www.psy-
chotherapy.org.uk

YoungMinds, 102-108 Clerkenwell Road, London EC1M 5SA Tel: 020
7336 8445 Fax: 020 7336 8446 Email:
enquiries@youngminds.org.uk Parents' Information Service: 0800
018 2138 Website: www.youngminds.org.uk

Youth Access, 19 Taylor's Yard, 67 Alderbrook Road, London SW12
8AB Tel: 020 8772 9900

Australia

Anorexia and Bulimia Nervosa Foundation of Victoria (Inc.), 1513
High Street, Glen Iris, 3146 Victoria Tel: 613 885 0318 Fax: 613
885 1153

ISMA, 44 Riverlea Waters Estate, 184 Nerang-Beaudesert Road,
Nerang OLD 4211,

Australia E-mail: Vmdrury@bizyweb.com.au

Oz Child: Children Australia, PO Box 1310, South Melbourne,
Victoria 3205 Tel: 03 9695 2211 Fax: 03 969 0790

Sleep Disorders Centre, Royal Prince Alfred Hospital, Missenden
Road, Camperdown, NSW, 2050, Australia Tel: 612 9515 8630
Fax: 612 9365 5612 E-mail: rrg@blackburn.med.su.oz.au

Tisserand Australia, PO Box 1081, Dandenong, Victoria 3175 Tel: 03
9706 7070 Fax: 03 9794 0833

Canada

Ontario Association of Children's Aid Societies, 75 Front Street East,
2nd Floor, Toronto, Ontario, CANADA 6 Tel: 416 366 8115 Fax:
416 366 8317 Email: info@oacas.org

New Zealand

Barnardos New Zealand, Private Box 6434, Wellington Tel: 64 4385 7560 Fax: 64 4385 3769

Canterbury College of Natural Medicine, PO Box 4529, Christchurch Tel: 03 366 0373 Fax: 03 366 5342

Kiwi Health website: www.kiwihealth.com

Mental Health Foundation of New Zealand, 62-64 Valley Road, Mt Eden, PO Box 10051, Dominion Road, Auckland 1003 Tel: 09 630 8573 Fax: 09 630 7190

New Zealand Bach Flower Remedies, P O Box 358, Waiuku Tel/Fax: 09 235 7057 E-Mail: bachnz@ps.gen.nz

New Zealand Herbal website: www.nzherbal.com

New Zealand Natural Health Practitioners Accreditation Board, PO Box 37–491, Auckland Tel: 09 625 9966

Touch for Health Association of New Zealand, 33 Gilshennan Valley, Red Beach, Orewa 1461 Tel/Fax: 09 426 7695

South Africa

Allergy Society of South Africa website: www.allergysa.org/resources.htm

The Centre for Natural Therapies and the School of Complementary Health, 475 Townbush Road, Montrose, Pietermaritzburg 3201 Or: P.O. Box 13559, Cascades 3202 Tel: 033 347 3937 Fax: 033 347 0680

Children's Inquiry Trust, PO Box 784678, Sandton 2146 Tel: 2711 884 2647 Fax: 2711 784 3142 Email: chit@wn.apc.org

The Eczema Society, A Geers, Schering (Pty) Ltd., Freepost, JHZ156

National Asthma Education Campaign (NAEP), Private Bag X3032, Randburg 2125 Tel: 011 886 1075 Fax: 011 787 3766

Nutrition Information Centre, Nicus, P.O. Box 19063, Tygerberg 7505 Tel: 021 933 1408 Fax: 021 933 1405

South Africa Homoeopaths, Chiropractors and Allied Professions Board, PO Box 17055, 0027 Groenkloof Tel: 246 6455

South African Federation for Mental Health, 210 Happiness House, PO Box 2587, Loveday. Johannesburg Tel: 725 5800 Fax: 725 5835

Index

Note: page numbers in *italics* refer to illustrations and page numbers in **bold** refer to tables.